THE GOSPEL
ACCORDING TO
THIS MOMENT

THE GOSPEL ACCORDING TO THIS MOMENT

The Spiritual Message of
Henry David Thoreau

BARRY M. ANDREWS

University of Massachusetts Press
Amherst and Boston

Copyright © 2024 by University of Massachusetts Press
All rights reserved
Printed in the United States of America

ISBN 978-1-62534-779-4 (paper); 780-0 (hardcover)

Designed by Sally Nichols
Set in Adobe Jenson Pro
Printed and bound by Books International, Inc.

Cover design by adam b. bohannon
Cover photo by Bethany Bourgault, *Crystal clear water at Walden Pond*, © 2018.
Courtesy of the photographer.

Library of Congress Cataloging-in-Publication Data

Names: Andrews, Barry M., author.
Title: The gospel according to this moment : the spiritual message of Henry
David Thoreau / Barry M. Andrews.
Description: Amherst : University of Massachusetts Press, [2024] | Includes
bibliographical references and index. |
Identifiers: LCCN 2023046460 (print) | LCCN 2023046461 (ebook) | ISBN
9781625347794 (paperback) | ISBN 9781625347800 (hardcover) | ISBN
9781685750503 (ebook)
Subjects: LCSH: Thoreau, Henry David, 1817–1862—Religion. | Christian
life.
Classification: LCC PS3057.R4 A53 2024 (print) | LCC PS3057.R4 (ebook) |
DDC 818/.309—dc23/eng/20231201
LC record available at https://lccn.loc.gov/2023046460
LC ebook record available at https://lccn.loc.gov/2023046461

British Library Cataloguing-in-Publication Data
A catalog record for this book is available from the British Library.

To my granddaughters, Maddie, Phoebe, and Fiona.

May they step to the music each of them hears,
however measured or far away.

Every author writes in the faith that his book is to be the final resting place of the sojourning soul, and sets up his fixtures therein as for a more than oriental permanence. But it is only a caravansery which we soon leave without ceremony. We read on his sign only, refreshment for man and beast, and a drawn hand directs us to Isphahan or Bagdad.

—Henry David Thoreau, September 25, 1840

CONTENTS

PREFACE

I was first introduced to Thoreau by Mr. Don Black, my high school English teacher, who assigned "Civil Disobedience" as class reading. This was in 1964, at the height of the civil rights movement. A year earlier, as the nation watched on television, Sheriff Eugene "Bull" Connor used high-pressure water hoses and police dogs on protesters, including children, in Birmingham, Alabama. Martin Luther King Jr. and other civil rights leaders had called for demonstrations there in April 1963. Several of them were arrested. During his incarceration King wrote his "Letter from Birmingham Jail," which was widely published. A few months later he delivered his famous "I Have a Dream" speech in Washington, DC. That September a Black church in Birmingham was bombed, killing four young girls.

Against that background, Mr. Black could tell that I was quite affected by reading "Civil Disobedience" and suggested that, in addition, I might consider another of Thoreau's essays, "Life without Principle." This essay took a different tack and stimulated my thinking about the purpose of my life. During my college years I was frequently drawn to Thoreau's writing. *Walden* was high on my countercultural reading list, along with Jack Kerouac's *On the Road*, Albert Camus's *The Rebel*, and, later, Robert Persig's *Zen and the Art of Motorcycle Maintenance*. All of the books on that list echoed, in one way or another, Thoreau's central message: "If a man does not keep pace with his companions, perhaps it is because he hears a different drummer. Let him step to the music which he hears, however measured or far away."[1]

In the late 1960s and early 1970s the Vietnam War cast a pall over the hopes of my generation as young men faced the prospect of being drafted into a war so many of us considered morally wrong. Thoreau's refusal to pay his taxes and the night he spent in jail as a result foreshadowed the resistance to the Vietnam War, in the course of which hundreds if not thousands of demonstrators were similarly arrested and jailed. Thoreau's protest, importantly, was in opposition not only to slavery but also to the unjust war the United States was waging in Mexico. The original title of his famous essay, "Resistance to Civil Government," was prophetic in light of all that happened at the time.

In the decades immediately following the war, environmentalism took center stage, powerfully captured by a public service video of what was apparently a Native American man shedding a tear as he beheld his garbage-strewn surroundings. Attention was given not just to cleaning up refuse and toxic wastes but also to preserving wilderness areas and limiting damage to the environment caused by mining, clear-cutting, and laying oil pipelines. Once again, Thoreau's legacy proved to be a potent stimulus. The Sierra Club, largest of all the organizations devoted to environmental preservation, adopted words from his essay "Walking" as their motto: "In wildness is the preservation of the world."[2] Thoreau's writings on nature provided a rationale for wilderness preservation while also imbuing nature with a sacred quality that made it inviolable.

Reacting to the overconsumption and waste that led to ecological damage, many people began looking for ways to simplify their lifestyle and lessen their impact on the environment. In response, Thoreau has often been regarded as both a model and a voice for simplicity and sustainability. "Most of the luxuries, and many of the so called comforts of life, are not only not indispensable, but positive hindrances to the elevation of mankind," he wrote in *Walden*, advising us to live below our means rather than above them.[3] In doing so, he inspired the back-to-the-land and tiny house movements, as well as efforts, for example, to ban single-use plastics and to encourage composting.

As consciousness was raised concerning environmental impacts, it suddenly became clear that the earth's temperature was rising to an alarming degree. This was contributing to rising sea levels and weather-related disasters leading to the extinction of species that cannot tolerate a warming planet. Thoreau's detailed phenological studies of plant and animal life surrounding his native town have proved useful in determining, for instance, that spring comes earlier to Concord now than it did in his day. In light of climate change, species extinction, and the careless extraction of natural resources, many scientists have concluded that we are entering a new era, the

Anthropocene—the age of humans' impact on the planet. Although Thoreau would be dismayed to see how quickly this change happened, he would not have been surprised that it has occurred. Many thoughtful people are turning to his writings for guidance in responding to the challenges of this new reality.

The recent COVID pandemic, resulting in the lockdown and social isolation of hundreds of millions of people, has significantly altered patterns of work and everyday life. Many of those who have grown accustomed to working from home no longer wish to tolerate lengthy commutes and claustrophobic office workspaces. It has also provided an opportunity to rethink the work–life balance, leading to what some have called a "Great Resignation." Freed from the oppressive demands of the workplace, many people are seeking more time for leisure and reflection, heeding Thoreau's admonition: "When [one] has obtained those things which are necessary to life, there is another alternative than to obtain the superfluities; and that is, to adventure on life now, his vacation from humbler toil having commenced."[4]

No writer has addressed the many challenges Americans have faced in my lifetime more directly and eloquently than Henry David Thoreau. For me he has been what the Greeks called a *daimon*, an inner voice guiding people through their lives, reminding them of the divine order they cannot see on their own. In this respect, I consider him a spiritual writer who viewed nature, human life, and the problems of the world often from a higher perspective than mine. I have written this book in the hope that others may find guidance and inspiration in his writing also.

I have been aided in my understanding of Thoreau's spirituality by many outstanding scholars, including David M. Robinson, Alan D. Hodder, Phyllis Cole, Robert D. Richardson, Lawrence Buell, Laura Dassow Walls, Jeffrey Cramer, and numerous others. I am also grateful for the encouragement of Matt Becker and Mary Dougherty at the University of Massachusetts Press, as well as many friends and loved ones, especially my wife, Linda, who has tolerated my obsession to get this book written. I have also been inspired by those who have participated in my workshops and classes over the years, for whom Thoreau and his writings have proved to be a precious spiritual resource. In this sense, writing about Thoreau is a collective enterprise. Any mistakes I may have made, however, are entirely my own.

THE GOSPEL
ACCORDING TO
THIS MOMENT

INTRODUCTION

In March 1847, Henry David Thoreau received a letter from the secretary of his Harvard class requesting information regarding his date and place of birth, his marital status, his occupation, and current employment. He replied to the letter later that year, on September 30. He wasn't sure how to answer the question about his occupation, but he described his employment as follows:

> I am a Schoolmaster, a Private Tutor, a Surveyor, a Gardener, a Farmer, a Painter, I mean a house painter, a Carpenter, a Mason, a Day-laborer, a Pencil-Maker, a Glass-paper Maker, a Writer, and sometimes a Poetaster. . . . Indeed, my steadiest employment, if such it can be called, is to keep myself at the top of my condition, and ready for whatever may turn up in heaven or on earth. For the last two or three years I have lived in Concord woods alone, something more than a mile from any neighbor, in a house built entirely by myself.[1]

Of course, he was many other things besides the occupations mentioned in his letter. He is best known today as a writer and poet, a naturalist, a social critic, and an advocate of simple living, civil disobedience, and environmental preservation. Since the celebration of the bicentennial of his birth in 2017, numerous books have been published on his studies of trees, flowers, and animals; his fascination with spirits and fairies; his river explorations; his role in the antislavery movement; his reading and embrace of Darwin's *On the Origin of Species*; his friendship with Ralph Waldo Emerson; and the grace with which he faced his own tragic and untimely death. In addition, we now have the most detailed account to date of his life, Laura Dassow Walls's biography *Henry David Thoreau: A Life*.

This scholarship is a boon to those who feel that Thoreau is worth the effort to understand him better and to discover more about his interests and subsequent influence on American life and culture. The danger we encounter amidst the welter of information produced in the wake of recent scholarship, as Rebecca Solnit points out in her essay "The Thoreau Problem," is that we will end up compartmentalizing him, as in Thoreau the surveyor, Thoreau the abolitionist, Thoreau the naturalist, and so on. Or, worse yet, bifurcating his life between the recluse of Walden Pond on the one hand and the activist in the Concord jail on the other; or between the dreamy Transcendentalist of his youth and the hardheaded scientist of his later years.[2] Thus, we fail to see how the myriad parts of his life are of a piece and hang together.

Much has been written about Thoreau's turn toward science in the last decade of his life. He grasped many truths about river hydrology, the succession of forest trees, and the dispersion of seeds, but he never ceased to be amazed at what he observed in the natural world and to express his sense of wonder in the language of myth and symbol. In this sense, there never was a dichotomy between his Transcendentalism and his scientific observations. As he once said in turning down an invitation to join the Association for the Advancement of Science, "The fact is I am a mystic, a transcendentalist, and a natural philosopher to boot."[3] His was one of the earliest voices rejecting the dualism of religion and science.

I believe that the thread on which all the beads of Thoreau's many-faceted life are strung is his idiosyncratic and unconventional religious faith—a dimension largely unexplored in Thoreau scholarship. His earliest religious views were informed by his Unitarian upbringing. He was baptized and catechized in Concord's First Parish Church. His mother and father were members there. But he "signed off" from the church when he was a young man. By the time he entered college in 1833, he was perhaps not a devout Unitarian, but his Harvard education was nevertheless steeped in Unitarian tradition, the school having been a training ground for a generation of Unitarian ministers.

As a student, however, he was drawn to certain countercultural ideas then in vogue—the so-called new views of religion, self, and society that were being entertained by a younger generation of Unitarian intellectuals and divines. He was tutored by proponents of these views, first by Orestes Brownson during a three-month hiatus in his junior year, and later by Ralph Waldo Emerson, whose Transcendentalist manifesto *Nature* Thoreau devoured in his senior year at Harvard.

Emerson continued to be a mentor in the years following Thoreau's graduation. It was Emerson who encouraged him to begin a journal, the best record we have of Thoreau's spiritual life. Emerson also introduced him to the scriptures of India, China, and other cultures, which were extremely influential in his religious development. The Transcendentalists, with whom he identified, were generally of the opinion that the religious sentiment is natural and universal in human experience, whereas religious institutions are but the parochial and limited forms that this sentiment takes. They also believed that religious truth is known by experience, intuitively, and thus does not depend on religious scriptures or church teachings. They conceived of a natural or absolute religion, shorn of sectarian elements.

Walls tells us that Thoreau's purpose in going to live at Walden Pond was "profoundly religious," and that in writing of his experience he was intending to produce a "new sacred book for the modern age."[4] To this I would add that *Walden* is not just a religious treatise; it is also a manual of spiritual practice. Self-culture played a central role in Transcendentalist spirituality. Sometimes termed "the art of life," for the Transcendentalists it meant the cultivation of the soul. "*The art of life!*" Thoreau wrote in his journal. "Was there anything memorable written upon it? By what disciplines to secure the most life—with what care to watch our thoughts." The disciplines he practiced and described in *Walden* and elsewhere include leisure, self-reliance, reading, contemplation, solitude, conversation, sauntering in nature, and simple living. By such practices we may, even today, attempt "to secure the most life."[5]

As for describing Thoreau's religion, we should perhaps heed his own admonition. "What is religion?" he once asked himself. "That which is never spoken," he replied.[6] Part of the difficulty we have in describing Thoreau's religion is that the word "religion" was only then in the process—one accelerated by the Transcendentalists themselves—of being considered apart from its historical manifestations in the various faith traditions.[7] What we can say, I believe, is that his religious views were experiential and nature-centered. God, for him, was immanent rather than transcendent. Thoreau was, if anything, a nature mystic and a pantheist. He was familiar with the Bible and frequently drew from biblical language, but—in my view at least—he was not a Christian in any meaningful sense of the word.

Leigh Eric Schmidt argues in his book *Restless Souls: The Making of American Spirituality* that the Transcendentalists were responsible for introducing the distinction between religion and spirituality, a prominent feature of religious life today. Thoreau eschewed religious institutions but was a deeply spiritual person. And this is one of the reasons why many people today find him so appealing. He may have been decried as a heretic and village atheist in his own time, but now he is revered as an avatar of an alternative way of being religious in the world.

Thoreau's god was in the woods, not in a church. "I feel that I draw nearest to understanding the great secret of my life in my closest intercourse with nature," he noted in his journal. "I suppose that what in other men is religion is in me love of nature."[8] His nature mysticism was coupled with an all-embracing religious cosmopolitanism. He sought and found wisdom in other religious traditions, including Hinduism, Confucianism, and Sufism. His interest in these traditions went beyond mere curiosity. He mined them for spiritual truths. And yet his religious views were uniquely his own; they were distinctive, not derivative.

To talk about Thoreau's religion is also difficult for the fact that the word "religion" is so often associated with creeds, rites, and institutions. These Thoreau had little use for. He was put off by the hypocrisy and absolutism of sectarian religion. "I do not prefer one religion or philosophy to another," he wrote in his journal. "I have no sympathy with the bigotry and ignorance which make transient and partial and puerile distinctions between one man's faith or form of faith and another's,—as Christian and heathen. I pray to be delivered from narrowness, partiality, exaggeration, bigotry. To the philosopher all sects, all nations, are alike. I like Brahma, Hari, Buddha, the Great Spirit, as well as God."[9]

For these reasons, I think it is more appropriate to speak of Thoreau's spirituality than his religion. The word "spirituality" has shortcomings too. Lacking the trappings of religion, spirituality seems vague and is given to different interpretations. His form of spirituality had primarily to do with transcendent experiences triggered by his encounters with the natural world: "to watch for, describe all the divine features which I detect in Nature," he wrote in his journal. "My profession is to be always on the alert to find God in nature—to know his lurking places, to attend all the oratorios, the operas, in nature." By transcendent, I do not mean supernatural or otherworldly but rather intuitive knowledge transcending sense experience. "If it is possible that we may be addressed, it behooves us to be attentive," he wrote. "If by watching all day and all night, I may detect some trace of the Ineffable, then will it not be worth the while to watch?"[10]

Given the large number of books written about Thoreau in recent years, one might wonder why I have written this one. Most of these books have been written by scholars for a scholarly audience. I am deeply appreciative of their efforts, and I have learned a great deal from their attention to important aspects of Thoreau's life and work. This book is intended to make the best scholarly insights accessible to the widest possible audience, while at the same time avoiding the superficiality of popular self-help books about Thoreau that shortchange the richness of his writing and the depth of his thought.

As in other books I have written on the Transcendentalists, what I seek to offer is not an interpretation or critique of his writings but an explanation of them. For the most part I am content to let Thoreau speak for himself and to take him at his word. While greatest attention will be given to his writings, it will be helpful to provide important biographical information, to set his ideas in their social and historical context, and to explore what he means by certain concepts. He loves wordplay, irony, and hyperbole, which may sometimes seem confusing or off-putting. These too will require some clarification. Where appropriate, I also draw attention to the contemporary relevance of his ideas.

In a letter written to a friend in Plymouth who was trying to arrange for one of his lectures there, Thoreau noted that some of his topics were profane or secular, implying that others were sacred in nature.[11] Nowhere does he indicate which of his writings were which, but it has seemed to me that, indeed, some deal with spiritual and moral issues more than others. In this book I have chosen to examine these to the exclusion of the others. In the case of his journal, which covers a wide variety of subjects, I have focused on entries most revealing of his views on spirituality and the art of life. It is what he calls the "Gospel according to this moment" that the majority of his readers find most compelling and which is my primary focus in this book. Thoreau is a terrific writer, offering insights on a great number of topics, but even more importantly, I believe, he is a spiritual guide to living a more flourishing and deliberate life.

My approach to Thoreau grows out of my experience as a minister and religious educator in two important ways. For many years I led classes and workshops for adults on the Transcendentalist writers, including Thoreau, Emerson, and Margaret Fuller. The participants were intelligent and discerning readers, drawn to these writers not only out of curiosity but also because they sensed these writers had something to teach them about the art of living. In addition to parsing their words, they wanted to understand how their message might have personal, even spiritual significance for them.

Second, I myself was drawn to these writers because, as a Unitarian minister, I was aware of their profound importance, theologically and historically, for the development of Unitarianism and liberal religion. Transcendentalism is a significant and continuing influence in Unitarian worship and church polity. The writings of the Transcendentalists, Emerson and Thoreau in particular, have informed my ministry, my writing, and my spiritual life. Historian David Robinson once observed that "Unitarians lament their vague religious identity, standing upon the richest theological legacy of any American denomination. Possessed of a deep and sustaining history of spiritual achievement and philosophical speculation, religious liberals have been, ironically, dispossessed of that heritage."[12] My mission has been to enliven this tradition for all religious seekers. In doing so, to paraphrase Emerson, I have sought to bring people not to Unitarianism but to themselves.

CHAPTER I

BECOMING HENRY DAVID THOREAU

D avid Henry Thoreau was born in Concord, Massachusetts, on July 12, 1817, to John and Cynthia Thoreau, the third of four children. He was the only one of the Transcendentalist circle, some of whom came to settle in Concord, who was actually born there. In search of a livelihood, the family moved to Chelmsford and then to Boston before returning to Concord after learning that Cynthia's brother Charles had stumbled upon a graphite deposit in New Hampshire. The discovery proved useful in the manufacture of pencils, which were marketed under the name John Thoreau & Co. Together with income from boarders living in the family home, the pencil business afforded the family a comfortable if modest lifestyle.[1]

A Religious Education

Thoreau's parents were members of the First Parish Church in Concord, where they owned a pew and regularly attended services. The Reverend Dr. Ezra Ripley ministered to the congregation during a remarkable tenure of sixty-three years. It was Ripley who christened and baptized their son David Henry.

Perhaps it is because Thoreau "signed off" from the rolls of the church in 1841 that little attention has been given to the extent to which Unitarianism shaped his thinking about religion. Barely a generation before his birth, liberal Christians—soon to be known as Unitarians for their disavowal of the doctrine of the Trinity—broke away from orthodox Calvinist churches of the Standing Order. They did so not only because of their denial of the

Trinity but also, and more importantly, for their estimate of human nature. The notions of total depravity, predestination, and election to salvation were articles of faith for the Calvinists. It was preordained whether humans were bound for heaven or hell; only the elect would be saved.

The liberal Christians were often referred to as Arminians after the Dutch theologian Jacobus Arminius, who believed that humans were capable of both sin and righteousness, and thus able to gain God's grace by living moral lives. In their view, Calvinism undercut the motivation to live a moral life since the outcome—whether one ended up in heaven or hell—was determined in advance.[2] As Arminian views gained favor, congregations in Massachusetts began calling liberal ministers to their pulpits, transforming their churches from orthodox to Unitarian almost overnight. In the end, even the church in Plymouth, Massachusetts, the first to be established in the New England colonies, became Unitarian.

Such was also the case in "Doctor Ripley's Church," as First Parish was commonly called. During his ministry in Concord, Ripley introduced liberal reforms, dropping strict tests of admission, ending public confessions of faith, and easing requirements for baptism. In reaction to such reforms, orthodox churches inserted creeds and confessions of faith into church covenants. The Arminians, Ripley among them, resisted this, deploring such creeds as unscriptural and insisting on the right of private judgment.[3]

It's hard to know the extent to which young David Henry was aware of these developments. Probably not very much. But an incident involving his mother must have made an impression on him. As previously noted, his parents were devoted members of First Parish Church. In 1826 a small group within the congregation, dissatisfied with Ripley's liberal preaching, broke away to establish an orthodox Trinitarian church in the town. Among them were three sisters-in-law of Thoreau's mother, Cynthia, who was implored to join them. Winning approval from First Church to do so, she was interviewed for admission to the orthodox congregation and pressed to affirm its covenant. Cynthia refused to compromise her beliefs. Despite the entreaties of her sisters-in-law, she could not swallow her reservations or go against her conscience. Dr. Ripley was delighted to welcome her back into the Unitarian fold, where she remained for the rest of her life.

Historian Robert A. Gross speculates on the impact this incident might have had on Cynthia's young son:

As a ten-year-old boy witnessing the religious struggles in the [Thoreau family] boardinghouse, he may well have drawn several conclusions. First, no one should ever sacrifice his conscience to the claims of others, whether family, friends, or fellow travelers in the world of reform. . . . The second lesson was to reject organized religion in all its denominational forms. In the pursuit of purity, Concord had become a battlefield of squabbling parsons and warring churches. Like many other observers, Thoreau was appalled by the vicious sectarianism.[4]

Thoreau entered Harvard College at the age of sixteen, which wasn't unusual at the time. While the curriculum included mathematics, science, rhetoric, and other secular subjects, the college was established in 1636 primarily to prepare young men for the ministry. When he enrolled in 1833, the school still served a religious purpose—that of instilling moral self-culture. By this time the school was solidly liberal, enlisting the ideas of the Scottish Enlightenment to establish moral philosophy as the basis of religion. As historian Daniel Walker Howe puts it, "Moral philosophy was, in a sense, the successor of theology." The emphasis on moral philosophy, Howe continues, "reflected a desire to supplement religious sanctions with natural bases for values."[5]

Another prominent feature of the curriculum was its reliance on the classics as a means of fostering moral development. Harvard moral philosophy, in keeping with the college's understanding of the Arminian view of human nature and its capacity for righteousness, held that humans possessed a moral sentiment or faculty that needed to be developed. The classical literature of ancient Greece and Rome seemed well suited to the purpose. While a student, Thoreau took courses in Latin and Greek, reading works by Horace, Sophocles, Cicero, Seneca, Virgil, Homer, and many other such writers.[6] He drew on this literature in composing his college essays and continued to do so throughout his career as a writer. His journals, books, and essays make countless references to classical literature. And as his spiritual horizons expanded, so did his references to classical literature from other religious and philosophical traditions.

Thoreau's religious education at Harvard was supplemented—and to a considerable degree undermined—by an encounter with Orestes Brownson, who was at the time a Unitarian minister in Canton, Massachusetts. Thoreau took advantage of Harvard's policy allowing students to take leave for a term in order to earn money to pay for college expenses. In 1836, during his junior year, he boarded with the Brownson family while he taught school in Canton. In addition to his teaching duties, he spent many hours with Brownson studying German language and literature and learning about "new views" of religion and philosophy coming to America from Europe and Britain.

Among such views were those of Victor Cousin and other French philosophers of what was called the Eclectic school. In his *Introduction to the History of Philosophy*, Cousin stated that truth is not the exclusive possession of any religion or philosophy but can be found in all of them. The comparative study of religions and philosophies reveals truths, such as the Golden Rule, that are commonly agreed upon. Moreover, individuals are able to perceive truth on their own, intuitively, by means of what the British poet and philosopher Samuel Taylor Coleridge called Reason, a claim that undercut the assertion of empiricists like John Locke that all knowledge comes to us through the senses from without.

During this time Brownson was writing his treatise *New Views of Christianity, Society, and the Church*, which drew on the ideas of Cousin and others in refuting the notion that faith could be sustained on empirical grounds. In Brownson's view, Locke's insistence that all knowledge comes from the senses leads to atheism: "Our senses take cognizance only of Matter; then we can know nothing but Matter. We can know nothing of the spirit or soul. . . . If nothing can be known but by means of our senses, God, then, inasmuch as we do not see him, hear him, taste him, smell him, touch him, cannot be known; then he does not exist for us. Hence Atheism."[7] The message was clear: if Unitarianism continued to be wedded to Locke's philosophy, it would be doomed to extinction.[8] As an indication of the significance of this encounter, Thoreau sent a letter of thanks to Brownson two years later in which he wrote that his days in Canton "were an era in my life—the morning of a new Lebenstag."[9]

For some time after his stay with Brownson, Thoreau continued to read Cousin and other writers on Brownson's countercultural reading list, including Coleridge, Thomas Carlyle, and Emerson, whose first book, *Nature*, had just been published. By the time he graduated from Harvard, Thoreau was well on his way to Transcendentalism. His senior year essays rehearsed themes he would enlarge upon in his subsequent writing. In a student paper on William Howitt's *Book of Seasons; or The Calendar of Nature*, written shortly after he returned to Harvard, he wrote: "No one, perhaps, possesses materials for happiness in such abundance, or has the resources of contentment and pure enjoyment so completely under his thumb, as the lover of Nature."[10] An essay written later in the year touched on the theme of self-culture: "The cultivation of the mind, then, is conducive to our happiness. But this cultivation consists in the cultivation of its several faculties. What we call the Imagination is one of these, hence does its culture, in a measure, conduce to the happiness of the individual."[11] Of all the means of promoting his own self-culture, none was more important than his cherished walks in nature. As he confessed in his Class Book autobiography written shortly before graduating: "Suffice it to say, that though bodily I have been a member of Harvard University, heart and soul I have been far away among the scenes of my boyhood. Those hours that should have been devoted to study, have been spent in scouring the woods and exploring the lakes and streams of my native village."[12]

As his graduation approached, Thoreau was assigned a topic to address in a commencement speech, "The commercial spirit of modern times, considered in its Influence on the Political, Moral, and Literary character of a Nation." Having two months to prepare, he returned home to Concord, where he participated in the dedication of the new Revolutionary War monument at the Old North Bridge. He also spent six weeks living in a cabin on Flint's Pond with his Harvard friend Charles Sterns Wheeler. Overshadowing this bucolic interlude was the Panic of 1837, up to that point the country's worst financial crisis. Banks and factories closed, property values collapsed, widespread unemployment ensued. The economy did not recover for the next ten years. The financial prospects were grim for the students of Thoreau's graduating class.

Facing an audience of hundreds, including the governor of Massachusetts, state legislators, the president and overseers of the college, as well as his classmates and their families, Thoreau observed that the commercial spirit reflected the busy-ness of the nation. "Man thinks faster and freer than ever before. He moreover moves faster and freer. He is more restless for the reason that he is more independent, than ever." Yet the influence of the commercial spirit on the moral character of the nation was unhealthy in that it infused all aspects of life with a degree of selfishness. Rather than merely pursuing the good things of this world, people should aspire "to lead a more intellectual and spiritual life." In a passage anticipating the message of *Walden*, Thoreau offered an alternative to the commercial spirit:

Let men, true to their natures, cultivate the moral affections, lead manly and independent lives; let them make riches the means and not the end of existence, and we shall hear no more of the commercial spirit. The sea will not stagnate, the earth will be as green as ever, and the air as pure. This curious world which we inhabit is more wonderful than it is useful—it is more to be admired and enjoyed then, than used. The order of things should be somewhat reversed,—the seventh should be man's day of toil, wherein to earn his living by the sweat of his brow, and the other six his sabbath of the affections and the soul, in which to range this widespread garden, and drink in the soft influences and sublime revelations of Nature.[13]

This would be the goal and pattern of his life in the years to come.

Thoreau's religious education did not cease with his graduation from Harvard. From here on out, however, it would be a lifelong self-guided pursuit, as we shall see. In summing up this phase of his religious education, it is important to note not only what he left behind but also what he took with him. Although he quit the Unitarian Church he'd grown up in, rejected the theology of orthodox Unitarianism, and criticized hypocritical ministers and their dull sermons, he retained much of what he had learned from his experience at First Parish Church and Harvard College. He took with him Unitarianism's insistence on the right of private judgment, its emphasis on the cultivation of the soul, its moral appeal to a higher law, its positive assessment of human nature, and its critical approach to the Bible.

A Transcendental Apprenticeship

During his senior year at Harvard, Thoreau read Ralph Waldo Emerson's book *Nature*, which he checked out of the library not once but twice. It's hard to say when the two first met. Emerson and his new wife, Lidian, moved to Concord in 1835, while Thoreau was still in college. But it was no doubt Emerson who encouraged Thoreau to keep a journal. In his first entry, dated October 22, 1837, he reported: "'What are you doing now?' [Emerson] asked, 'Do you keep a journal?'—So I make my first entry today."[14]

Emerson had begun to make a name for himself as a lecturer in the Boston area. Formerly a Unitarian minister serving Boston's Second Church, he resigned from the pulpit in 1832 following a spiritual crisis and the death of his first wife. After spending nine months traveling in Europe and Britain, he returned to Boston and offered several series of lectures on various topics. He published his first book, *Nature*, in 1836 and the following year was invited to deliver the annual Phi Beta Kappa address at Harvard. He was an integral member of what came to be called the Transcendental Club, a gathering of Unitarian ministers, friends, and former classmates at Harvard Divinity School who met from time to time to discuss "new views" in religion, philosophy, and literature coming to America from abroad.

Emerson was fourteen years Thoreau's senior and for several years served as a mentor to his young friend, inviting him to meetings of the Transcendental Club, offering him the use of his substantial library, and, on one significant occasion, giving him tickets to his lecture series in the winter of 1837–38. Emerson was impressed to learn that Thoreau had walked eighteen miles to Boston in the dead of winter to attend his first lecture and invited him to join Lidian and several family friends to hear him read the lectures at home after they had been delivered in Boston.[15]

The occasion was significant not only for the kind gesture on Emerson's part but also for the fact that the topic of the lecture series was self-culture. Although it sounds a bit quaint to the modern ear, the term "self-culture" was a familiar one in the nineteenth century. Access to learning beyond a few years of formal education was limited, especially for women. For many people, lectures offered an opportunity for personal development and professional advancement. The lyceum movement and working-class institutes, similar in some ways to TED talks today, were popular venues for continuing education. Such lectures served moral purposes as well as practical ones.

For the Unitarians, who broke with Calvinist churches over the issue of human agency, the formation of character was substituted for the doctrine of divine election. Self-culture was thus a means of moral development. William Ellery Channing, minister of the Federal Street Church in Boston, was a prominent spokesperson for the Unitarian point of view. In 1838 he delivered a lecture on self-culture to an audience of laborers and artisans at the Franklin Institute in Boston. As he expressed it, self-culture was "the care which every man owes to himself, to the unfolding and perfecting of his nature." All are capable of pursuing it and benefiting from it both spiritually and practically, he said, "not only because we can enter into and search ourselves. We have a still nobler power, that of acting on, determining and forming ourselves."[16]

While today we might associate culture with art museums and opera-going, it meant something different to Channing, Emerson, and other proponents

of the practice. Channing likened culture to the agrarian notion of cultivation. "To cultivate anything, be it a plant, an animal, a mind, is to make
grow," he said. "Growth, expansion, is the end. Nothing admits culture, but
that which has the principle of life, capable of being expanded. He, therefore,
who does what he can to unfold all his powers and capabilities, especially
his nobler ones, so to become a well-proportioned, vigorous, excellent, happy
being, practices self-culture."[17] It was not seen as an elitist activity; it was promoted as a benefit for everyone.

For Unitarians like Channing, steeped in the moral philosophy of Harvard
College, self-culture served an important purpose. Arminian theology, as we
have seen, held that human beings could gain divine grace through righteous
living. Central to Harvard moral philosophy was faculty psychology, a notion
borrowed from the Scottish Enlightenment which insisted that individuals
possessed innate faculties or sentiments that needed to be developed. The
moral sense or faculty was deemed the most important of these. In Channing's words, "It is a real principle in each of us, and it is the supreme power
within us, to be cultivated above all others."[18] Unitarian self-culture wedded
Arminian theology to faculty psychology, substituting the cultivation of
character for the experience of conversion.

Emerson and the Transcendentalists took the understanding of self-
culture further than Channing did. For Channing the goal of self-culture was
to cultivate a "likeness to God." As he described it in a sermon by that title,
"religious instruction should aim chiefly to turn men's aspirations and efforts
to that perfection of the soul, which constitutes it a bright image of God."[19]
Emerson also believed that the goal of self-culture was spiritual awakening
and personal transformation, but for him the practice had a much greater
range of application than it did for Channing.

Over the course of ten lectures, Emerson outlined a rationale and program
for his understanding of self-culture. "His own culture,—the unfolding of
his nature, is the chief end of man," Emerson declared in the first lecture. "A
divine impulse at the core of his being, impels him to this." He believed that
we live superficial lives, going about our daily routines as if asleep. "There is
very little life in a lifetime," he declared. "So much of our time is preparation,
so much is routine, and so much is retrospect that the real pith of each man's
genius seems to contract itself to a very few hours."[20]

Occasionally—perhaps only once or twice in a lifetime—we catch a vision
of a higher life to which we might aspire, which reveals our present condition

as trivial and superficial. Immediately, however, we are confronted with a paradox. On the one hand, such visions are spontaneous. "The mind that grows could not predict the times, the means, the mode of that spontaneity," Emerson observed. "God comes in by a private door into every individual: thoughts enter by passages which the individual never left open." Passive receptivity seems to be the key. And yet, on the other hand, these visions are so compelling, so potentially life-changing, that we wish to seek them out:

> We say, I will walk abroad and the truth will take form and clearness to me. We go forth but cannot find it. It seems as if we only needed the stillness and composed attitude of the library to seize the thought. But we come in and are still as far from it, as at first. Then in a moment and without observation the truth we sought appears. A certain wandering light comes to us and is the distinction, the principle we wanted. But the oracle comes to us because we had previously laid siege to the shrine.[21]

We wish not merely to seek them out but to make them continuous and live according to the wisdom gained from the experience. "Can we give permanence to the lightnings of thought which lick up in a moment these combustible mountains of sensation and custom, and reveal the moral order after which the earth is to be rebuilt anew?"[22] Self-culture was the means Emerson suggested for laying siege to the shrine. He recommended several spiritual exercises designed to put us into a receptive frame of mind.

The first of these spiritual exercises was to cultivate an awareness of the miraculous in the common. We are infinitely related to all that is, Emerson insisted. Everywhere objects solicit our senses and yield new meanings. "There is no trifle in nature," he said. "Our culture comes not alone from the grand and beautiful but also from the trivial and sordid." Even the smallest thing can symbolize the spirit that animates and pervades the universe. Next, he recommended periods of silence and solitude:

> The simple habit of sitting alone occasionally to explore what facts of moment lie in the memory may have the effect in some more favored hour to open to the student the kingdom of spiritual nature. He may become aware that there around him roll new at this moment and inexhaustible the waters of Life; that the world he has lived in so heedless, so gross, is illumined with meaning, that every fact is magical; every atom alive, and he is the heir of it all.[23]

He also encouraged the discipline of keeping a journal. "Pay so much honor to the visits of Truth to your mind as to record those thoughts that have shone therein." he advised. "It is not for what is recorded . . . , but for the habit of rendering account to yourself of yourself in some more rigorous manner and at more certain intervals than mere conversation or casual reverie of solitude require." Nature also plays an important role in Emerson's spiritual regimen. "We need Nature," he argued, "and cities give the human senses not room enough. The habit of feeding the senses daily and nightly with the open air and firmament, presently becomes so strong that we feel want of it like water for washing."[24]

Conversation is yet another important exercise: "In able conversation we have glimpses of the universe, perceptions of immense power native to the soul, fardarting lights and shadows of a mountain landscape, such as we cannot at all attain unto in our solitary studies."[25] We are stimulated and enriched by joining in conversation with others on high topics. Finally, Emerson recommended walks in nature and reading as vital practices for cultivating the soul.

It is difficult to know how much of an impression these lectures made on Thoreau at the time. He doesn't mention them in his journal. But as Robert D. Richardson tells us, "Self-culture became a major concern, perhaps the major concern of his life, and increasingly he tried to reach behind the metaphor of cultivation to the reality."[26] Meanwhile, there were more pressing issues at hand. Most importantly, he needed to find a job. Shortly after his graduation he was offered a position as teacher in Concord's grammar school. This was a stroke of good fortune, considering the recent collapse of the economy. But shortly into his tenure he was directed by a member of the school committee to flog his students for disobedience. This he refused to do and resigned the post. After unsuccessful attempts to find similar work elsewhere, he joined his father in the family pencil business. He put his mind to improving the quality of pencils currently being manufactured. He soon introduced innovations in both the composition of lead and the assembly of the pencils, making Thoreau pencils the best on the market.

He was not done with teaching, however, and in 1838 partnered with his brother John to take over the Concord Academy. The two Thoreau brothers introduced numerous innovations in teaching methods and a curriculum based on the notion of self-culture. According to this notion, education was the unfolding of one's inward spiritual nature. The teacher's role was to draw this out. The school was soon enrolled to capacity. Henry—he had recently insisted on switching his given and middle names—taught Latin and Greek, mathematics, and natural philosophy. His older brother taught classes in English studies.

They dispensed with the common practice of rote memorization, recitation, and drills. No student was ever flogged or physically disciplined, although the teachers were strict in their demands. Some of the teaching was done out of doors—learning botany on field trips to Walden Pond, mathematics by surveying land, regional history by studying the remnants of Native American settlements, and so on. Students were required to write compositions every week, drawing on their own experience. By all accounts the school was a great success.

Even so, Henry fretted over his lack of accomplishments, itching to get on with his life. In an early draft of a poem published later as "The Poet's Delay," he wrote:

> Two years and twenty now have flown;
> Their meanness time away has flung;
> These limbs to man's estate have grown,
> But cannot claim a manly tongue.
>
> Amidst such boundless wealth without
> I only still am poor within;
> The birds have sung their summer out,
> But still my spring does not begin.[27]

At the same time, he was getting to know more people in Emerson's circle of friends and fellow intellectuals, including Bronson Alcott and Margaret Fuller. He and his brother enjoyed floating on the Concord River in a boat they had built. In 1839, both brothers fell for young Ellen Sewall, the daughter of a Unitarian minister in another town, on a visit to Concord. Both courted her, and John even proposed. It is said that she would have preferred Henry, but the matter was moot since her father refused to let her marry either of them. Henry never had a serious love interest after this. Their rivalry over winning the affection of Ellen Sewall did not prevent the brothers from taking a two-week boat trip together later that summer down the Concord River, up the Merrimack River to the White Mountains in New Hampshire, and then back again. This excursion, as Henry would call it, was the subject of his first book, *A Week on the Concord and Merrimack Rivers*, published ten years later.

The brothers resumed teaching in the fall, but soon thereafter John's health was weakened by a bout of tuberculosis. Henry tried to carry on without his invalid brother but could not bear the burden. He closed the school in April 1841. At loose ends, he cast about for alternatives to teaching, going so far as to purchase an old farm. After the farmer backed out of the deal, Emerson invited Thoreau to join his household. He became a live-in gardener and handyman and tutor to the Emerson children. Best of all, he had access to Emerson's library with its treasures of ancient wisdom and modern knowledge.

With his protégé now living under his roof, Emerson encouraged Thoreau's literary efforts. *The Dial* magazine, edited at first by Margaret Fuller and later by Emerson, was published as a vehicle for sharing Transcendentalist ideas with a wider audience. Although Thoreau and Fuller became friends, he was stung by her rejection of his poetry for publication in the magazine. Nevertheless, he continued to hone his craft as a writer, getting her approval to publish an essay on the Roman satirist Aulus Persius Flaccus, which appeared in the July 1840 issue. After the first two years, Emerson succeeded Fuller as editor of the magazine and looked more favorably on Thoreau's submissions, publishing twenty-three of his young friend's poems and essays. Emerson initiated "Ethnical Scriptures," a feature that he and Thoreau worked on together.

Thoreau's first real break as a writer came with Emerson's invitation to review for *The Dial* several reports on plants and animals commissioned by the state legislature. The resulting essay, "Natural History of Massachusetts," which appeared in the July 1842 issue, is the first example of his nature writing. In it he sounds notes of a refrain that would become increasingly familiar to readers of his subsequent work. In addition to detailed descriptions of flora and fauna, there are paeans in praise of the beauties and benefits of nature:

> In society you will not find health, but in nature. Unless our feet at least stood in the midst of nature, all our faces would be pale and livid. Society is always diseased, and the best is the most so. There is no scent in it more wholesome as that of the pines, nor any fragrance so penetrating and restorative as the life-everlasting in high pastures. I would keep some book of natural history always by me as a sort of elixir, the reading of which should restore the tone of the system. To the sick, indeed, nature is sick, but to the well, a fountain of health. To him who contemplates a trait of natural beauty no harm nor disappointment can come. The doctrines of despair, of spiritual or political tyranny or servitude, were never taught by such as shared the serenity of nature.[28]

He is cheered by the sights and sounds and superabundance of nature. "The spruce, the hemlock, and the pine will not countenance despair," he writes. Only those "of sick and diseased imaginations" would fail to recognize that "joy is the condition of life." Walks in nature give us "a sense of greater space and freedom" and show us that the universe is not piecemeal and haphazard but whole and complete. Nature "has no interstices; every part is full of life," he tells us.[29]

Robert Richardson calls our attention to the line "Surely joy is the condition of life," noting that this essay was written within six months of his brother's death in January 1842. The tragic event affected Henry deeply, leaving a gap of five weeks in his journal. Richardson believes Emerson tossed Thoreau a lifeline when he asked him to review these reports for *The Dial*. He comments, "To understand the deep trouble out of which, and against which, this piece was written, ask yourself why this sentence needs the word *surely*."[30] In one sense, the word underscores the rest of the sentence, confirming that, yes, "joy is the condition of life." Yet in another sense, it seems to be asking for reassurance that this is indeed the case. Writing this essay was an important step in his self-recovery, moving from a condition of despair to one of acceptance and joy.

Turning to the substance of the state's reports on fishes, birds, mammals, insects, and vegetation, Thoreau describes in considerable detail the life of birds through the cycle of the seasons. Next he turns to a description of the variety of quadrupeds, lamenting the disappearance of bears, wolves, lynxes, and other animals. He then gives us descriptions of fishes, tortoises, and snakes. He is amazed by the sheer exuberance of life in the woods, fields, ponds, and rivers. "Nature is mythical and mystical always," he asserts, "and works with the license and extravagance of genius."[31]

Thoreau notes that the volumes provide measurements and considerable detail but fail to capture the vitality of the natural world. In a sentence that encapsulates his approach to science he says, "Let us not underestimate the value of a fact; it will one day flower into a truth." For him, facts were not merely symbols, as they were for Emerson; they were "traces of the Ineffable," leading the patient observer to spiritual truths. The true scientist is one who seeks a rapport with the object under examination and not mere empirical knowledge of it. "We do not learn by inference and deduction, and the application of mathematics to philosophy, but by direct intercourse and sympathy. It is with science as with ethics, we cannot know truth by contrivance and method."[32]

In another important contribution to *The Dial*, Thoreau selected quotations from "The Laws of Menu," the "Sayings of Confucius," the "Chinese Four Books," "Hermes Trismegistus," and the "Gulistan of Saadi" for the ongoing "Ethnical Scriptures" column. No doubt it was Emerson who introduced him to the literature of Asian religion and philosophy. Thoreau first mentions these ancient traditions in his journal in 1838. Once he joined the Emerson household in 1841, it is fair to say that he devoured his mentor's considerable collection of books on these subjects. After reading Emerson's copy of *Institutes of Hindu Law*, he wrote in his journal, "When my imagination travels eastward and backward to those remote years of the gods, I seem to draw near to the habitation of the morning, and the dawn at length has a place. I remember the book as an hour before sunrise."[33]

Thoreau was an inveterate walker, by his own account spending a good part of each day hiking in the woods, hills, and fields surrounding his native village. His favorite word for this activity was sauntering. Occasionally he went on longer hikes, often accompanied by a friend for companionship. These he referred to as excursions. Writings about journeys, whether by foot, coach, or boat, were a popular literary genre. Typically, descriptions of the countryside were interspersed with philosophical reflections or information gleaned from various sources. Johann Wolfgang von Goethe's book *Italian Journey* was a model for this type of writing and one with which Thoreau was quite familiar.

His first work of this kind was an essay, "A Walk to Wachusett," describing a journey taken with a friend in July 1843 to Mount Wachusett, thirty miles to the west of Concord. Although in one sense it is a prosaic account of a three-day journey by foot, passing through villages and the countryside, culminating in the ascent of the mountain and then back again, it is in another sense a mythic journey through space and time in search of transcendence and renewal.

Thoreau introduces these themes in the first paragraph of the essay, invoking the epic poets Homer and Virgil and the legendary mountains of Greece and Italy. The two travelers are drawn to the blue wall of mountains on the horizon, traversing the streams and valleys in between, sharing passages from the ancient poets as they go along. Wild raspberries plucked and eaten remind them of "ambrosial fruits" that grow at higher elevations and "the springs that gush out from the mountain sides," leading them to conclude that "the gross products of the plains and valleys are for such as dwell therein," whereas pristine "juices of this berry had relation to the thin air of the mountaintops."[34]

Although Mount Wachusett is modest by comparison with the fabled mountains of Greece and the Lake District of England, the summit offers "an immense landscape to ponder on a summer's day. We could see how ample and roomy is nature." Civilization creeps along the sides of mountains, Thoreau observes, but the heights offer "a barrier to prejudice and fanaticism." In the thin atmosphere of the mountains, "the follies of the plain are refined and purified."[35]

Descending to the plain below, they were sustained for a time "by the more ethereal hues, which the mountain assumed." Eventually their thoughts became as dusty as the roads they plodded along, until at length they "proceeded only passively in a sort of rhythmical cadence of the confused material of thought." The traveler, "though weary and travel-worn," takes consolation from the experience of beholding the heavens and the horizon from the mountain's summit. In retrospect, Thoreau concludes:

> And now that we have returned to the desultory life of the plain, let us endeavor to import a little of that mountain grandeur into it. We will remember within what walls we lie, and understand that this level life too has its summit, and why from the mountain top the deepest valleys have a tinge of blue; that there is elevation in every hour, as not part of the earth is so low that the heavens may not be seen from it, and we have only to stand on the summit of our hour to command an uninterrupted horizon.[36]

Since 1842 Thoreau had been making notes on the writings of Thomas Carlyle for an essay he intended to write. As previously mentioned, he had been introduced to the Scottish essayist while a student at Harvard. Thoreau liked the directness and vigor of Carlyle's writing. This contrasted with the more mannered diction he was schooled in at Harvard and which characterized his early essays. He also admired the distinctive persona that Carlyle adopted as a writer, especially his penchant for exaggeration.[37] "He who cannot exaggerate is not qualified to utter truth. No truth we think was ever expressed but with this sort of emphasis, so that for the time there seemed to be no other," Thoreau writes. "Moreover, you must speak loud to the hard of hearing, and so you acquire a habit of shouting to those who are not."[38]

Carlyle, along with Coleridge, was an important influence in the development of Transcendentalism in America. Both writers helped to make the philosophy of Immanuel Kant intelligible for English-speaking readers. And both decried the influence of empiricism and materialism on contemporary thought and life. For his part, Carlyle first attracted the attention of Emerson and his like-minded friends through a series of articles in the *Edinburgh Review*.

In one of these, "Signs of the Times," which appeared in 1829, Carlyle declared this to be the Mechanical Age. "It is the Age of Machinery, in every outward and inward sense of that word; the age which, with its whole undivided might, forwards, teaches and practises the great art of adapting means to ends." Its influence is felt everywhere. "Not the external and physical alone is now managed by machinery, but the internal and spiritual also." Owing to the insidious philosophy of John Locke, "what cannot be investigated and understood mechanically, cannot be investigated and understood at all." The implications for faith are especially devastating: "The truth is, men have lost their belief in the Invisible, and believe, and hope, and work only in the Visible; or, to speak it in other words: This is not a Religious age. Only the material, the immediately practical, not the divine and spiritual, is important to us. The infinite, absolute character of Virtue has passed into a finite, conditional one; it is no longer a worship of the Beautiful and Good; but a calculation of the Profitable."[39] This refrain, in an American idiom, was also sounded by the New England Transcendentalists, Emerson and Thoreau especially. Like Carlyle, they argued that instrumental values had replaced intrinsic ones, to the detriment of religion and morality.

Thoreau speaks approvingly of Carlyle's *Sartor Resartus* in his essay. The title is Latin, meaning "the tailor re-tailored." He admired the practical philosophy of the book's central character, Professor Diogenes Teufelsdrockh, who has written a treatise on the theory of clothes. The book is essentially a satire focusing on the mutability of truth through the metaphor of changing fashions; hence the title. Similar to *Pilgrim's Progress*, it tells the story of the professor's progression from the Everlasting No to the Everlasting Yea, or from skepticism to belief. Clearly, the comments on clothing in *Walden* owe something to the influence of *Sartor Resartus*.

Especially important were two additional notions adopted from the book. The first is the need for what Carlyle calls a new "mythus." As the professor observes: "The Mythus of the Christian Religion looks not in the eighteenth century as it did in the eighth. . . . But what next? Wilt thou help us to embody the divine Spirit of that Religion in a new Mythus, in a new vehicle and vesture, that our Souls, otherwise too like perishing, may live?" The second notion, related to the first, is that of Natural Supernaturalism. As the professor explains:

> We speak of the Volume of Nature: and truly a Volume it is,—whose Author and Writer is God. To read it! Dost thou, does man, so much as well know the Alphabet thereof? With its Words, Sentences, and grand descriptive Pages, poetical and philosophical, spread out through Solar Systems, and Thousands of Years, we shall not try thee. It is a volume written in celestial hieroglyphs, in the true Sacred-writing; of which even Prophets are happy that they can read here a line and there a line.[40]

For Unitarians such as Emerson and Thoreau, the notion of Natural Supernaturalism had special meaning. The Unitarians of Thoreau's day held to a doctrine called Supernatural Rationalism which distinguished between Natural Religion and Revealed Religion. Natural Religion entailed all that could be known from the study of nature and the use of reason concerning the existence of God. The Unitarians argued, however, that Natural Religion needed to be reinforced and supplemented by Revealed Religion, that is, by the Christian revelation contained in the Bible, shown to be of divine origin by virtue of the divinity of Christ.[41]

Emerson and Thoreau understood Carlyle's Natural Supernaturalism to mean that nature alone was sufficient to ground faith and morals. The new mythus, in their view, was nature religion as conceived by the Transcendentalists. Typical of Thoreau's position is this 1842 journal entry: "I feel that I draw nearest to understanding the great secret of my life in my closest intercourse with nature. There is a reality and health in nature which is not to be found in any religion. . . . I suppose that what in men is religion is in me love of nature."[42] Thoreau's first book, *A Week on the Concord and Merrimack Rivers*, gives voice to Carlyle's call for a new mythology.

Thoreau continued to struggle in making a name for himself as a writer. His essays caught the attention of Nathaniel Hawthorne, who remarked of "Natural History of Massachusetts": "Methinks this article gives a very fair image of his mind and character,—so true, innate, and literal in observation, yet giving the spirit as well as the letter of what he sees, even as a lake reflects its wooded banks, showing every leaf, yet giving the wild beauty of the whole scene."[43] Horace Greeley, editor of the *New York Daily Tribune*, also took note, offering his help in getting Thoreau's articles published.[44] Thoreau even accepted a position tutoring the children of Emerson's brother William on Staten Island, with the ulterior purpose of making contact with New York publishers. This plan came to naught and, feeling homesick, he returned to Concord.

Despite his difficulties, it is clear that by this time he had become a confirmed Transcendentalist. In a journal entry dated June 7, 1851, he wrote, "I begin to be transcendental and show where my heart is."[45] But as early as July 1838 he was making entries that demonstrated a Transcendentalist proclivity even if they did not mention the word itself:

> If with closed ears and eyes I consult consciousness for a moment, immediately are all walls and barriers dissipated, earth rolls from under me, and I float, by the impetus derived from the earth and the system, a subjective, heavily laden thought, in the midst of an unknown and infinite sea, or else heave and swell like a vast ocean of thought without rock or headland, where are all riddles solved, all straight lines making their two ends to meet, eternity and space gamboling familiarly through my depths. I am from the beginning, knowing no end, no aim. No sun illumines me, for I dissolve all lesser lights in my own intense and steadier light. I am a restful kernel in the magazine of the universe.[46]

CHAPTER 2

THE ART OF LIFE

⌣

Prior to the Walden years, Emerson's tutelage was the most significant factor in Thoreau's development both as a Transcendentalist and as a writer. Robert Sattelmeyer, in his study of Thoreau's reading, writes, "Chiefly under Emerson's guidance he had read selections from the idealistic tradition of ancient philosophy, Oriental scriptures, modern eclectic philosophy, Anglicized articulations of German Transcendental thought, and contemporary essayists like Carlyle and Emerson himself." As we have seen, Thoreau had begun to read some of this literature on his own and through his acquaintance with Orestes Brownson. "Nevertheless," Sattelmeyer writes, "Emerson's own habits of voluminous and eclectic reading, his impressive library, and his kindness in sharing his books and his thoughts with Thoreau made a powerful impression on the younger man's training and cast of mind."[1]

Emerson was also Thoreau's instructor in the practice of self-culture. As mentioned previously, Thoreau was invited to attend Emerson's lectures on human culture, which were given in Boston in the winter of 1837–38 and then repeated at the Emerson home, where Thoreau heard them. He had already been exposed to the notion of self-culture through his Unitarian upbringing and his education in the Greek and Roman classics and Scottish common sense philosophy at Harvard. But it was Emerson who introduced Thoreau to the spiritual writings of India, China, and the Middle East, which contributed significantly to his ongoing self-culture. Emerson first delved into Hindu writings in preparation for a Harvard senior class poem, "Indian Superstition," delivered in 1821. His opinion of Indian spirituality steadily rose as he read an increasing number of classical texts newly translated by British and European scholars. Soon thereafter, he was also drawn to writings of the Confucian tradition in China and the Sufi poetry of Persia. By the time Thoreau came under Emerson's roof, his mentor had one of the largest private collections of this literature in the country.

Aside from satisfying his curiosity, what drew Thoreau to this literature? And what did he learn from it? There are several reasons why these writings appealed to him. For one thing, the spiritual traditions of India and China seemed ancient, more so for India than China. But in either case, it was wisdom handed down from an earlier time, closer to the origins of philosophy and religion, and therefore more authentic in a way. Taken together with the philosophies of classical Greece and Rome, these works embodied wisdom that was both perennial and universal. They also aligned closely with the notions of self-culture and virtue ethics associated with his Unitarian background and Harvard education.

Typically, the spiritual traditions he was drawn to exhibited both a metaphysics and a praxis, that is, a diagnosis of the human condition and a prescription for improving it. It was not just for the wisdom they embodied but also for their practical application in everyday living that he found them valuable. As Caleb Smith explains: "Thoreau took an interest in the tradition of spiritual exercises, developed over many centuries by mystics and philosophers. Spiritual exercises are practices designed to detach people's minds from the passions and dramas of everyday social life so they can focus on higher, more enduring realities."[2] These were not the hair-shirted austerities he describes in *Walden* but rather exercises intended to enhance his awareness of the world and make him feel more alive.

Philosophy as a Way of Life

As mentioned in the preceding chapter, a distinctive feature of *The Dial* magazine, beginning in 1843, was an ongoing column under the heading "Ethnical Scriptures," featuring quotations taken from various philosophical and religious traditions. Choices for several of these selections were assigned to Thoreau, including "The Laws of Menu," "Sayings of Confucius," and the "Chinese Four Books."

The Institutes of Hindu Law, or what he calls "The Laws of Menu," was one of the first Hindu texts Thoreau read. That it made a deep impression is shown in several journal entries, including one dated May 31, 1841: "They are the laws of you and me, a fragrance wafted down from those old times, and no more to be refuted than the wind."[3] Thoreau tells us that Menu (today known as Manu) was the son or grandson of the Hindu god Brahma and the first human. Brahma is said to have taught his laws to Menu, who was instructed to convey them to primitive humanity. Succeeding chapters focus on the duties and proper conduct of those in various stages of life, punishments for a variety of offenses, and customs regarding inheritance, property, and divorce. The selections he chose dealt primarily with the education and training of the Brahmin priesthood. Brahmins are told how to eat their food, how to conduct sacrifices, how to treat their bodies, and whom to marry. They are enjoined from receiving gifts and honors. And they are advised to abandon all earthly attachments, to withdraw from the world, to seek solitude, and to practice meditation.[4]

His next selection of "Ethnical Scriptures" was taken from the Analects of Confucius, translated by Joshua Marshman in 1836, and from *The Phenix: a Collection of Old and Rare Fragments*, published in 1835. These selections depict the proper conduct of would-be followers of Confucius. Some of them, like those taken from *The Laws of Menu*, prescribe certain types of behavior. Others offer ethical advice more generally, as in this example: "Chee [Confucius] says, if in the morning I hear about the right way, and in the evening die, I can be happy."[5]

Another group of selections was taken from the Four Books of Confucian literature: the Analects of Confucius, the Great Learning, the Doctrine of the Mean, and the book of Mencius. The last three of these are revisions of the original canon of Confucian literature, reflecting the teachings of the neo-Confucian tradition that arose some 1,300 years later. These selections have primarily to do with the cultivation of virtue. Some of the advice given is in the form of parables. Other selections deal with rules for proper conduct. All of them relate to the notion of the superior man, by which is meant a person exhibiting moral excellence, as in this example: "The superior man's nature consists in this, that benevolence, justice, propriety, and wisdom, have their root in his heart, and are exhibited in his countenance."[6]

The fourth group of selections are taken from Hermes Trismegistus and the *Gulistan* of Saadi, a collection of writings by one of the greatest of Persian (Sufi) poets. The writings of Hermes Trismegistus, Thoreau tells us, were "written, or at least interpolated, by the new Platonists in the third or fourth century of our era." His selections from Saadi consist of brief moral tales such as this one: "Saadi was troubled when his feet were bare, and he had not wherewithal to buy shoes; but soon after meeting a man without feet, I was thankful for the bounty of Providence to me, and submitted cheerfully to the want of shoes."[7]

Why did he choose these particular extracts? To understand the meaning of these four groups of selections and why Thoreau chose them, we need to view them in the context of what he says about philosophers in the opening chapter of *Walden*. "There are nowadays professors of philosophy, but not philosophers," he writes. "To be a philosopher is not merely to have subtle thoughts, nor even to found a school, but so to love wisdom as to live according to its dictates, a life of simplicity, independence, magnanimity, and trust. It is to solve some of the problems of life, not only theoretically, but practically." He likens professors of philosophy to courtiers "who make shift to live merely by conformity." The true philosopher "is not fed, sheltered, clothed, warmed, like his contemporaries," but maintains "his vital heat by better methods than other men."[8] The "better methods" he alludes to amount to a spiritual practice that he developed and described—under the rubric of self-culture—not only in *Walden* but throughout his essays, journal, and letters as well.

Thoreau views "the ancient philosophers, Chinese, Hindoo, Persian, and Greek," as proponents of philosophy as a way of life. The selections chosen for the "Ethnical Scriptures" offer examples of what may be termed self-cultivation philosophies. In an essay on these philosophies, Christopher W. Gowans offers us an interpretive framework. He summarizes his topic as follows:

> Self-cultivation philosophies propound a program of development for improving the lives of human beings. On the basis of an account of human nature and the place of human beings in the world, they maintain that our lives can and should be substantially transformed from what is judged to be the problematic, untutored condition of human beings into what is put forward as an ideal state of being. As such, self-cultivation philosophies are preeminently practical in their orientation: their primary purpose is to change our lives in fundamental ways.[9]

According to Gowans, these philosophies share two general characteristics. First of all, they promote a cultivation of the self that is radically different from ordinary conceptions of the self. Second, such philosophies have a practical orientation in teaching their followers how to live a good life. More specifically, he identifies a fourfold pattern typical of these philosophies. They begin with a baseline understanding of human nature. They conclude that the existential condition of human beings is problematic. They posit an ideal state of being—often the opposite of our present unsatisfactory condition—that we should aspire to attain. And finally, they prescribe a spiritual regimen designed to achieve a transformation of the self.

We can see this pattern in the writings of the Stoic and Epicurean philosophers of ancient Greece and Rome. One of the foremost authorities on these philosophies is Pierre Hadot, author of *Philosophy as a Way of Life*. He stresses the point that in antiquity, to be a philosopher meant living a philosophical life rather than engaging in abstract theoretical discourse. The philosophical life was achieved by means of spiritual exercises. According to Hadot: "In all philosophical schools, the goal pursued in these exercises is self-realization and improvement. All schools agree that man, before his philosophical conversion, is in a state of unhappy disquiet. Consumed by worries, torn by passions, he does not live a genuine life, nor is he truly himself. All schools also agree that man can be delivered from this state."[10] Philosophy is an art of living that alleviates suffering by teaching a radically new way of life.

The central tenet of Epicureanism is the enjoyment of life in the here and now. "Pleasure," said Epicurus, "is the beginning and end of a blessed life."[11] By pleasure he did not mean wanton self-indulgence but rather a serenity of spirit that comes from plain living and high thinking. One maximizes pleasure by minimizing wants and by engaging in certain kinds of spiritual disciplines. One of these was the exercise of leisure, not in the form of idleness but in the pursuit of friendship and the practice of the arts. Other disciplines included conversation, reading, proper diet and exercise, and the contemplation of nature. Moreover, the Epicureans sought to transcend the ego by cultivating a cosmic consciousness, as suggested by Lucretius in *The Way Things Are* (*De Rerum Natura*):

> Look up at the pure bright color of the sky,
> The wheeling stars, the moon, the shining sun!
> If all these, all of a sudden, should arise
> For the first time before our mortal sight,
> What could be called more wonderful, more beyond
> The heights to which aspiring mind might dare?[12]

The Stoics sought happiness through harmony with nature. In the words of Seneca, "Not to stray from Nature and to mould ourselves according to her law and pattern—this is true wisdom."[13] Happiness was defined as tranquility, or the well-being of the soul, and was achieved by means of spiritual exercises. These included leisure, solitude, contemplation, simplicity, walks in nature, companionship, and the practice of philosophy—accompanied, Seneca adds, by drinking copious amounts of good wine![14] If the Epicureans sought to transcend the ego by imagining the immensity of space, the Stoics sought the same by experiencing the timelessness of the present moment. Marcus Aurelius writes, "Remember also that each of us lives only in the fleeting present moment, and that all the rest of our lives has already been lived or is undisclosed."[15]

In September 1851, Thoreau made this entry in his journal:

> The *Art of life*! Was there anything memorable written upon it? By what disciplines to secure the most life, with what care to watch our thoughts. To observe not what transpires in the street, but in the mind and heart of me! I do not remember any page which will tell me how to spend this afternoon. I do not so much wish to know how to economize time, as how to spend it, by what means to grow rich, that the day may not have been in vain.[16]

If he hadn't yet found anything memorable written on the art of life, it wasn't for lack of trying. As noted, his earliest education was in the classical literature of Greece and Rome. His classical education had commenced with his studies at the Concord Academy, under the tutelage of Phineas Allen, who schooled him in the Greek and Latin languages. He continued these studies at Harvard College and for a number of years after he graduated.

It's hard to say how well acquainted Thoreau was with the writings of the Epicureans and the Stoics, but he does mention Zeno, the founder of Stoicism, in his journal in 1838:

> Zeno, the Stoic, stood in precisely the same relation to the world that I do now. He is, forsooth, bred a merchant—as how many still!—and can trade and barter, and perchance higgle, and moreover he can be shipwrecked and cast ashore at Piraeus, like one of your Johns or Thomases.
> He strolls into a shop and is charmed by a book by Xenophon—and straightaway he becomes a philosopher. The sun of a new life's day rises to him,—serene, unclouded,—which looks over *stoa* [Greek for portico, from which Stoicism took its name]. And still the fleshly Zeno sails on, shipwrecked, buffeted, tempest-tossed; but the true Zeno sails ever a placid sea. Play high, play low,—rain, sleet, or snow,—it's all the same with the Stoic.[17]

In this passage he has captured the gist of Stoicism and likens Zeno's condition to his own and that of his contemporaries. Zeno reads a book by Xenophon, a student of Socrates, and is converted to a life of philosophy, giving serenity to his storm-tossed life. It's easy to imagine Thoreau seeking the same outcome for himself.

While a student at Harvard he read works by the Stoics, Seneca and Cicero, and the writings of Horace and Plutarch, who espoused similar views. He also read a number of anthologies of classical literature in which he would have encountered Stoic and Epicurean philosophers. Even if his knowledge of these schools of philosophy was limited, it is clear that Thoreau shared a similar outlook on life. For instance, in the "Economy" chapter of *Walden* he describes our habitual existence as one of ceaseless toil, burdened by debt and the pressures of conformity. "The mass of men lead lives of quiet desperation," he insists.[18] They have no time for leisure, necessary for peace of mind and the cultivation of the soul. The remedy he prescribes for this dis-ease combines elements of both Epicureanism and Stoicism. Like the Epicureans, he advocates simple living. When we have secured the necessities of life—food, shelter, clothing, and warmth—"there is another alternative than to obtain the superfluities," he writes, "and that is to adventure on life now, [our] vacation from humbler toil having commenced."[19] And, like the Stoics, he seeks serenity through harmony with nature, as described in a passage from the chapter "Solitude": "This is a delicious evening, when the whole body is one sense, and imbibes delight through every pore. I go and come with a strange liberty in Nature, a part of herself."[20]

The spiritual exercises Thoreau engages in are also in accord with those of the Stoics and Epicureans: reading, solitude, contemplation, proper diet, journal-keeping, walks in nature, and the pursuit of leisure. Such practices are intended to achieve awareness, transcend the ego, and transform the self. "We must learn to reawaken and keep ourselves awake, not by mechanical aids," he writes, "but by an infinite expectation of the dawn, which does not forsake us in our soundest sleep. I know of no more encouraging fact than the unquestionable ability of man to elevate his life by a conscious endeavor."[21] Finally, he describes transcendence in terms of both cosmic consciousness and the eternity of the present moment, sometimes in the same passage, as in this example:

> Time is but the stream I go a-fishing in. I drink at it; but while I drink I see the sandy bottom and detect how shallow it is. Its thin current slides away, but eternity remains. I would drink deeper; fish in the sky, whose bottom is pebbly with stars. I cannot count one. I know not the first letter of the alphabet. I have always been regretting that I was not as wise as the day I was born.[22]

In a perceptive paper, "There Are Nowadays Professors of Philosophy, but Not Philosophers," Hadot finds that Thoreau's account of his life in the woods "bears a remarkable analogy to Epicurean philosophy, but also to certain aspects of Stoicism."[23] He says Thoreau may not have been conscious of the fact that there were elements of Stoic and Epicurean philosophies in his writings, but he thinks "that he found, perhaps spontaneously and unintentionally, perhaps under the influence of certain writings of the Ancients or of the Moderns," what adepts of these philosophical schools had practiced and taught. "One could say that in the same way that there exists a sort of universal Stoicism, there also exists a sort of universal Epicureanism, that is to say an attitude always possible for, and always open to, man, and that consists, through a certain discipline and reduction of desires, in returning pleasures mixed with sorrow and pain, to the simple and pure pleasure of existing."[24]

As a historian of philosophy, Hadot focuses on the ancient philosophies of Greece and Rome, but his remarks on Thoreau suggest that his understanding of philosophy as a way of life has much broader application and relevance, even today. For the ancients, *philosophia* meant the love of wisdom, not in the abstract, but in relation to the art of living. As Hadot explains it, the wisdom they sought "was a way of life which brought peace of mind (ataraxia), inner freedom (autarkia), and a cosmic consciousness." As we have seen, these philosophies and others like them were therapeutic in nature, intended to relieve fear, anxiety, and stress. They also offered a means or method for achieving spiritual freedom and self-reliance. And finally, they issued in an awareness of one's self as an integral part of the cosmos. "At each instant," Hadot says, "the ancient sage was conscious of living in the cosmos, and he placed himself in harmony with the cosmos."[25]

Thoreau was perceptive in distinguishing between discourse about philosophy and philosophy itself. There were aspects of theory to these ancient philosophies, but what mattered most was their practical application to the problems of life. As the Stoic Epictetus once said:

> The builder does not come forward and say, "Listen to me deliver a discourse about the art of building"; but he takes a contract for the house, builds it, and thereby proves that he possesses the art. Do something of the same sort yourself too; eat as a man, drink as a man, adorn yourself, marry, get children, be active as a citizen; endure revilings, bear with an unreasonable brother, father, son, neighbour, fellow-traveller. Show us that you can do these things, for us to see that in all truth you have learned something of the philosophers.[26]

These philosophies aimed to cultivate attention or awareness so one might live fully in the present, neither troubled by the past nor fretful about the future. We can be happy right now in "the bloom of the present moment," as Thoreau so beautifully put it in *Walden*. "The time which we spend in living is but a point, nay, even less than a point. But this point of time, infinitesimal as it is," is all that we truly possess, Seneca observes in his epistle "On the Shortness of Life."[27]

With the passage of time, philosophy became increasingly abstract, theoretical, and academic. It was no longer a way of life offering spiritual exercises geared to attaining wisdom. Hadot concurs with Thoreau's assessment, noting that from the end of the eighteenth century onwards, philosophy was captured by the university. With few exceptions, philosophy is no longer a way of life but an academic discipline. "Ancient philosophy proposed to mankind an art of living," Hadot writes. "By contrast, modern philosophy appears above all as the construction of a technical jargon reserved for specialists."[28]

With few exceptions, academic philosophy is largely dismissive of the idea that Thoreau should seriously be considered a philosopher. Even Stanley Cavell, his most sympathetic critic, focuses more on Thoreau's use of language than he does on the practical application of his philosophy.[29] Moreover, the impression persists that the pursuit of self-culture is both individualistic and escapist, without due consideration not only of its ethical and therapeutic value but also of its contribution to political discourse. Again, what Hadot says about ancient philosophy applies just as well to Thoreau's, namely, "an essential place is accorded to the duty always to act in the service of the human community, that is, to act in accordance with justice. . . . In other words, the philosophical life normally entails a community engagement."[30]

Ex Oriente Lux!

Thoreau's notion of self-culture has affinities with Indian and Chinese philosophies of self-cultivation also. His access to the spiritual classics of India and China was limited since only a few of these had been translated at the time. But he felt a deep sympathy with those he was able to find and study. Emerson's library was the primary source for this literature, and Thoreau drew on it in making selections for the "Ethnical Scriptures" column in *The Dial*. There are countless references to this literature throughout his books and journal.

With regard to Indian teachings, he read, in addition to William Jones's translation of the Ordinances of Menu, William Ward's treatise on the six systems of Indian philosophy; Henry Colebrooke's translation of the Sankhya Karika, a major text of the Sankhya school; a selection of the Upanishads translated by the Hindu reformer Rammohun Roy; and, most importantly, the Bhagavad Gita, translated by Charles Wilkins.[31] (In 1855 he received a trove of Hindu texts from Thomas Cholmondeley, a British admirer, but he seems to have made little use of them.)

Generally speaking, these Hindu texts follow the pattern of self-cultivation philosophies. Human beings suffer and feel pain, caused, on the one hand, by desires and, on the other, by a misapprehension of the true nature of reality. Liberation, or freedom from suffering, therefore depends on stilling desires and dispelling the illusions that keep us trapped in a desperate condition. Those seeking release are advised to engage in spiritual practices known as yogas. These may include physical exercises, austerities of various kinds, mental concentration, the performance of certain rituals, and the study of sacred scriptures.

Thoreau acknowledged his indebtedness to this tradition in a letter to his friend H. G. O. Blake written in 1849:

> Free in this world, as the birds in the air, disengaged from every kind of chains, those who have practiced the *yoga* gather in Brahma the certain fruit of their works.
>
> Depend on it that rude and careless as I am, I would fain practice the *yoga* faithfully.
>
> The yogin, absorbed in contemplation, contributes in his degree to creation. He breathes a divine perfume, he hears wonderful things. Divine forms traverse him without tearing him, and united to the nature which is proper to him, he goes, he acts, as animating original matter.
>
> To some extent, and at rare intervals, even I am a yogin.[32]

In this letter he quoted the Harivansa, a part of a much longer work, the Mahabharata, the classic epic of ancient India. The Bhagavad Gita, which played an even greater role in Thoreau's self-cultivation philosophy, is also a part of this epic story. It was Emerson's copy of the Gita that Thoreau took with him to Walden Pond, and he mentions the book in the "Pond in Winter" chapter of *Walden*: "In the morning I bathe my head in the stupendous and cosmogonical philosophy of the Bhagavat-Geeta, since whose composition years of the gods have elapsed, and in comparison with which our modern world and its literature seem puny and trivial; and I doubt if that philosophy is not to be referred to a previous state of existence, so remote is its sublimity from our conceptions."[33]

Most Americans today associate yoga with the posture-based practices of hatha yoga, a type of yoga Thoreau would not have been familiar with. His introduction to yoga came primarily from his reading of the Bhagavad Gita, which depicts three types of yoga: karma yoga, the yoga of action; bhakti yoga, the yoga of devotion; and jnana yoga, the yoga of knowledge. No doubt he would have been drawn to passages such as this one from the sixth chapter of the Gita, which extols the discipline of action:

A man of discipline should always discipline himself, remain in seclusion, isolated, his thought and self well controlled, without possessions or hope.

He should fix for himself a firm seat in a pure place, neither too high nor too low, covered in cloth, deerskin, or grass.

He should focus his mind and restrain the activity of his thought and senses; sitting on that seat, he should practice discipline for the purification of the self.[34]

Two notions common to Indian self-cultivation philosophies are *maya*, or illusion, and *ahimsa*, the principle of nonviolence toward all living things. These play a part in Thoreau's philosophy as well. "Shams and delusions are esteemed for soundest truths, while reality is fabulous," he insists. "When we are unhurried and wise, we perceive that only great and worthy things have any permanent and absolute existence,—that petty fears and petty pleasures are but the shadow of the reality. This is always exhilarating and sublime. By closing the eyes and slumbering, and consenting to be deceived by shows, men establish and confirm their daily life of routine and habit everywhere, which still is built on purely illusory foundations."[35] Whether or not prompted by his reading of Hindu scriptures, Thoreau, in the "Higher Laws" chapter of *Walden*, declares his growing aversion to hunting and eating meat on the grounds that such practices are unclean and not in accord with a higher law governing human behavior.

Thoreau was also attracted to the Confucian classics of Chinese philosophy. In Emerson's library, that treasure trove of ancient wisdom, he found copies of Joshua Marshman's *Works of Confucius*, David Collie's *The Chinese classical work, commonly called The Four Books*, and Jean-Pierre-Guillaume Pauthier's *Confucius et Mencius*.[36] As we have seen, he drew on these in compiling quotations for two issues of *The Dial*. They are also the source for numerous quotations in *A Week on the Concord and Merrimack Rivers, Walden*, and several essays, including "Civil Disobedience."

Thoreau didn't study the Chinese classics to the same extent that he did the Hindu scriptures. Thus it is difficult to know how much his understanding of this literature contributed to his own philosophy. Nevertheless, self-cultivation was central to Confucianism. Like other self-cultivation philosophies, it emphasized practice over theory. In particular, it focused on becoming a moral person. The concept of virtue—how one develops and exhibits it—played a central role in this regard. Virtue had an ethical dimension, but it also was a form of personal power or influence. The epitome of Confucian self-cultivation was the sage, a person who internalized and exhibited virtue.[37] The methods used to achieve sage-hood included, first and foremost, the study of the Confucian canon, especially the four basic books: the Analects of Confucius, the book of Mencius, the Great Learning, and the Doctrine of the Mean.

Scholar Arthur Christy, in *The Orient in American Transcendentalism*, insisted that "there was nothing Confucian in Thoreau's temperament." No Confucian would have been an exponent of civil disobedience or would ever have gone to Walden Pond.[38] This remark overlooks two important ways in which Confucian philosophy appealed to him. First of all, we must recall that Thoreau was a Unitarian—if not a very observant one—steeped in the moral philosophy of Harvard College. He was taught that the highest faculty was that of conscience and that the aim of education was the fullest development of one's faculties, including conscience, through a conscious effort of study and self-reflection. The teachings of Harvard College and Confucian philosophy are both examples of virtue ethics, prioritizing the cultivation of moral character over the following of rules. And it is on this basis that the moralism of Confucius would have had some appeal.

Second, the aphorisms of Confucius and his disciple Mencius offered Thoreau concrete examples of moral behavior that resonated with his own inclinations. Consider, for example, the selections chosen for the first group of Confucian texts in the April 1843 issue of *The Dial*. These emphasize concrete behavior, in this case the importance of simple living:

> A man's life is properly connected with virtue. The life of the evil man is preserved by mere good fortune.
> Coarse rice for food, water to drink, and the bended arm for a pillow—

happiness may be enjoyed even in these. Without virtue, riches and honor seem to me like a passing cloud.

A wise and good man was Hooi. A piece of bamboo was his dish, a cocoanut his cup, his dwelling a miserable shed. Men could not sustain the sight of his wretchedness; but Hooi did not change the serenity of his mind. A wise and good man was Hooi.[39]

Another example, from the selections in the October issue of the same year, reflects the tradition of scholar as moral hero who goes into reclusion during times of evil and corruption. Mencius cites the famous example of Bo Yi, transliterated as Pih E in Thoreau's version:

In times of good government, he went into office, and in times of confusion and bad government, he retired. Where disorderly government prevailed, or where disorderly people lived, he could not bear to dwell. He thought that to live with low men was as bad as to sit in the mud with his court robes and cap. In the time of Chou, he dwelt on the banks of the North Ka, watching til the Empire should be brought to peace and order. Hence, when the fame of Pih E is heard of, the stupid become intelligent and the weak determined.[40]

It takes no stretch of the imagination to suppose that going into reclusion at Walden Pond was at least in part occasioned by Thoreau's aversion to the corrupting influences of politics and the market economy.[41]

Many of Thoreau's readers have lamented the fact that he did not discover Taoism in the course of his Chinese studies, convinced that he would have had more in common with Zhuangzi, for example, than with Confucius.[42] This is undoubtedly true. He would have found the Taoists' nature mysticism, disdain of convention, and love of simplicity quite appealing. Like Zhuangzi, in whom he would have found a kindred soul, Thoreau extolled the enjoyment of life, the pleasures of free and easy wandering, the cultivation of the self, communion with nature, simple living, nonconformity, and detachment from worldly concerns. In a passage that could have been taken from the "Economy" chapter of *Walden*, Zhuangzi says, "To labor without ceasing all life, and then, without living to enjoy the fruit, worn out with labor, to depart, one knows not whither,—is not this a just cause for grief?"[43] In Chinese culture, Taoism and Confucianism are not mutually exclusive philosophical orientations. If Thoreau's views are more Taoist than Confucian, they nevertheless exhibit characteristics of both.[44]

The extracts from the writings of Hermes Trismegistus, dating from the third or fourth century CE, are said to be the teachings of Pymander, a godlike figure representing *nous*, or the eye of the mind. Catherine L. Albanese explains that his "discourses present the individual religious seeker as agonist. Longing for illumination, the intuitive wisdom-knowledge of the divine, the Hermetic seeker searches for salvation—but this without the personal God or redeemer of Christian teaching. Instead . . . salvation comes from the seeker's own work, from the effort that yields the wisdom-knowledge itself."[45]

This so-called Hermetic literature was more widely read in Thoreau's time than ours, having been popularized by Romantic writers, including Goethe and Coleridge. Emerson possessed a copy of *The Divine Pymander* in his own library, given him by his friend Bronson Alcott. Hermes Trismegistus, or Thrice-Greatest Hermes, was named for a figure in Greek mythology noted for the ability to move freely between the worlds of the mortal and the divine. He was a guide of souls to the afterlife and a revealer of what Carlyle called "the Open Secret" of the universe.[46] Emerson includes Hermes among a "band of grandees," including Heraclitus, Plato, and Plotinus, who were, in his view,

> so vast in their logic, so primary in their thinking, that it seems antecedent to all the ordinary distinctions of rhetoric and literature, and to be at once poetry and music and dancing and astronomy and mathematics. I am present at the sowing of the seed of the world. With a geometry of sunbeams the Soul lays the foundations of nature. The truth and grandeur of their thought is proved by its scope and applicability; for it commands more even than our dear old bibles of Moses and Swedenborg.[47]

Given Thoreau's predilection for the earliest expressions of past revelation, he must have felt the same way.

Thoreau first mentions "The Gulistan; or, Flower Garden" of Saadi in one of his college essays. The author is considered one of the greatest of the Persian, or Sufi, poets. The book is a manual for the conduct of life, conveyed primarily in the form of aphorisms, moral fables, and poetry. Here too he was especially attracted to passages that emphasized living simply: "Ardishir Babagan asked an Arabian physician, what quantity of food ought to be eaten daily. He replied, Thirteen ounces. The king said, What strength can a man derive from so small a quantity? The physician replied, so much can support you, but in whatever you exceed that, you must support it."[48]

Poetry was the primary medium for conveying Sufi wisdom. Emerson, in his essay "Persian Poetry," wrote that such poetry consisted of "gnomic verses, rules of life, conveyed in lively image, especially in an image addressed to the eye, and contained in a single stanza," as in this poem by Hafiz:

> See how roses burn!
> Bring wine to quench the fire!
> Alas! The flames come up with us,—
> We perish with desire.[49]

Sufi teaching, like that of other philosophies of moral self-culture, stressed attaining virtue rather than obeying rules, often exhibiting a transgressive quality, as in this example:

> Ask me not, as Muftis can,
> To recite the Alkoran;
> Well I love the meaning sweet,—
> I tread the book beneath my feet.[50]

There were two types of Sufism, drunk and sober. The first entailed the revelation of an all-embracing unity and the immanence of God, the second a vision of differentiated multiplicity and God's transcendence. The Persian poets were drunken Sufis, believing that religion is neither law nor theology, neither creed nor ritual, but rather the means by which one transcends the ego and becomes one with the Absolute. According to Omar Khayyam they were seekers "who do not seek knowledge intellectually or discursively, but by the cleansing of their inner self and through the purgation of their morals, they have cleansed their rational soul from the impurities of nature and incorporeal body." This is the best path, he says, "for it becomes known to the servant of God that there is no perfection better than the presence of God [in the soul], and in that state, there are no obstacles or veils. For all that man lacks is due to the impurities of nature, for if the [spiritual] veil is lifted and the screen and the obstacle is removed, the truth of things as they really are becomes apparent."[51]

In November 1837, at the outset of his own spiritual journey, Thoreau wrote in his journal, "My desire is to know *what* I have lived, that I may know *how* to live henceforth."[52] The conduct of life is the constant theme in all of his writing. Literary scholar Sherman Paul tells us that "Thoreau was chiefly interested in self-cultivation; he wanted the warrant to stand outside of anyone's world, and thereby make his own—he wanted to try the universe on his pulses, to live only on that which he had certified by his sovereign reason to be true. Such a moral life was to his mind a life of daring; its superiority over the conformities of the lives of the majority of men was in its necessity for bravery of self-determination."[53] He was drawn to those spiritual traditions and philosophical schools of thought that similarly promoted self-cultivation, as shown in his selections for the "Ethnical Scriptures" and those frequently mentioned in his subsequent writings.

Thoreau may not have been fully knowledgeable about the spiritual traditions of India, China, and Persia, but—with the possible exception of Emerson—he was better informed about them and more sympathetic toward them than anyone else in his day. I would not argue that any one of these or any combination of them necessarily shaped his own views. He, like his Transcendentalist colleagues, believed that such teachings represented a form of perennial wisdom just as true in their day as it was in ancient times. In this literature they found inspiration, guidance, and a confirmation of their own intuitions. As previously indicated, self-culture was a defining characteristic of Transcendentalist spirituality. Reading was an essential practice, along with the embrace of a wide-ranging religious cosmopolitanism. In the "Reading" chapter of *Walden*, Thoreau envisions gathering the literature of all of these traditions in one vast library:

> That age will be rich indeed when those relics which we call Classics, and the still older and more than classic but even less known Scriptures of the nations shall have still further accumulated, when the Vaticans shall be filled with Vedas and Zendavestas and Bibles, with Homers and Dantes and Shakespeares, and all the centuries to come shall have successively deposited their trophies in the forum of the world. By such a pile we may hope to scale heaven at last.[54]

Like many people today, Thoreau was a religious seeker—curious, open-minded, and in search of wisdom, which is to say, peace of mind, inner freedom, and a cosmic consciousness. For generations of people, not only in this country but in other times and places as well, Thoreau has been a spiritual guide whose writings—*Walden* especially—belong with those I have mentioned here. He modeled the art of life, encouraging others not to follow him but to find and pursue their own way. Contemporary seekers have been drawn to the teachings of Buddhism and Stoicism and have practiced yoga, tai chi, and mindfulness meditation in the same spirit as Thoreau. The lesson of these philosophies and religious practices is the same, in Hadot's words: "an invitation to each human being to transform himself. Philosophy is a conversion, a transformation of one's way of being and living, and a quest for wisdom."[55]

This way is not for the faint of heart or those seeking amusement rather than enlightenment. It takes dedication and discipline. The philosopher Spinoza indicated as much in his *Ethics*: "If the way which I have pointed out as leading to this result seems exceedingly hard, it may nevertheless be discovered. It must indeed be hard, since it is so seldom found. How would it be possible, if salvation were easy to find, and could without great labor be found, that it should be neglected by almost everybody? But all excellent things are as difficult as they are rare."[56]

CHAPTER 3

OF TIME AND THE RIVER

While still living with the Emersons in January 1841, Thoreau suffered the devastating loss of his brother John, who had cut himself while shaving. The wound became infected, and he succumbed to lockjaw, dying in Henry's arms at the age of twenty-six. A week later Henry, too, developed symptoms of the disease, a sympathetic reaction to John's terrible end, from which he slowly recovered. For months afterward he felt weak and depressed. Soon after his brother's passing, he experienced another blow when he learned that Emerson's five-year-old son, Waldo Jr., had died from scarlet fever. Henry had been very close to the boy, playing with him nearly every day.

He struggled to find emotional footing. When he returned to his journal he wrote: "My life, my life—why will ye linger? Are the years short, are the months of no account? How often has long delay quenched my aspirations. . . . Can heaven be postponed with no more ado? Why were my ears given to hear those everlasting strains—which haunt my life—and yet to be prophaned much more by these perpetual dull sounds!"[1] He seems to have hit bottom the following year, lamenting in his journal: "What am I at present? A diseased bundle of nerves standing between time and eternity like a withered leaf that still hangs shivering on its stem. A more miserable object one could not well imagine—but still very dull, very insipid to think of. I suppose I may live on not a few years, trailing this carcass after me, or perhaps trailing after it."[2]

Returning from his six-month sojourn in New York in 1843, where he had tutored William Emerson's son and sounded out the New York literary market, he took up residence once again in the family home, still uncertain as to his next move. He had published several essays in *The Dial* and elsewhere, but felt he needed to write a book in order to secure his literary reputation.

Beginning with notes he had taken on the boat trip with his brother in 1839, he compiled additional writings from his journal and other sources in hopes of making a book out of these bits and pieces. John's death provided both a theme for the work and an impetus for writing it.

Reading the finished book, *A Week on the Concord and Merrimack Rivers*, finally published in 1849, we feel as though we are entering a mythical world, announced, as the ancient poets did, by an invocation of one's muse—in this case, Henry's deceased brother, John:

> Where'er thou sail'st who sailed with me,
> Though now thou climbest loftier mounts,
> And fairer rivers dost ascend,
> Be now my Muse, my Brother—.[3]

Their trip on the rivers in the late summer of 1839 is recounted as a voyage through space and time in search of healing and renewal. The elegiac mood of the book and Thoreau's frequent mention of myth and fable reinforce this impression.

As Robert Richardson observed in his book *Myth and Literature in the American Renaissance*, of all the Transcendentalist writers, Thoreau made "the most deliberate, extensive, original, and successful use of myth." Most importantly, Richardson noted, "he tried to recover for himself the original conditions in which the early creators of the great myths found themselves."[4] Thoreau himself muses on myth at great length in the "Sunday" chapter of the book, citing numerous examples from Greek literature. The narrative of the two brothers on the river conjures up the legendary figures of Damon and Pythias and the mythic voyage of Jason and the Argonauts. References to the subject are so prevalent as to suggest that myth itself provides the ordering framework of the entire book.

Scholars have examined at considerable length both the structure and the construction of the book.[5] It was not published until May 1849, after numerous revisions. Ostensibly an account of a trip taken ten years before, it includes material from a later date, together with discourses on a variety of topics, including religion, books, friendship, Native Americans, and Eastern philosophy. Readers then and since have been bewildered by Thoreau's digressions and some have been outraged by his opinions, especially on the subject of Christianity. As James Russell Lowell wrote in his review of the book, "We were bid to a river-party,—not to be preached at."[6]

A Week on the Rivers

Their boat, which they built themselves, was named *Musketaquid* after the Native name for the Concord River. It was equipped with sails and wheels. The sails served as shelter during the chilly nights; the wheels made for easier portage when necessary. On the eve of their departure, they invited friends and neighbors to a melon party. Well laden with provisions for their journey, they set off on Saturday morning, August 31, under a gloomy sky. From the beginning, their voyage displays a nostalgia for the past—for the Native peoples who named the river and the farmers who first raised hay along its banks. The river itself is likened to legendary rivers—the Nile, the Euphrates, and the Ganges.

As they glide down the stream in the "Saturday" chapter, Thoreau muses on the lives of the fishes, the original inhabitants of the river. He has an unusual rapport with them, so much so that they allow him to take them in his hand and bring them to the surface. He describes the various species that are found in the river, but is especially drawn to the plight of the shad, whose migrations upstream were prevented by a dam at Billerica.[7] "Still patiently, almost pathetically, with instinct not to be discouraged, not to be *reasoned* with, revisiting their old haunts, as if their stern fates would relent, and still met by the Corporation with its dam. Poor shad! where is thy redress?" Anticipating today's eco-warriors, he imagines taking a crowbar to the dam in their defense. Poignantly, he asks, "Who hears the fishes when they cry?" (36–37).

Putting in for the night, they feasted on huckleberries, bread, and cocoa and listened to sounds of the summer night, especially the barking of dogs in the distance. "Even in a retired and uninhabited district like this," he writes, "it was a sufficiency of sound for the ear of night, and more impressive than any music" (41). Far from annoying, Thoreau found the voice of the hounds sweet and melodious. As we shall see—not only in *A Week* but also in his journal and his other writings—sensuousness is a springboard to rapture.

They awoke on Sunday morning to the sight of fog on the river, which was soon dispersed as the sun rose. The day felt as if it were "a natural Sabbath," and the world seemed adorned with the trappings of a holy day. As Thoreau humorously describes the scene, "the frogs sat meditating, all sabbath thoughts, summing up their week, with one eye out on the golden sun, and one toe on a reed, eying the wonderful universe in which they act their part;

the fishes swam more staid and soberly, as maiden go to church; shoals of golden and silver minnows rose to the surface to behold the heavens, and then sheered off into more sober aisles" (49). This lead-in to his thoughts about religion and the church is reminiscent of Emerson's prelude to his "Divinity School Address." Like Emerson, he contrasts nature religion with historical Christianity.

The chapter highlights several such contrasts, the second being that of Native American life with the lives of white settlers, illustrated in the following two passages:

> The white man comes, pale as the dawn, with a load of thought, with a slumbering intelligence as a fire raked up, knowing well what he knows, not guessing but calculating; strong in community, yielding obedience to authority; of experienced race; of wonderful, wonderful common sense; dull but capable, slow but persevering, severe but just, of little humor but genuine; a laboring man, despising game and sport; building a house that endures, a framed house. He buys the Indian's moccasins and baskets, then buys his hunting grounds, and at length forgets where he is buried, and plows up his bones. (53)

This is not a flattering portrait. By contrast, he finds much to admire in Native American culture:

> We talk of civilizing the Indian, but that is not the name for his improvement. By the wary independence and aloofness of his dim forest life he preserves his intercourse with his native gods, and is admitted from time to time to a rare and peculiar society with Nature. He has glances of starry recognition to which our saloons are strangers. The steady illumination of his genius, dim only because distant, is like the faint but satisfying light of the stars compared with the dazzling but ineffectual and short-lived blaze of candles. (55)

Another contrast is drawn between the wild and the cultivated. "I am convinced that my genius dates from an older era than the agricultural," he tells us. "There is in my nature, methinks, a singular yearning toward all wildness. . . . What have I to do with plows? I cut another furrow than you see." Gardening, by comparison, "is civil and social, but it wants the vigor and freedom of the forest and the outlaw" (54). In each case he privileges the first item of the contrast.

Thoreau is especially attracted to the notions of the wild and the primitive. He admires not only the ways of Native peoples but also the myths and fables of antiquity. In light of the distinction Coleridge made between imagination and understanding—central to the thinking of the Transcendentalists—he states that myth satisfies the imagination even if it perplexes the understanding. From the perspective of the understanding, myths are patently false. When we read, for example, that Bacchus turned mariners into dolphins, "we are not concerned about the historical truth of this, but rather a higher poetical truth," he insists. "We seem to hear the music of a thought, and care not if the understanding be not gratified" (58). Far from being false, myth "contains only enduring and essential truth, the I and you, here and there, the now and then, being omitted" (60). In his view, myths express primordial and universal truths: "In the mythus a superhuman intelligence uses the unconscious thoughts and dreams of men as its hieroglyphics to address men unborn. In the history of the human mind, these glowing and ruddy fables precede the noonday thoughts of men, as Aurora the sun's rays" (61).

Thoreau's reflections on wildness, Native life, and myth are a prologue to a longer discourse on religion. Ethel Seybold tells us that, for Thoreau, the classical literature of Greece and Rome were "the most pertinent and valuable source of past revelation."[8] Classical writers and their works are frequently alluded to or quoted in *A Week*. Given his predilection for myth and classical literature, it should not be surprising that he prefers Jove to Jehovah. "Jehovah, though with us he has acquired new attributes, is more absolute and unapproachable, but hardly more divine, than Jove. He is not so much a gentleman, not so gracious and catholic, he does not exert so intimate and genial an influence on nature, as many a god of the Greeks" (64). As if such blasphemy were not bad enough, he embraces an unbridled pantheism: "In my Pantheon, Pan still reigns in his pristine glory, with his ruddy face, his flowing beard, and his shaggy body, his pipe and his crook, his nymph Echo, and his chosen daughter Iambe; for the great god Pan is not dead, as was rumored. No god ever dies. Perhaps of all the gods of New England and of ancient Greece, I am most constant at his shrine" (65).

Thoreau enjoys being provocative, but it is understandable that he should choose to worship a deity of nature rather than the judgmental God of the Bible. Moreover, people have fashioned gods to suit their own purposes. "It seems to me that the god that is commonly worshipped in civilized countries is not at all divine, though he bears a divine name, but is the overwhelming authority and respectability of mankind combined" (65). His quarrel is not with religion per se, nor with the simple teachings of Jesus, but with the bigotry and distortions of Christianity: "It is necessary not to be Christian to appreciate the beauty and significance of the life of Christ. I know that some will have hard thoughts of me, when they hear their Christ named beside my Buddha, yet I am sure that I am willing they should love their Christ more than my Buddha, for love is the main thing, and I like him too. . . . Why need Christians be still intolerant and superstitious?" (67–68).

Most people seem content with a cut-and-dried scheme of the universe. They cling to their creeds. "But in all my wanderings I never came across the least vestige of authority for these things," he writes. "The wisest man preaches no doctrines; he has no scheme; he sees no rafter, not even a cobweb, against the heavens." The Christian scheme is an obstacle to our understanding of one another. "You did not invent it; it was imposed on you," he insists. "Examine your authority. Even Christ, we fear, had his scheme, his conformity to tradition, which slightly vitiates his teaching." Such schemes may satisfy the understanding, but they cannot capture the mysteries of the universe: "Can you put mysteries into words? Do you presume to fable of the ineffable? Pray, what geographer are you, that speak of heaven's topography?" (70).

Although he concedes that the New Testament is an important book, Thoreau was somewhat prejudiced against it in his youth by the church and the Sabbath school. He came to find more charm in it later on but preferred to read the scriptures of other religious traditions—the Hindus, the Chinese, and the Persians—instead. Despite its popularity, the New Testament isn't taken seriously. "Let but one of [Jesus'] sentences be rightly read, from any pulpit in the land, and there would not be left one stone of the meeting-house upon another." Yet Jesus had his shortcomings because "his thoughts were all directed toward another world" (73). We have serious problems to solve in this world without worrying about the next one. The sort of morality that proceeds from fear of punishment in the afterlife is not worthwhile.

In a markedly uncharitable description of ministers and churches, Thoreau recalls being reproved by a minister for skipping church on the Sabbath while on his way to climb a mountain in New Hampshire. The minister was certain that God was watching and would surely punish him for disobeying the fourth commandment. "The country is full of this superstition," Thoreau counters,

> so that when one enters a village, the church, not only really but from association, is the ugliest looking building in it, because it is the one in which human nature stoops the lowest and is most disgraced. . . . There are few things more disheartening and disgusting than when you are walking

the streets of a strange village on the Sabbath, to hear a preacher shouting like a boatswain in a gale of wind, and thus harshly profaning the quiet atmosphere of the day. (75–76)

He views churches as hospitals for religious cripples. "One is sick at heart of this pagoda worship," he says. "The sound of the Sabbath bell far away . . . does not awaken pleasing associations, but melancholy and somber ones rather." As for Christianity, it "only hopes. It has hung its harp on the willows, and cannot sing a song in a strange land. It has dreamed a sad dream, and does not yet welcome the morning with joy" (77). Its creeds are never in actuality adopted even though believers anxiously cling to them.

By the time he wrote this chapter, Thoreau was well within the Transcendentalist orbit. As we have seen, he studied for a time with Orestes Brownson, one of the original members of the so-called Transcendental Club and author of *New Views of Christianity, Society, and the Church*, an early manifesto of the movement. He was well aware of the controversy surrounding Theodore Parker's sermon "The Transient and Permanent in Christianity," as a result of which Parker was shunned by many of his colleagues in the Unitarian ministry. And then there was Emerson's address at the Divinity School in 1838 which had stirred similar controversy. In each case the attempt was made to separate the life and teachings of Jesus from the doctrines and rituals of the Christian church. Thoreau is making a similar argument in this chapter. But while Brownson, Parker, and even Emerson wished to reform the church, Thoreau dismissed it entirely. Most of the members of the group were or had been Unitarian ministers who still had ties to the church, but after Thoreau withdrew from the First Parish Church in 1841, he had no further need of it.

Despite quitting First Parish and his negative feelings about churches, Thoreau was a deeply spiritual person. Like others in his own time and many more since then, he found religion in nature. When Franklin Sanborn, a younger contemporary of Thoreau, arrived in Concord in 1855, he asked his landlord what religious societies there were in the town. "'Three,' was his answer, 'the Orthodox, the Unitarian, and the Walden Pond Association.'"[9] No doubt Thoreau was a high priest of the last. He was an early adopter of a religious stance outside of what he termed "the Christian scheme."

Before Thoreau's time it was difficult to think outside that framework. To be sure, there were religious freethinking outliers such as Abner Kneeland, a Universalist minister in Boston who was convicted and jailed for blasphemy in 1838. Nevertheless, as James Turner argues, "Before the middle of the nineteenth century, atheism or agnosticism seemed almost palpably absurd; shortly afterward unbelief emerged as an option fully available within the general contours of Western culture, a plausible alternative to the still dominant theism." Turner credits the Transcendentalists, including Thoreau, for making it possible "to realize that one could abandon Christianity without losing morality, spirituality, reverence, and the larger hope."[10] As noted previously, Thomas Carlyle, in his book *Sartor Resartus*, had called for a new mythus, which he termed "Natural Supernaturalism," dressing religion in the cloak of nature. In a way, *A Week* was Thoreau's response to Carlyle's call.

The brothers arose on Monday morning in the midst of a fog which dispersed as they made their way on the river. Occasionally they put in for a while to rest in the shade of trees along the shore and contemplated at their leisure "the lapse of the river and of human life" (124). The spiritual teachings of the ancient philosophers counsel us to avoid the world's busy-ness in favor of contemplation and detachment, he muses. "There are moments when all anxiety and stated toil are becalmed in the infinite leisure and repose of nature. All laborers must have their nooning, and at this season of the day, we are all, more or less, Asiatics, and give over all work and reform" (125–26). Reformers, in his view, are too restless. Instead, the reform they propose "can be undertaken any morning before unbarring our doors. We need not call any convention" (127). For Thoreau, the reformation of society begins with the reformation of the individual.

Thoreau pursues this line of argument in his comments on the Bhagavad Gita, a book that made an enormous impression on him. In the text, Arjuna, a warrior, is reluctant to kill family and friends fighting for an opposing army. His charioteer, the god Krishna in disguise, tells him he must fight, detaching his feelings from his actions. Thoreau contrasts the "pure morality" of the New Testament with the "pure intellectuality" of the Bhagavad Gita. Of the Gita he says, "It is unquestionably one of the noblest and most sacred scriptures which have come down to us" (137).

Although he is moved by the contemplative nature of the Gita, Thoreau finds Krishna's argument unsatisfactory. Having seen him express dissatisfaction with Christianity in the "Sunday" chapter, we may find it somewhat surprising that he considers the social teachings of the New Testament superior to those of the Gita. "This teaching is not practical in the sense in which the New Testament is. . . . The Brahman never proposes courageously to assault evil, but patiently to starve it out. His active faculties are paralyzed by

the idea of cast [*sic*], of impassable limits, of destiny and the tyranny of time"
(140). The difference between the ethics of the Gita and the New Testament
is that, while the former may be unconcerned about the consequences of
one's actions, the latter cannot be.

Despite his criticism of the Gita on moral grounds, Thoreau finds much
to admire in the spiritual literature of the East. "In comparison with the philosophers of the East, we may say that modern Europe has yet given birth
to none. Beside the vast and cosmogonal philosophy of the Bhagavat-Geeta,
even our Shakespeare seems sometimes youthfully green and practical
merely. . . . *Ex oriente lux* may still be the motto of scholars, for the Western
world has not yet derived from the East all the light which it is destined to
receive thence" (143) He envisions gathering together the sacred writings of
China, India, Persia, as well as those of the Jews and Christians. The inter-
sectionality of these scriptures has a liberalizing effect. As his references to
the Bhagavad Gita indicate, he especially prizes the sacred writings of the
Hindus, including the moral tales of the Vishnu Sharma, the Puranas, the
Laws of Manu, the Dharma Shastra, and of course the Gita.

These writings are both timely and timeless. They represent the perennial
wisdom of the human race. "There has always been the same amount of light
in the world," Thoreau tells us. "Always the laws of light are the same, but the
modes and degrees of seeing vary. The gods are partial to no era, but steadily
shines their light in the heavens, while the eye of the beholder is turned to
stone. There was but the sun and the eye from the first. The ages have not
added a new ray to the one, nor altered a fibre of the other" (157). They are the
world's inheritance bequeathed to us from the dawn of time.

Bedding down for the night, Thoreau hears the sound of a distant drummer. As is so often the case, sounds such as those of a guitar, a piano, or in
this case a drum trigger mystical reveries: "I stop my habitual thinking, as if
the plough had suddenly run deeper in its furrow through the crust of the
world" (173). What follows is a meditation on time and eternity. "Suddenly
old Time winked at me,—Ah, you know me, you rogue,—and news had
come that IT was well. That ancient universe is in such capital health, I think
undoubtedly it will never die" (173). We live in the virtual world of time, but
there is another world or dimension or mode of being that lies beyond what
the eye can see and the ear can hear. He shares lines from a poem he wrote
titled "Inspiration," perhaps the most apt expression of Thoreau's Transcendental philosophy. I quote at length the middle portion of the poem:

Always the general show of things
    Floats in review before my mind,
And such true love and reverence brings,
    That sometimes I forget that I am blind.

But now there comes unsought, unseen,
    Some clear divine electuary;
And I who had but sensual been,
    Grow sensible, and as God is, I am wary.

I hearing get, who had but ears,
    And sight, who had but eyes before,
I moments live who lived but years,
    And truth discern who knew but learning's lore.

I hear beyond the range of sound,
    I see beyond the range of sight,
New earths and skies and seas around,
    And in my day the sun doth pale his light.

A clear and ancient harmony
    Pierces my soul through all its din,
As through its utmost melody,—
    Farther behind than they—farther within.

More swift its bolt than lightening is,
    Its voice than thunder is more loud,
It doth expand my privacies
    To all, and leave me single in the crowd.

It speaks with such authority,
    With so serene and lofty tone,
That idle Time runs gadding by,
    And leaves me with Eternity alone.

Then chiefly is my natal hour,
    And only then my prime of life,
Of manhood's strength it is the flower,
    'Tis peace's end and war's beginning strife.[11]

An electuary is a form of herbal medicine, laced with honey to make it palatable. As we know, drugs of all kinds have been consumed for the purpose of stimulating mystical visions. In Thoreau's case, sounds seem to have produced a similar result, namely, the perception of a rupture in "the crust of the world," revealing a previously unknown dimension of existence. We discover that the life we have been living is but a virtual existence, not a real one. Beyond the range of sight and sound lie "new earths and skies and seas." The mundane world seems pale in comparison. A sense of harmony pierces "the soul through all its din." From behind or within, a voice "speaks with such authority" that time is stopped, leaving us "with Eternity alone." We feel at once newly born and in "the prime of life."

Thoreau's description is in keeping with the four characteristics William James attributed to mystical experiences. They have a *noetic* quality: "They are states of insight into depths of truth unplumbed by the discursive intellect. They are illuminations, revelations, full of significance and importance, all inarticulate though they remain; and as a rule they carry with them a curious sense of authority for after-time." They are *transient*; they cannot be sustained for long. But insofar as they may recur from time to time, they add a cumulative richness to life. They are *passive*. Although they may be stimulated—as in Thoreau's case, by sounds—"the mystic feels as if his own will were in abeyance, as if he were grasped and held by a superior power." Finally, they are *ineffable*. The experience cannot be adequately described, nor can it be imparted or transferred to others.[12] One need not claim that Thoreau was a thoroughgoing (Thoreau-going?) mystic to maintain that he had numerous experiences of a mystical nature, as shown in this poem and elsewhere in his writings.

As to the ineffable quality of such experiences, recall that in the "Sunday" chapter Thoreau wrote: "Can you put mysteries into words? Do you presume to fable of the ineffable?" (70). This is one of the paradoxes of mysticism. The experience is life-altering. "I see, smell, taste, hear, feel, that everlasting Something to which we are allied, at once our maker, our abode, our destiny, our very Selves," he writes; "the one historic truth, the most remarkable fact which can become the distinct and uninvited subject of our thought, the actual glory of the universe; the only fact which a human being cannot avoid recognizing, or in some way forget or dispense with" (173–74). And yet it eludes our ability to adequately describe it.

There is a tinge of sadness that comes with such experiences, the result of yet another paradox. Thoreau likens it to a strain of music that comes to us from a remote distance, conveying both beauty and serenity. But, he says, "we feel a sad cheer when we hear it. Perchance because we that hear are not one with that which is heard" (175). Not only are we locked inside the consciousness that enables us to experience the mystery, but also we are unprepared to fully surrender to its demands, since it calls us to live a life so different from that which we commonly lead.

Mountains play a significant role in Thoreau's mythologizing. Two well-known examples are Mount Wachusett, which I discussed in chapter 1, and Mount Katahdin, described in his excursion to the Maine woods in 1846. In the "Tuesday" chapter Thoreau gives a lengthy account of climbing Saddleback Mountain (also known as Mount Greylock) in 1844. He describes the path to the mountain as "a road for the pilgrim to enter upon who would climb to the gates of heaven" (181). Making his way to the summit, he discovered an observatory erected by students from nearby Williams College. After spending the night on the mountain, he climbed atop the observatory to survey the morning scene:

> As the light increased I discovered around me an ocean of mist, which by chance reached up exactly to the base of the tower, and shut out every vestige of the earth, while I was left floating on this fragment of the wreck of a world, on my carved plank in cloudland; a situation which required no aid from the imagination to render it impressive. As the light in the east steadily increased, it revealed to me more clearly the new world into which I had risen in the night, the new *terra firma* perchance of my future life.... It was such a country as we might see in dreams, with all the delights of paradise. (188)

The earth below had become ephemeral, an apparition veiled by the mist, passing away like "the phantom of a shadow . . . and this new platform was gained." As the sun "began to rise on this pure world," he found himself "a dweller in the dazzling halls of Aurora, into which poets have had but a partial glance over the eastern hills, drifting amid the saffron-colored clouds, and playing with the rosy fingers of the Dawn, in the very path of the Sun's chariot, and sprinkled with its dewy dust, enjoying the benignant smile, and near at hand the far-darting glances of the god." The inhabitants of the mundane world below seem only the "dark and shadowy under-side of heaven's pavement." Before long, he "sank down again into that 'forlorn world'" from which he had emerged (189).

It seems odd that Thoreau would drop an account of this experience, which occurred on a different occasion, into his narrative of the boat trip. But we must remember that the book is not a factual account of the journey. It is an act of mythmaking. Coming roughly midway in the book, the episode is the climax of the narrative. As David Robinson explains, "The climbing of Saddleback seems a parable of enlightenment in which the pilgrim's struggle is rewarded with illumination." Thoreau's reentry into the world below marks "a point of renewal in which [he] is reintroduced to a world whose newness and complexity are constantly revealed as he advances upstream."[13]

Thoreau is sometimes portrayed as a loner and a misanthrope.[14] While it is difficult to prove what one is not, there is ample evidence that he had many friends and few enemies. That said, he could be prickly at times and critical of others who did not share his views.[15] He often had companions on his walks and carried on an extensive correspondence with those he considered his soulmates, and, following his death in 1862, it was his friends who were instrumental in fostering his literary reputation. His friend Franklin Sanborn, one of his first biographers, wrote, "Of all the thousand topics about which he thought and wrote . . . none returned to his thought and his anxieties so often as Friendship."[16]

Friendship is the major theme of the "Wednesday" chapter. In his musings on the river, Thoreau is reminded of the kindness of friends who "treated us not as what we were, but as what we aspired to be" (259). As valuable as these memories are, they are fleeting. We seldom appreciate the importance of friendship. "There is on the earth no institution which Friendship has established," Thoreau tells us; "it is not taught by any religion; no scripture contains its maxims. It has not temple, nor even a solitary column" (263). Although we seek friendship, we aren't sure where to find it. He quotes the Chinese philosopher Mencius, who says: "If one loses a fowl or a dog, he knows well how to seek them again; if one loses the sentiments of his heart, he does not know how to seek them again. . . . The duties of practical philosophy consist only in seeking after those sentiments of the heart which we have lost; that is all" (264).[17]

His anxieties regarding friendship, such as they were, stem from the fact that he was an idealist who had expectations of his friends that were hard to meet. We dream "that our Friends are our *Friends*, and that we are our Friends' *Friends*," but we discover that in reality they fail to measure up. "How often we find ourselves turning our backs on our actual Friends, that we may go and meet their ideal cousins" (265). And yet friendship is important for the fact that it makes us better people. "A Friend is one who incessantly pays us the compliment of expecting from us all the virtues, and who can appreciate them in us" (267). We stand in true relation to our friends when we give our best to them and they in turn give their best to us. "Between whom there is hearty truth there is love; and in proportion to our truthfulness and confidence in one another, our lives are divine and miraculous, and answer to our ideal" (268).

True friends are those with whom we share a natural bond. "They cherish each other's hopes," Thoreau says. "They are kind to each other's dreams" (270). Friendship is a relationship of equality and mutual respect. Friends confide in each other and hold each other to a higher standard. They do not stand on ceremony, nor do they demand proofs of their love. "A true friendship is as wise as it is tender," he writes. "The parties to it yield implicitly to the guidance of their love, and know no other law or kindness" (274). While friendship is mutual, it is not exclusive. "Indeed we cannot have too many friends; the virtue which we appreciate we to some extent appropriate, so that thus we are made at last more fit for every relation of life" (277). Although its foundations are private, its benefits are public. Friendship is a delicate plant, even if it is a native one. It is vulnerable to faults and suspicions. Friends sometimes complain that we do not appreciate them enough, "as if they expected a vote of thanks for every fine thing which they uttered or did" (278). The danger is that misunderstandings may lead to silence.

"For a companion," Thoreau insists, "I require one who will make an equal demand on me with my own genius" (279). Such friends value our aspiration over our performance and tolerate our shortcomings. We appreciate them for who they are rather than what they can do for us. Inevitably, we will find faults in our friend. "Constitutional differences" always exist, he says, and "are obstacles to a perfect Friendship." In the end, however, "we must accept or refuse one another as we are" (283). In spite of difficulties and misunderstandings that may arise between friends, he wholeheartedly endorses the ideal of Friendship:

> As surely as the sunset in my latest November shall translate me to the ethereal world, and remind me of the ruddy morning of youth; as surely as the last strain of music which falls on my decaying ear shall make age to be forgotten, or, in short, the manifold influences of nature survive during the term of our natural life, so surely my Friend shall forever be my Friend, and reflect a ray of God to me, and time shall foster and adorn and consecrate our Friendship, no less than the ruins of temples. As I love nature, as I love singing birds, and gleaming stubble, and flowing rivers, and morning and evening, and summer and winter, I love thee my Friend. (285)

Thoreau's paean of praise to the value of friendship would be tested in his relationship with Emerson following the publication of *A Week*. When the book failed to sell, Thoreau was on the hook for the printing costs and blamed his friend for putting him up to it. He confided his bitterness toward Emerson in his journal: "I had a friend, I wrote a book, I asked my friend's criticism, I never got but praise for what was good in it—my friend became estranged from me and then I got blame for all that was bad,—and so I got at last the criticism which I wanted."[18] Commenting on the rift in their relationship, Jeffrey Cramer writes, "It is unlikely that Thoreau knew all that Emerson had done to promote the book, nor that Emerson knew of Thoreau's criticisms."[19] They remained civil toward each other but seldom afterwards enjoyed the camaraderie they once felt.

At the end of the day that Wednesday, Henry and John sat on the bank and witnessed the reflection in the water of trees lit by the setting sun, enjoying "so serene an evening as left nothing to describe." All too often we think that there are few degrees of sublimity, such that the highest is only a bit higher than what we see. But we are mistaken: "Sublimer visions appear, and the former pale and fade away" (291). At such times we feel that we have come face to face with reality. "This world is but canvas to our imaginations," Thoreau tells us. We tend to our bodies, but not our imaginations. "But what avails all other wealth if this is wanting?" (292). We settle for too little. We walk on our particular path as though fate would have it so. "We are hedged about, we think, by accident and circumstance," he says (293). We find it hard to believe that any other kind of life is possible, and yet there is a path for us that, if taken, will lead us to the "unexplored Pacific Ocean of Futurity" (294).

On Thursday the boatmen reach the turning point of their voyage. (In fact, their two-week journey—not all of it by boat—had taken them all the way to Mount Washington before heading back.) As they turn toward home, a wind from the north catches their sail and they are rapidly carried downstream. Passing a certain point, Thoreau is reminded that almost 150 years previously, two white women and a boy hastened along the same part of the river in flight from Native tribesmen who had enslaved them. One of the women, Hannah Duston, had been captured when Natives raided her settlement, killing her infant child. Duston, together with her nurse and a boy who had been captured some time before, killed their captors as they slept, and, after taking scalps, made a hasty getaway, eventually reaching home in safety.

As happens so often in the book, historical events such as this one conjure up thoughts of the distant past. Referring to Hannah Duston's escape, he writes, "From this September afternoon, and from between these now cultivated shores those times seemed more remote than the dark ages" (324). Such events are homologized with those of antiquity. Earlier in the chapter he observed that "the life of a wise man is most of all extemporaneous, for he lives out of an eternity which includes all time. The cunning mind travels farther back than Zoroaster each instant, and comes quite down to the present with its revelation" (311–12). By extemporaneous he does not mean spontaneous or unscripted but rather *ex tempore*, out of time. Paradoxically, the past continues to exist in the timeless present.

The two sailors awakened the next morning to a change of seasons. They "had gone to bed in summer, and . . . awoke in autumn" (334). A steady wind filled the sail and blew them on toward home and the end of their journey. The change of seasons reflects a change of moods as well. As autumn is a prelude to winter, Thoreau's writing takes on a slightly melancholy tone, occasioned perhaps by the memory of his brother's death.

With the onset of autumn, the rhythm of life changes. The activities of summer days give way to "the stillness and longer nights of autumn and winter" (377). The harvest is gathered in, "but behind the sheaves, and under the sod, there lurks a ripe fruit, which the reapers have not gathered, the true harvest of the year" (378). What is this true harvest of the year? What knowledge or insight has Thoreau gleaned from his voyage?

> Men nowhere, east or west, live yet a *natural* life, round which the vine clings, and which the elm willingly shadows. Man would desecrate it by his touch, and so the beauty of the world remains veiled to him. He needs not only to be spiritualized, but *naturalized*, on the soil of earth. Who shall conceive what kind of roof the heavens might extend over him, what seasons minister to him, and what employment dignify his life! . . . The winds should be his breath, the seasons his moods, and he should impart of his serenity to Nature herself. But such as we know him he is ephemeral like the scenery which surrounds him, and does not aspire to an enduring existence. When we come down into the distant village, visible from the mountain-top, the nobler inhabitants with whom we have peopled it have departed, and left only vermin in its desolate streets. (379)

Once again, we have a vision of the mountaintop and descent to the world below, a transition from the sacred to the mundane. Paradoxically, however, the sacred is not transcendent but immanent. The vision of the mountaintop must be imported to the world below. We must be born again, though not in the Christian sense of the term. "We have need to be earth-born as well as heaven-born, γηγενεις, as was said of the Titans of old, or in a better sense than they"[20] (380). Having searched for heaven, we fail to realize that it is here and nowhere else. "We need pray for no higher heaven than the pure senses can furnish, a *purely* sensuous life" (382). As it is, our senses have become atrophied. They are used for trivial, mundane purposes.

How, then, are the senses purified? Thoreau asks. "Where is the instructed teacher? Where are the *normal* schools?" (382).[21] The schools of ancient philosophy, with which he was quite familiar, were therapeutic in that they offered both a diagnosis and a cure for our spiritual anemia. It is easier to look outward than within. "But there is only necessary a moment's sanity and sound senses, to teach us that there is a nature beyond the ordinary, in which we have only some vague" awareness. "We live," he says, "on the outskirts of that region" (383).

He is "not without hope that we may, even here and now, obtain some accurate information concerning that OTHER WORLD which the instinct of mankind has so long predicted" (385). Science gives us knowledge of the material, temporal world. But "we are provided with senses as well fitted to penetrate the spaces of the real, the substantial, the eternal, as these outward are to penetrate the material universe" (386). Scientists show us the world as it appears; mystics, seers, and poets show us the world as it truly is. We seek reality, a "bottom" that will sustain us. Common sense has its uses, but "uncommon sense, that sense which is common only to the wisest, is as much more excellent as it is more rare" (387).

As the sun sets on the last day of their journey, Thoreau is led to conclude that, while poets may "presume to fable of the ineffable," in the end there is only Silence. Silence "is when we hear inwardly, sound when we hear outwardly" (391). For thousands of years we have tried to translate the Silence, but "still she is little better than a sealed book."

> A man may run on confidently for a time, thinking he has her under his thumb, and shall one day exhaust her, but he too must at last be silent, and men remark only how brave a beginning he made; for when he at length dives into her, so vast is the disproportion of the told to the untold that the former will seem but the bubble on the surface where he disappeared. Nevertheless, we will go on, like those Chinese cliff swallows, feathering our nests with the froth which may one day be bread of life to such as dwell by the seashore. (393)

A Natural Life

What are we to make of *A Week*, this narrative with so many digressions? It is easy to get lost among the trees in Thoreau's writing, but we mustn't lose our vision of the forest itself. This vision was perhaps best expressed by Ethel Seybold: "The truth, the quite incredible truth about Thoreau, the truth that we resist in spite of his own repeated witness, is that he spent a quarter of a century in a quest for transcendental reality, in an attempt to discover the secret of the universe."[22] This transcendental reality was a mythical realm lurking behind, below, and above the ordinariness of everyday life. It was a search for this realm that he was embarked upon:

> I am bound, I am bound, for a distant shore,
> By a lonely isle, by a far Azore,
> There it is, there it is, the treasure I seek,
> On the barren sands of a desolate creek. (3)

Historian of religions Mircea Eliade helps us see how myth functions in *A Week*. In *The Sacred and the Profane: The Nature of Religion*, Eliade describes the sacred and profane as two modes of being in the world.[23] We become aware of the sacred because it reveals itself as something entirely different from the profane. People living in premodern societies sought to live as much as possible in the realm of the sacred because, Eliade says, "the sacred is pre-eminently the *real*, at once power, efficacity, the source of life and fecundity. Religious man's desire to live *in the sacred* is in fact equivalent to his desire to take up his abode in objective reality, not to let himself be paralyzed by the never-ceasing relativity of purely subjective experiences, to live in a real and effective world, and not in an illusion."[24]

The sacred is manifested in both space and time. It constitutes a break in the uniformity of space, an opening to another, transcendent dimension of existence. It establishes a center and a point of reference in an otherwise dimensionless and chaotic world and, in Eliade's words, "makes possible ontological passage from one mode of being to another."[25] The sacred represents a break in time as well as in space, arresting profane temporal duration. Moreover, sacred time is reversible. By means of festivals, liturgies, and spiritual practices, sacred events that occurred in the mythical past may be reactualized, as they were in the beginning. "Religious man lives in two kinds of time," Eliade observes, "of which the more important, sacred time, appears under the paradoxical aspect of a circular time, reversible and recoverable, a sort of eternal mythical present that is periodically regenerated by means of rites."[26] Taken together, the notions of sacred space and time demonstrate a longing for paradise and eternity.

Thoreau was not a member of a primitive society, of course, but he did possess a religious sensibility akin to that of traditional peoples to the extent that he felt trapped in the present, a profane time of endless mundane duration. Like the Native peoples Eliade describes, his writing displays a nostalgia for paradise and a desire to live in the sacred. Examples of this are the myriad references to classical literature—Greek most of all, but also Roman, Indian, Chinese, and Persian. Seybold reminds us that to Thoreau, the classics were "the most pertinent and valuable source of past revelation." As she further explains:

> All antiquities had a great attraction for Thoreau. They seemed to him not so much old as early, not so far removed from the present as near to the beginning. There is, to be sure, a slight inconsistency between the belief that all things are everywhere and always the same and the suspicion that the farther back you are in time, the closer you are to reality. But that suspicion was always with Thoreau. He fancied that the message shone a little clearer in the beginning.[27]

Classical literature transports him to a distant time and place—the origin of things, as Eliade would say—radically different from his prosaic, mundane existence. "Reading the classics or conversing with those old Greeks and Latins in their surviving works," he writes, "is like walking amidst the stars and constellations, a high and by way serene to travel" (226).

This nostalgia for the distant past is also shown in the way Thoreau identifies familiar settings with ancient and mythical ones, such as when he likens the Concord River to the Nile and the Euphrates. Even calling the river by its original name, the Musketaquid, displays a preference for the mythic past, when the Natives first named it. Farmers are likened to men out of Homer, or Chaucer, or Shakespeare. In the "Wednesday" chapter is a lengthy meditation on rocks worn smooth by the river. "With such expanse of time and natural forces are our very paving-stones produced," he writes. "They teach us lessons, these dumb workers; verily there are 'sermons in stones, and books in the running brooks'" (248). They remind him of the monuments of antiquity, of the ruins of Athens and Rome, and the temples at Karnak.

In the "Tuesday" chapter he vividly describes a transcendent vision he had atop Saddleback Mountain. "The symbolic and religious significance of mountains is endless," Eliade writes in *Patterns in Comparative Religion.* "Mountains are often looked on as the place where sky and earth meet, a 'central point' therefore, the point through which the *Axis Mundi* goes, a region impregnated with the sacred, a spot where one can pass from one cosmic zone to another."[28] Elsewhere he notes that "the act of climbing or ascending symbolizes *the way towards the absolute reality.*"[29]

In addition to the polarity of sacred and profane are those of the wild and the cultivated and of Native and civilized. As we saw in the "Sunday" chapter, Thoreau expressed a "yearning toward all wildness" in preference to gardening, which lacks "the vigor and freedom of the forest and the outlaw" (55). He also contrasted Native and village life. In these polarities, the sacred is identified with what is wild and Native, while the tame and the civilized are profane.

Certain structural elements in *A Week* also contribute to the book's mythic quality. As Eliade points out, sacred time is circular; it can be repeated by such means as rituals and storytelling. In this manner, the cosmos is re-created and life is renewed. In keeping with this circular pattern, Thoreau compresses a two-week trip into one, just as he reduces his two-year life in the woods to one in *Walden;* in the first instance, the cycle of the week, in the second, the cycle of the year. Moreover, each chapter in *A Week* describes the diurnal course of a day from sunrise to sunset.

Another mythic element is the quest and return pattern of the journey, like that of the excursion to Saddleback Mountain, which is akin to the shaman's quest for a vision.[30] In Eliade's view the shaman's quest "is equivalent to a *journey back to the origins,* a regression into the mythical time of the Paradise lost."[31] It expresses the desire to recover the state of freedom and restore the sense of connection with nature that existed *in illo tempore,* at the beginning.

The polarity of the sacred and the profane is unmistakable in Thoreau's description of his ascension of Saddleback Mountain. As he climbs the mountain, he leaves behind the profane "wreck of a world" below. The summit is clearly the realm of the sacred: a pure world, the abode of the gods, "such a country as we might see in dreams, with all the delights of paradise." This is reality, whereas the earth beneath is but "the phantom of a shadow" (188–89). Having gained this "new platform," he descends the mountain and sinks down again into that forlorn, profane world from which he had emerged, disconsolate perhaps, but comforted in the knowledge that another mode of existence is attainable.

The chapter also includes an homage to Greek poets and poetry. "When we have sat down to them," Thoreau writes, "life seems as still and serene as if it were very far off, and I believe it is not habitually seen from any common platform so truly and unexaggerated as in the light of literature" (226). Here again he uses the word "platform," which is suggestive of a familiar theme in classical literature, "the view from above." Consider these lines from *The Way Things Are* by Lucretius:

> But nothing is more sweet than full possession
> Of those calm heights, well built, well fortified
> By wise men's teaching, to look down from here
> At others wandering below, men lost,
> Confused, in hectic search for the right road.[32]

For the Stoic philosophers, too, Seneca and Marcus Aurelius in particular, taking the view from above was a spiritual exercise.[33] It was a means of transcending the messiness and discord of the mundane world.

Thoreau's journey was an attempt to return to the origins in search of healing and renewal not only for himself but also for his imagined readers. He was aware that his world was rapidly becoming more secularized and disenchanted. He worried, as did others among the Transcendentalists, that the Understanding—in the form of science, technology, and capitalism—was predominating over the Reason, an intuitive awareness of the wholeness and sacrality of the natural world. The profane was eclipsing the sacred. And yet he was confident that, as Emerson had avowed in *Nature*, "a correspondent revolution in things will attend the influx of the spirit."[34]

The book narrates Thoreau's mythic encounter with the sacred as experienced on Saddleback Mountain. This was a vision of a new world. It is the same world he had left and to which he returned but is viewed from a transcendent perspective. "Here or nowhere is our heaven," he writes, but this is true only in so far as we are able to purify our senses and live a more naturalized life.

CHAPTER 4

BEGINNING TO LIVE

It was a chilly morning in late March. The ice on the water had recently broken up. A light flurry of snow was falling. And yet it seemed a pleasant spring day. A young man walked out to Walden Pond from Concord village, two miles distant, carrying an axe borrowed from a friend. Seeking a suitable site to build a small house, he spotted a hillside covered with pine woods through which was a view of the pond. Hefting the axe, he began to cut down a few trees for timber. Sometime in May, friends from the village helped him raise the frame of the house. For siding, he bought a shanty from an Irish laborer who had worked on the Fitchburg Railroad.

On the fifth of July 1845, Henry Thoreau noted in his journal, "Yesterday I came here to live."[1] He insisted it was only coincidental that he moved in on Independence Day, and yet going to live at Walden Pond did signal a new-found sense of freedom. He had been frustrated that his efforts at getting published had largely come to naught. Several years earlier, in April 1841, he had written in his journal: "I only ask a clean seat. I will build my lodge on the southern slope of some hill, and take there the life the gods send me. Will it not be employment enough to accept gratefully all that is yielded me between sun and sun?"[2] He returned to this thought later in the year, on Christmas Eve: "I want to go soon and live away by the pond where I shall hear only the wind whispering among the reeds. It will be success if I shall have left myself behind. But my friends ask what I will do when I get there? Will it not be employment enough to watch the progress of the seasons?" The next day he added, "I don't want to feel as if my life were a sojourn any longer. That philosophy cannot be true which so paints it. It is time now that I begin to live."[3]

The opportunity presented itself after Emerson purchased several parcels of property around the pond and invited Thoreau to build his cabin there in exchange for cutting firewood and clearing some land for planting. In addition to his musings in the journal, Thoreau had practical reasons for moving to the pond. He needed some peace and quiet to write a book he had envisioned about the boat trip he and John had taken before his brother's untimely death. What with boarders and a voluble mother, the family home offered little of that. According to his friend Ellery Channing, the cabin at the pond was "a writing case," an "inkstand" in the woods.[4] While there he wrote two drafts of *A Week*, one of *Walden*, and two lengthy essays, "Ktaadn, and the Maine Woods" and "Thomas Carlyle and His Works." He composed several lectures as well, accomplishing all of this in a span of twenty-six months.[5]

His stated aim was to conduct an experiment in living deliberately. He wished "to front only the essential facts of life" and discover what it had to teach,

> to live deep and suck out all the marrow of life, to live so sturdily and Spartan-like as to put to rout all that was not life, to cut a broad swath and shave close, to drive life into a corner, and reduce it to its lowest terms, and, if it proved to be mean, why then to get the whole and genuine meanness of it, and publish its meanness to the world; or if it were sublime, to know it by experience, and be able to give a true account of it in [his] next excursion.[6]

It was essentially a spiritual exercise in pursuit of self-culture, driven by a desire to live life on his own terms, and not at the behest of others.

An added attraction of living at the pond was the nearness of nature. He had always enjoyed his daily forays into the woods and fields surrounding Concord. Now he could live amidst the flora and fauna, immersed in the natural world. He is rightly regarded as a naturalist and nature writer, but his love of nature went deeper than mere botanizing. The Japanese have a word for what he sought: *shinrin-yoku*, which means bathing in nature, or taking in nature through our senses. The sights and sounds of nature, the sunlight through the trees, the sound of water lapping the shore—these have a therapeutic quality. They ease our stress and worry and help us to relax. They restore our vitality, refreshing and rejuvenating our spirits.

Thoreau relished the solitude he found in going to the pond, but he was far from the hermit he is so often portrayed as. He made frequent trips to the village, visiting with friends and shooting the breeze with the locals. He dined with his family most weekends. He entertained curious visitors and went boating with children on the pond. He traveled with a cousin to the

Maine woods, delivered several lectures at the Concord Lyceum and else-where, and, famously, spent a night in jail for refusing to pay his taxes.

Another reason why he might have wanted to go out to the pond to live is suggested by his reading of Confucian literature. As I mentioned in chapter 2, the notion of the recluse as moral hero is a long-established tradition in Chinese culture. Although he was probably unaware of this tradition, Tho-reau did cite one well-known example of it in the selections he chose for *The Dial*. By going into reclusion and withholding allegiance to the state, the sage engages in a form of protest, of action from principle, the very notion that underlies Thoreau's argument in "Civil Disobedience."

Walden was finally published on August 9, 1854, having gone through a course of seven major revisions. J. Lynden Shanley, who made a detailed account of these revisions, tells us: "It is not a book which he had practically finished in 1849 but did not publish until 1854 because of external circum-stances. The full expression of the joy and confidence of *Walden* depended greatly upon the work Thoreau did after 1851."[7] The work he refers to is Thoreau's journal, which I examine in the following chapter. Many passages from it were incorporated in the final revisions of the book. Not only did they enliven the finished version, but also they demonstrate that *Walden* is not simply an account of what transpired while he was living at the pond. They indicate that, like *A Week*, it is a product of Thoreau's imaginative mythmaking. By his own admission, facts were only the frame of his pictures, the "material to the mythology which I am writing."[8] Contrary to the com-mon view that myth is falsehood, "'myth' means a 'true story,'" Mircea Eliade writes, "and, beyond that, a story that is a most precious possession because it is sacred, exemplary, significant."[9] This is because myth deals with *realities*, with the sacred as opposed to the profane. Hence *Walden* is not a fictional version of his time at the pond but rather a *true* account, as Thoreau would insist.

His mythmaking is most obvious in the fact that he conflated his two years living at the pond into a single year, from one spring to the next. The cycle of the seasons is symbolic of a pattern of death and rebirth and of the cosmog-ony, or the creation of a new world out of the old one. In Thoreau's view, industrial society, driven by commerce and materialism, has desacralized the world. We must restore the sacred dimension of existence by undertaking the creation of a new world, one that we would desire to inhabit.

Walden is not only an example of Thoreau's mythmaking; it is also a philosophical treatise, not in the modern sense of a closely reasoned set of propositions, but in the manner of ancient philosophies of moral development, such as those described in the second chapter. Recall what I quoted from *Walden* in that chapter: "To be a philosopher is not merely to have subtle thoughts, nor even to found a school, but so to love wisdom as to live according to its dictates, a life of simplicity, independence, magnanimity, and trust. It is to solve some of the problems of life, not only theoretically, but practically" (14–15). These philosophies are essentially therapeutic in nature. Martha Nussbaum's description of Hellenistic philosophy also applies to other schools of this type. They "all conceived of philosophy as a way of addressing the most painful problems of human life. They saw the philosopher as a compassionate physician whose arts could heal many pervasive types of human suffering. They practiced philosophy not as a detached intellectual technique dedicated to the display of cleverness but as an immersed and worldly art of grappling with human misery."[10] This is amply described in the "Economy" chapter of the book.

The dichotomy between the misery experienced by so many of his contemporaries and the flourishing life they might have should they choose to live more simply and deliberately is most pronounced in the tonal difference between the first and second chapters of the book. The first, written in expository language, is didactic and often judgmental. Conversely, the second, written in the language of metaphor and poetry, is uplifting and inspirational. Another dichotomy is that between society and solitude, as shown in chapters 5 and 6. This back-and-forth pattern is repeated throughout, often expressed in the dualities of the actual and the real, the factual and the mythic, the profane and the sacred, materialism and spirituality, and civilization and nature. In each case, the second term in the polarity redeems or transforms the first one.

The therapy Thoreau prescribes for others applies to him as well. By his own admission, he dwelled too much and too long in the profane quotidian. *Walden* touches on many topics, but it is fundamentally a narrative of Thoreau's search for the sacred, for ultimate reality, eloquently expressed in this passage from the second chapter:

> Let us settle ourselves, and work and wedge our feet downward through the mud and slush of opinion, and prejudice, and tradition, and delusion, and appearance, that alluvion which covers the globe, through Paris and London, through New York and Boston and Concord, through church and state, through poetry and philosophy and religion, till we come to a hard

bottom and rocks in place, which we can call reality, and say, This is, and no mistake.... Be it life or death, we crave only reality. (97–98)

On Walden Pond

It might seem odd that Thoreau begins his book on life in the woods with a chapter on economics. But Thoreau loves wordplay, and for him economy means something more than pinching pennies. The book as a whole is an "accounting" of his two-year stay at the pond. And in this chapter he examines the way people are "spending" their lives. All around him, "in shops, offices, and fields," people appear "to be doing penance in a thousand remarkable ways" (4). They seem so burdened with cares and labors that they cannot enjoy the finer fruits of life. Lacking leisure, they have no time to be anything but a machine. Worst of all, they are driving themselves as though they had no other choice.

One might assume that people had deliberately chosen to live this way, thinking there was no alternative. But, Thoreau insists, "it is never too late to give up our prejudices" (8). Change *is* possible. It's just that we're too timid and unsure of what might happen if we followed his advice. Our capacity for change hasn't been measured because it hasn't been tested. He insists we may safely trust a good deal more than we do. "How vigilant we are!" he says,

> determined not to live by faith if we can avoid it; all the day long on the alert, at night we willingly say our prayers and commit ourselves to uncertainties. So thoroughly and sincerely are we compelled to live, reverencing our life, and denying the possibility of change. This is the only way, we say; but there as many ways as there can be drawn radii from one center. All change is a miracle to contemplate; but it is a miracle which is taking place every instant. (11)

Thoreau spends a good part of the chapter examining what he calls "the necessaries of life" and what it takes to attain them. He identifies these as food, shelter, clothing, and fuel. A problem arises once we have obtained them, since having done so, we are never satisfied. We reach for the luxuries besides, which he considers positive hindrances to our spiritual elevation. There is an alternative, however, and that is to "adventure on life now, [our] vacation from humbler toil having commenced" (15). When we have met our physical needs, it is time to seek a more spiritual kind of fulfillment. He doesn't quarrel with those who feel well employed. He is mainly concerned with those who feel otherwise, complaining of their lot in life when they might actually improve it, those who feel trapped out of a sense of duty, and those who have accumulated possessions and are now feeling burdened by them.

In offering himself as an example, Thoreau tells us how he has spent his own life. As much as possible, he has tried to live extemporaneously, in the present moment: "In any weather, at any hour of the day or night, I have been anxious to improve the nick of time, and notch it on my stick, too; to stand at the meeting of two eternities, the past and the future, which is precisely the present moment; to toe that line." What follows is a cryptic but intriguing passage: "I long ago lost a hound, a bay horse, and a turtle-dove, and am still on their trail. Many are the travellers I have spoken concerning them, describing their tracks and what calls they answered to. I have met one or two who had heard the hound, and the tramp of the horse, and even seen the dove disappear behind a cloud, and they seemed as anxious to recover them as if they had lost them themselves" (17). Thoreau delights in such enigmatic fables, and there are several in *Walden*. This one, it seems to me, is emblematic of his elusive search for transcendent reality. From time to time he catches a glimpse of it, but it always seems just out of reach. In his journal he wrote: "I was always conscious of sounds in nature which my ears could never hear,—that I caught but the prelude to a strain. She always retreats as I advance. Away and behind is she and her meaning. Will not this faith and expectation make to itself ears at length? I never saw to the end; but the best part was unseen and unheard."[11]

Thoreau prescribes simple living as the remedy to overdosing on consumption. He gives us a detailed description of building his cabin and the cost of maintaining himself there, down to the last half cent! He figures that he has supported himself for the past five years on the earnings of six weeks per year.[12] The rest of the time he had free and clear to pursue the project of his own self-culture, convinced "both by faith and experience, that to maintain one's self on this earth is not a hardship but a pastime, if we will live simply and wisely" (70). But he cautions others against imitating his mode of life—or that of their parents or neighbors—insisting that each person find and follow his or her own path.

If we recall Hadot's comments on Stoic and Epicurean elements in Thoreau's philosophy, it would seem that in this chapter, his writing displays elements of the Epicurean way of life. A central tenet of this philosophy is the enjoyment of life in the here and now. Epicurus famously said that pleasure is the beginning and end of a blessed life. By pleasure, however, he did not mean hedonistic self-indulgence but rather serenity of spirit that comes from plain living and high thinking. One maximizes pleasure by minimizing wants, as Thoreau himself advises in this chapter. One need not be a student of Greek philosophy to come to the same conclusion.

There is a mythic quality to Thoreau's writing in the second chapter, "Where I Lived, and What I Lived For"—similar to that in *A Week*—as if to suggest that he is dealing with timeless truths. As he begins to describe where he lived, he observes that every spot might be the site of a house, and that wherever one lives, that place becomes the center of the cosmos. Eliade points out that "every dwelling stands at the 'centre of the world,' so that its construction was only possible by means of abolishing profane space and time and establishing sacred space and time."[13] Thoreau's description of the location and surroundings of his cabin at Walden Pond is homologized with mythical times, places, and people such as Mount Olympus, the steppes of Tartary, classical and Eastern writers, and constellations of stars. Elaborating on the symbolism of the center, Eliade insists that "every place that bore witness to an incursion of the sacred into profane space, was ... regarded as a 'centre.' These sacred spaces could also be constructed; but their construction was, in its way, a cosmogony, a creation of the world."[14] It is no exaggeration to suggest that Thoreau's modest cabin stands in the center of the world and that its construction exemplifies the creation of a cosmos out of chaos: "This was an airy and unplastered cabin, fit to entertain a travelling god, and where a goddess might trail her garments. The winds which passed over my dwelling were such as sweep over the ridges of mountains, bearing the broken strains, or celestial parts only, of terrestrial music. The morning wind forever blows, the poem of creation is uninterrupted; but few are the ears that hear it. Olympus is but the outside of the earth every where" (85).

"Both time and place were changed," he writes, "and I dwelt nearer to those parts of the universe and to those eras in history which most attracted me" (87). This is the eternal present, contemporaneous with the Golden Age of innocence and bliss—which we too might recover if we could only wake up and become more fully aware. Waking his neighbors up to this reality is precisely what Thoreau aims to do. "I do not propose to write an ode to dejection," he says, "but to brag as lustily as chanticleer in the morning, standing on his roost, if only to wake my neighbors up" (84). The morning is the temporal correlative to the cabin site at the pond. In the same way that his cabin in the woods is a gateway to Mount Olympus, "morning brings back the heroic ages." Every morning creates the world anew, giving promise of spiritual awakening and self-renewal. It is a sacred time, a time of innocence and simplicity:

> Every morning was a cheerful invitation to make my life of equal simplicity, and I may say innocence, with Nature herself. I have been as sincere a worshipper of Aurora as the Greeks. I got up early and bathed in the pond; that was a religious exercise, and one of the best things which I did. They say that characters were engraven on the bathing tub of king Tching-thang to this effect: "Renew thyself completely each day; do it again, and again, and forever again." (88)

For Thoreau, the morning is the "awakening hour" when there is the "least somnolence in us." Most of the time we seem to be asleep. We must rouse ourselves from our spiritual lethargy, not by artificial means, but by aspirations from within which summon us to a higher mode of life. For those able to do so, "the day is a perpetual morning" (89). But few are thus awakened. Most are alert enough only for physical labor, considerably fewer for intellectual exertion, fewer still for "a poetic or divine life." It is only when we are awake that we are alive. Thoreau says he has never yet met anyone who was entirely awake. "We must learn to reawaken and keep ourselves awake, not by mechanical aids, but by an infinite expectation of the dawn" (90). Although this may prove difficult, he is convinced that we have the ability to elevate ourselves if we make a conscious endeavor:

> It is something to be able to paint a particular picture, or to carve a statue, and so to make a few objects beautiful; but it is far more glorious to carve and paint the very atmosphere and medium through which we look, which morally we can do. To affect the quality of the day, that is the highest of arts. Every man is tasked to make his life, even in its details, worthy of the contemplation of his most elevated and critical hour. (90)

Sadly, we live meanly, like ants, our lives frittered away on detail. We should slow down and live more simply. "Why should we live with such hurry and waste of life?" he asks (93). People say they want to hear the news, but what passes for news is merely gossip. Most of our communications, including our correspondence, are superficial. (No doubt the same can be said of social media and emails today.) Infinitely more important is that which is timeless and real. "Shams and delusions are esteemed for soundest truths, while reality is fabulous." We should observe realities only and not allow ourselves to be distracted by appearances. When we are "unhurried and wise, we perceive that only great and worthy things have any permanent and absolute existence, that petty fears and petty pleasures are but the shadow of the reality" (95–96). We are like the prince in the Hindu fable who was raised by a forester, ignorant of his true estate. He imagined himself to belong to a lowly caste until one of the king's ministers discovered him and revealed to him who he truly was, thereby dispelling the misconception about his character. We think that our estate, too, is mean, but only because our vision does not penetrate the surface of things.

The concluding paragraphs of this chapter are a summons to wake up and become aware of the marvelous reality that lies about us wherever we are. We think that truth is remote, existing perhaps in some distant place and far-off time, but "all these times and places and occasions are now and here," Thoreau says. "God culminates in the present moment, and never will be more divine in the lapse of all the ages. And we are enabled to apprehend at all what is sublime and noble only by the perpetual instilling and drenching of the reality that surrounds us." He urges us to spend the day "as deliberately as Nature," determined not to be distracted (97). Instead of attending to the many trivial demands on our time, we should seek more depth in our lives; rather than the delusions of prejudice and appearance, we should seek only reality.

If the first chapter displays elements of the Epicurean way of life, this one conveys Stoic sentiments. A central tenet of Stoicism is living in the present. For the Stoics, happiness and peace of mind are to be gained only by experiencing the timelessness of the present moment In pointing out elements of Epicureanism and Stoicism in *Walden*—and there are some of each—we mustn't lose sight of the broader picture. As Hadot tells us, "In choosing to live in the woods for some time, Thoreau wanted to perform a philosophical act, that is to say, to devote himself to a certain mode of philosophical life that included, at the same time, manual labor and poverty, but also opened up to him an immensely enlarged perception of the world."[15]

Walden is both a mythic narrative of Thoreau's quest for reality and a manual of spiritual practice. The ancient schools of philosophy offered not only a diagnosis of our troubled condition but also the means for improving it. As we have seen, for Thoreau and the Transcendentalists this practice was self-culture, or the art of life. Following his description of the ideal way of life in the second chapter, in succeeding chapters he gives us the means of achieving it.

Reading is the first of several practices he proposes in *Walden*. But the reading he advises is not for idle minds in idle hours: "To read well, that is, to read true books in a true spirit, is a noble exercise, and one that will task the reader more than any exercise which the customs of the day esteem. It requires a training such as the athletes underwent, the steady intention almost of the whole life to this object. Books must be read as deliberately and reservedly as they were written" (100–101). His recommended reading consists chiefly of the classics and religious scriptures, for they represent the treasured wealth and cumulative wisdom of the human race. We will be truly enriched when we have filled our libraries with "Vedas and Zendavesta and Bibles, with Homers and Dantes and Shakespeares, and all the centuries to come shall have successively deposited their trophies in the forums of the world. By such a pile we may hope to scale heaven at last." Most people read for trivial reasons and know little of reading in the high sense, "as a noble and intellectual exercise" (104).

In Thoreau's day as in ours, potboilers and romantic novels seem to have been the most popular literature. The books he has in mind are those that address our condition, whatever it may be, and that would be beneficial to us:

> How many a man has dated a new era in his life from the reading of a book! The book exists for us, perchance, which will explain our miracles and reveal new ones. The at present unutterable things we may find somewhere uttered. These same questions that disturb and puzzle and confound us have in their turn occurred to all the wise men; not one has been omitted; and each has answered them, according to his ability, by his words and his life. (107–8)

Many of his readers, from his time to ours, have believed *Walden* to be just this sort of book.

We consider ourselves modern and think we are making great progress, but look how little we do for our self-culture. We need to be provoked, goaded into expanding our horizons of learning. Our communities provide common schools for children but, aside from the local lyceum and public library, little in the way of adult education. "It is time," Thoreau argues, "that we had uncommon schools, that we did not leave off our education when we begin to be men and women. It is time that villages were universities, and their elder inhabitants the fellows of the universities, with leisure . . . to pursue the liberal studies the rest of their lives" (108–9).

Self-culture was "the defining characteristic of the age," according to literary scholar Mark G. Vasquez, referring to the middle decades of the nineteenth century.[16] Under this rubric, scores of institutions, including lyceums and libraries, sprang up to advance self-culture primarily among young working-class people.[17] These were a means of cultivating civic participation in the newly formed republic and of improving the capacities of working people in a rapidly expanding economy. For Unitarians like Channing, it was also a means of advancing moral development. Self-culture and the leisure to pursue it had been the prerogative of the upper classes. Thoreau wants to make this possible for everyday people, not simply for the purposes of moral and economic betterment, but also, and especially, for their spiritual growth. Reading, of the type that he recommends, is one means of furthering this process.

Contemplation is another spiritual practice Thoreau advises. Books, for all their timeless wisdom, are abstract, dealing with experience at second hand. They cannot "supersede the necessity of being always on the alert." No course of study, including history, philosophy, or poetry, can compare with the practice of awareness, the discipline of attending to what may be seen at first hand. "Will you be a reader, a student merely," Thoreau asks, "or a seer? Read your fate, see what is before you, and walk on into futurity" (111).

He didn't have much time for reading his first summer at the pond since he was raising a crop of beans. But when he was not tending his garden, he seems to have spent a lot of time in contemplation:

> There were times when I could not afford to sacrifice the bloom of the present moment to any work, whether of the head or hands. I love a broad margin to my life. Sometimes, in a summer morning, having taken my accustomed bath, I sat in my sunny doorway from sunrise till noon, rapt in a revery, amidst the pines and hickories and sumachs, in undisturbed solitude and stillness, while the birds sang around or flitted noiseless through the house, until by the sun falling in at my west window, or the noise of some traveller's wagon on the distant highway, I was reminded of the lapse of time. I grew in those seasons like corn in the night, and they were far better than any work of the hands would have been. They were not time subtracted from my life, but so much over and above my usual allowance. I realized what the Orientals mean by contemplation and the forsaking of works. (111–12)

He required a "broad margin" to his life, he says, meaning by this that it needed to include periods of leisure as well as study and physical labor.[18] For it is in these contemplative interludes that he experienced spiritual growth. As suggested in this passage, contemplation and leisure are important disciplines in the cultivation of the soul.

The time spent in contemplation cannot be reckoned in days of the calendar nor hours of the clock. Though his neighbors might have considered it sheer idleness, by the standards of the birds and flowers it was time well spent. Living his life in such a mindful way, in full awareness of himself and his surroundings, Thoreau came to the following conclusion:

> I had this advantage, at least, in my mode of life, over those who were obliged to look abroad for amusement, to society and the theatre, that my life itself was become my amusement and never ceased to be novel. It was a drama of many scenes and without an end. If we were always indeed getting our living, and regulating our lives according to the last and best mode we had learned, we should never be troubled with ennui. Follow your genius closely enough, and it will not fail to show you a fresh prospect every hour. (112)

Thoreau describes in great detail the flora and fauna surrounding his cabin, scenes from his window and along the footpath through the woods. He notices the many kinds of berries growing nearby and the great variety of birds in the area. His reverie is interrupted, however, by the sound of the train as it passes by on the far shore of the pond. The noise is intrusive and disconcerting, drowning out the sounds of nature and disturbing his reverie. The whistle of the locomotive is a metaphor for the troublesome aspects of civilization and commerce, signaling the arrival of "restless city merchants" within the "circle of the town," heedless of the rhythms of nature and village life (115). The railroad has seemingly set the whole world in motion and speeded everything up, including conversation. There is no stopping it. "We have constructed a fate," he says, "that never turns aside" (118).

With the passing of the train, and "all the restless world" with it, Thoreau feels "more alone than ever" (122). But he is never lonely. He is serenaded by the agreeable sounds of the church bells in the surrounding villages, the lowing of cattle in the fields, the chanting of the whippoorwills, the rumbling of wagons over the bridge, the baying of dogs, and so many other sounds. "All sound heard at the greatest possible distance produces one and the same effect," he says, "a vibration of the universal lyre." As noted in the previous chapter, he was especially attentive to sounds. Very often they were a physical stimulus to transcendent experiences, to a realm beyond the senses: "no gate,—no front yard,—and no path to the civilized world" (128).

We get the impression, from the opening words of the "Solitude" chapter, that Thoreau has settled into life at Walden Pond and has come to feel at one with his surroundings. "I go and come with a strange liberty in Nature, a part of herself" (129). Aside from occasional visitors who leave flowers and other mementos as calling cards, he enjoys a great deal of solitude in his woodland retreat. His nearest neighbor is a mile distant, and Thoreau is, by his own reckoning, the sole inhabitant of Walden Woods.[19] "I have, as it were, my own sun and moon and stars, and a little world all to myself" (130). In spite of his isolation he "never felt lonesome, or in the least oppressed by a sense of solitude" except once, and then only briefly (131). Some of his most pleasant hours were those spent indoors during lengthy rainstorms or on long winter evenings "in which many thoughts had time to take root and unfold themselves" (132).

To those who think he might be lonesome he replies: "Why should I feel lonely? is not our planet in the Milky Way?" It is not mere distance that separates us from others. "What do we want most to dwell near to?" Thoreau asks. "Not to many men surely, the depot, the post-office, the bar-room, the meeting-house, the school-house, the grocery, Beacon Hill, or the Five Points, where men most congregate, but to the perennial source of our life, whence in all our experience we have found that to issue; as the willow stands near the water and sends out its roots in that direction" (133).[20]

Solitude allows us to stand apart from worldly affairs. We "may be either the driftwood in the stream, or Indra in the sky looking down on it." We become "sensible of a certain doubleness" by which we may stand remote from ourselves and one another (134–35). The reference to Indra may be traced to the Vishnu Purana, a work Thoreau was reading as he revised this portion of the *Walden* manuscript. It points to the distinction between appearance and reality. In the trancelike state induced by the appearance of driftwood floating in the stream, he becomes aware of a larger Self that transcends the self which is watching the scene below. Commenting on this passage in his book *The Magic Circle of Walden*, Charles R. Anderson remarks, "What had begun as a simple retreat to the woods to find solitude for writing has become involved in probing the meaning of nature, of reality itself, and through that a search for God and the discovery of Self."[21] Accordingly, solitude is another of Thoreau's spiritual practices.

Thoreau compares his own solitude with that of nature. He is no lonelier, he says, than the loon, or even Walden Pond for that matter. He alludes to visits he has had from the spirits of Pan, the Greek god of all the inhabitants of the countryside, and Mother Nature, in communion with which he feels part and parcel of the earth and the elemental forces of nature. "Shall I not have intelligence with the earth?" he asks. "Am I not partly leaves and vegetable mould myself?" For those who feel lonely, he prescribes "a draught of undiluted morning air," the morning being a metaphor for spiritual awakening (138).

The "Visitors" chapter is paired with the preceding one in expressing the dichotomy between solitude and society. Thoreau is actually seeking a balance in our need for both. Contrary to what readers might conclude from reading "Solitude," he says that he loves society "as much as most" and that he is "naturally no hermit." He has three chairs in his house, he says, "one for solitude, two for friendship, three for society," suggesting by this that a balanced life entails the use of all three (140). In her commentary on the metaphor of the three chairs in *Walden*, sociologist Sherry Turkle, author of *Reclaiming Conversation: The Power of Talk in a Digital Age*, explains:

> In order to feel more, and to feel more like ourselves, we connect. But in our rush to connect, we flee solitude. In time, our ability to be separate and gather ourselves is diminished. If we don't know who we are when we are alone, we turn to other people to support our sense of self. This makes it impossible to fully experience others as who they are. We take what we need from them in bits and pieces; it is as though we use them as spare parts to support our fragile selves.[22]

Solitude is essential in developing reliance on oneself rather than dependence on others.

In truth, Thoreau had many visitors to his cabin, curious, no doubt, to see what he was up to. He tells us that he once entertained a gathering of "twenty-five or thirty souls, with their bodies," referring to a meeting of the Concord Women's Anti-Slavery Society, which gathered at the cabin to celebrate the West Indian emancipation just a week after his night in jail (140). One of his visitors was a runaway slave whom he assisted in escaping to Canada. Children, including the Alcott girls, were welcome visitors. He feels that he met some of his visitors under more favorable circumstances at the pond than elsewhere, not only because of the natural surroundings, but also because at that distance from town, fewer came to see him on trivial business.

The impression persists that Thoreau was an antisocial hermit. Nothing could be further from the truth. Even while at the pond, where he lived for barely more than two years, he frequently walked to town to catch up on the latest gossip, to dine with his family or with the Emersons, and to do odd jobs, including surveying, for townsfolk. Especially curious is the accusation that his mother did his laundry. The implication is that he was cheating somehow, or that he was a hypocrite for extolling self-reliance while letting others do the dirty work. The fact is, he often did chores around the family home, a house, we might add, that he had helped to build the year before he went to the pond. Doing his laundry in exchange seems fair enough. In any case, in *Walden* he says that washing and mending were usually done out of the house (60). Thus it's likely that his mother didn't do it either. It is nevertheless a niggling criticism that doesn't seem to go away.[23]

In "The Bean-Field," Thoreau writes at length about planting two and a half acres of beans during his first year at the pond. "It was a singular experience that long acquaintance which I cultivated with beans," he tells us, "what with planting, and hoeing, and harvesting, and thrashing, and picking over, and selling, and hardest of all,—I might add eating, for I did taste. I was determined to know beans" (161). The cultivation of beans is a metaphor for the cultivation of the soul. "Why concern ourselves so much about our beans for seed," he asks, "and not be concerned at all about a new generation of men?" (164). Husbandry was once a sacred art, but now, owing to "avarice and selfishness, and a grovelling habit, from which none of us is free, of regarding the soil as property chiefly, the landscape is deformed, husbandry is degraded with us, and the farmer leads the meanest of lives" (165). Thoreau planted beans but did not reap their true harvest.

On one of his visits to Concord, recounted in the "Village" chapter, he was put in jail for refusing to pay his local poll tax. This incident is described at greater length in his essay "Civil Disobedience." Rather than running "amok" against society, as Emerson thought, Thoreau insists that society ran amok against him, he being the more virtuous of the two. He was convinced "that if all men were to live as simply" as he was doing, "thieving and robbery would be unknown. These take place only in communities where some have got more than is sufficient while others have not enough" (172). He quotes Confucius, who said: "Love virtue, and the people will be virtuous. The virtues of a superior man are like the wind; the virtues of a common man are like the grass; the grass, when the wind passes over it, bends" (168). This Confucian saying, well known in China, stresses the importance of leading by example, which Thoreau claims to do in refusing to pay the tax.

In the next chapter Thoreau describes the ponds in the area, Walden Pond in particular. The chapter is interesting for the fact that it lies midway

through the book. Walden Pond occupies a similar position in relation to
the landscape. "Lying between the earth and the heavens," Thoreau says, "it
partakes of the color of both" (176). And, like the image of the stream at the
end of the second chapter, the pond is a gateway to the soul. "A lake is the
landscape's most beautiful and expressive feature," he writes. "It is earth's eye;
looking into which the beholder measures the depth of his own nature" (186).

As happens so often in his writing, prose turns into poetry. He gives us
information about the pond—its clarity, its depth, its fishes, and its geo-
logical features—and then rhapsodizes over its mythic quality, once again
homologizing distant times and places. "Perhaps on that spring morning
when Adam and Eve were driven out of Eden Walden Pond was already in
existence," Thoreau writes. "Who knows in how many remembered nations'
literatures this has been the Castalian Fountain? or what nymphs presided
over it in the Golden Age? It is a gem of the first water which Concord wears
in her coronet" (179). The pond is a symbol of purity. "Sky water," he calls it.
"It is a mirror which no stone can crack, whose quicksilver will never wear
off, whose gilding Nature continually repairs" (184).

Eliade tells us that water has mythic significance. "Water purifies and
regenerates because it nullifies the past, and restores—even if only for a
moment—the integrity of the dawn of things."[24] Thoreau's daily immersion
in the pond was an important ritual for him. Recall that in the second chapter he told us he "got up early and bathed in the pond," calling it "a religious
exercise," and quoted the words of a Chinese emperor telling him, "Renew
thyself completely each day." In the "Sounds" chapter he wrote, "Having taken
my accustomed bath, I sat in my sunny doorway, from sunrise till noon, rapt
in a revery." For him, the ritual of bathing in the pond was symbolic not only
of cleansing but also of regeneration. He is baptized, which is to say purified
and reborn, in the pure waters of the pond.

Thoreau has a personal relationship with the pond, which he first witnessed at four years of age. "It struck me again tonight, as if I had not seen
it almost daily for more than twenty years—Why, here is Walden, the same
woodland lake that I discovered so many years ago" (193). "Here," Charles
Anderson observes, "Thoreau found his ideal Self in that symbol of perfection which was the exact opposite of all the imperfections he had inveighed
against in the life of society."[25] Viewing his reflection in his pond, he asks,
"Walden, is it you?" He speaks of his identity with it in a poem:

It is no dream of mine,
To ornament a line;
I cannot come nearer to God and Heaven
Than I live to Walden even.
I am its stony shore,
And the breeze that passes o'er;
In the hollow of my hand
Are its water and its sand,
And its deepest resort
Lies high in my thought. (193)

The summer chapters seem to end with Thoreau's visit to Baker Farm. It lies a short distance south of Walden Pond, and he once considered the possibility of living there. Visiting the area now, he comes upon an Irish family, John Field, his wife, and several children. "Field," he says, is "an honest, hard-working, but shiftless man" (204). His son is an emaciated brat, and his wife is saddled with chores, though one day hopes to improve her condition. He offers a bit of unsolicited advice, telling them that if they live simply and plan well, they might enjoy a better life.

Leaving the Fields' home, Thoreau hurries in the rain back to his cabin at the pond. Looking behind him, he sees a rainbow and hears "some faint tinkling sounds" from an unknown source. An inner voice seems to say:

Go fish and hunt far and wide day by day—farther and wider—and rest thee by many brooks and hearth-sides without misgiving.... Rise free from care before the dawn, and seek adventures.... Grow wild according to thy nature.... Let not to get a living be thy trade, but thy sport. Enjoy the land, but own it not. Through want of enterprise and faith men are where they are, buying and selling, and spending their lives like serfs. (207–8)

By contrast there is John Field, "with his horizon all his own, yet he is a poor man, born to be poor," destined "not to rise in this world" (209). Clearly, Thoreau is contrasting the plight of lives lived in quiet desperation with his own, lived deliberately. Nevertheless, it is hard to understand why Thoreau denigrates the condition of Field and his family. In juxtaposing their miserable existence with the upbeat message of his own "Good Genius," he seems callous toward their misfortune. Prejudice against the Irish was common in his day. Although his attitude changed as he came to know his Irish neighbors better, it is disappointing to read his remarks here.

On October 13, 1851, Thoreau wrote in his journal: "The alert and energetic man leads a more intellectual life in winter than in summer. In summer the animal and vegetable in him are perfected as in a torrid zone—he lives in his senses mainly. In winter cold reason and not warm passion has her sway. He lives in thought and reflection. He lives a more spiritual and less sensual life."[26] This passage is an apt prelude to the chapter "Higher Laws," as his thoughts begin to turn inward.

He begins the chapter with the rather shocking admission that he was once tempted to eat a woodchuck raw, not because he was hungry, but because he wished to consume the wildness that the animal represented. He confesses: "I found in myself, and still find, an instinct toward a higher, or, as it is named, spiritual life, as do most men, and another toward a primitive rank and savage one, and I reverence them both. I love the wild not less than the good" (210). Thoreau wished to be faithful both to nature, which is essentially wild, and to the higher spiritual life. This is not surprising, since he believes the way to the spiritual life is through the medium of the natural world.

Those who spend time in the out-of-doors, such as hunters, fishermen, and woodchoppers, have the advantage that their work brings them closer to nature. Those who would aspire to a higher life, however, must cease to kill. If the hunter or fisherman has "the seeds of the better life in him," he soon "leaves the gun and fish-pole behind" (213). Thoreau used to fish himself until he lost his self-respect in doing so. Not only did he cease to fish, but also he attempted to become a vegetarian. He even swore off coffee and tea because they did not agree with his "imagination." In his abstinence from meat and stimulating drinks, he pursued an asceticism that he hoped would transform him from a "grosser" form of existence into a more spiritual one.

Thoreau believed that we come into the world with our own special genius, a sort of guiding light or guardian angel. This is why he was confident that in following the promptings of our genius we are inevitably led along the path to a higher life. He expressed the idea this way:

> If one listens to the faintest but constant suggestions of his genius, which are certainly true, he sees not to what extremes, or even insanity, it may lead him; and yet that way, as he grows more resolute and faithful, his road lies. . . . No man ever followed his genius till it misled him. Though the result were bodily weakness, yet perhaps no one can say that the consequences were to be regretted, for these were a life in conformity to higher principles.

Describing the revelation that awaits those who persist in pursuing their genius, he writes: "If the day and the night are such that you greet them with joy, and life emits a fragrance like flowers and sweet-scented herbs, is more elastic, more starry, more immortal,—that is your success. All nature is your congratulation, and you have cause momentarily to bless yourself." The experience is so contrary to ordinary everyday experience that it is easily doubted and soon forgotten. And yet it represents the highest reality. Paradoxically, what is most important is also the hardest to express. "The true harvest of my daily life is somewhat as intangible and indescribable as the tints of morning or evening. It is a little star-dust caught, a segment of the rainbow which I have clutched" (216–17).

At the same time, Thoreau is honest about his own limitations. He admits to eating "a fried rat with good relish" on occasion (217). He practices sobriety but does not consider himself a thoroughgoing ascetic. More important than one's appetite for meat and drink is the mental attitude that accompanies it. "Our whole life is startlingly moral," he says. There is never an instant's truce between virtue and vice" (218). Whether virtue or vice, it matters what our intentions are.

His asceticism, such as it was, also contributed to the cultivation of his soul. Always we are aware of the animal in us, "which awakens in proportion as our higher nature slumbers." It cannot wholly be expelled. "Yet the spirit can for a time pervade and control every member and function of the body" he says, "and transmute what in form is the grossest sensuality into purity and devotion" (219). In the discussion of chastity that follows, Thoreau lapses into a dualism of spirit and body, arguing that only through cleanliness, or purity, can sensuality be overcome. In a reference to Paul's first letter to the Corinthians, he observes that "every man is the builder of a temple, called his body, to the god he worships, after a style purely his own, nor can he get off by hammering marble instead" (221).

Thoreau often ends his chapters with a fable, this one about John Farmer. Undoubtedly he means John the farmer, that is to say, everyman rather than a real individual.[27] This person has worked hard all day, his mind still absorbed in his labors. Bathing, he takes his ease and begins to think of more serious matters. He soon becomes aware of the sound of a flute, the music of which begins to play in his head and makes his mundane thoughts seem less important than they were. The notes of the flute come to him from "a different sphere from that he worked in, and suggest work for certain faculties which slumbered in him." The everyday realities of his life—where he lived and what he did for a living—cease to matter so much. A voice speaks to him, saying: "Why do you stay here and live the mean and moiling life, when a glorious existence is possible for you? Those stars twinkle over other fields than these." But how is he to depart from his customary way of life and take up residence in this new, more spiritual realm? "All he could think of was to practice some new austerity," Thoreau writes, "to let his mind descend into his body and redeem it, and treat himself with ever increasing respect" (222).

Thoreau raises two important issues in this chapter, the first of which has to do with the relationship between wildness and spirituality. There is a tension between the two notions that Thoreau wants to preserve. We might think that spirituality necessitates taming the wild. While he is willing to give up hunting and fishing, he believes there is a vital principle in wildness that is a necessary part of his own spiritual life. The second issue, related to the first, is a distinction between sensuality and sensuousness. Thoreau has keen senses, hearing most of all. As we have seen, sounds, sights, and smells often trigger experiences that transcend the senses. They are like springboards to the infinite. Whereas Emerson's spirituality, for example, is intellectual, Thoreau's is very sensuous. Commonly, sensuousness is confused with sensuality. He embraces chastity, calling it "the flowering of man." But such purity cannot be allowed to cancel out sensuousness or he would have no access to the divine. He seeks assurances that "the animal is dying out in him . . . and the divine being established" (219–20). But how can this happen if he also wishes to preserve the wild? This is possible only if we recognize the difference between sensuality and sensuousness.[28]

As if to counter the lofty abstractions of the "Higher Laws" chapter, "Brute Neighbors" deals with Thoreau's animal neighbors. He tells the story of a mouse who built a nest under his cabin and would visit him at lunchtime to pick up a few crumbs that fell to the floor. It would also run up his clothes, down his sleeve, and nibble at some cheese held in his hand. Birds of various kinds nest nearby. Many creatures live in the woods, though hidden from view.

In the battle of the ants, a satiric fable, Thoreau describes at length and in great detail warfare between red and black ants, comparing it to the Trojan War, the Battle of Austerlitz, and the "Concord Fight." "They fought with more pertinacity than bulldogs. Neither manifested the least disposition to retreat. It was evident that their battle-cry was 'Conquer or die'" (229). He observes this *bellum* with fascination. "I never learned which party was victorious, nor the cause of the war; but I felt for the rest of that day as if I had my feelings excited and harrowed by witnessing the struggle, the ferocity and carnage, of a human battle before my door" (231).

Comparing the life of humans with that of ants is a familiar trope in ancient philosophy. For example, in *Meditations* Marcus Aurelius writes, "The vain pomp of a procession, plays on a stage, flocks, herds, skirmishes, a meager bone tossed to puppies, a scrap of bread tossed in a fish tank, the toiling of ants with their burdens, the scurrying of nervous mice, puppets pulled by their strings". This comparison is indicative of the spiritual exercise that consists in looking down from above. As Marcus puts it, "Observing things on earth as if from on high is especially important for anyone who wants to discuss human life."[29] This is a recurring theme in Thoreau's writing, as evidenced, for example, in his experience atop Saddleback Mountain in *A Week*. According to Hadot, the exercise "teaches us to relocate human existence within the immeasurable dimensions of the cosmos," that is, to transcend the confusion and messiness of everyday life.[30]

Another brute neighbor capturing his attention is a loon whose dives below the surface of the water were teasingly evasive. "While he was thinking one thing in his brain, I was endeavoring to divine his thought in mine. It was a pretty game, played on the smooth surface of the pond, a man against a loon." The game he plays with the loon exemplifies his quest for reality in the same way that the fable of the hound, bay horse, and turtledove does. Although he comes tantalizingly close to "capturing" the loon, he is mocked for his efforts: "Again and again, when I was straining my eyes over the surface one way, I would suddenly be startled by his unearthly laugh behind me" (234–35).

In titling the next chapter "House-Warming," Thoreau enjoys a play on words. A housewarming is commonly understood to be a party celebrating a move into a new home. Here it refers to making his home warm for the coming winter. He began building the chimney to his cabin in November. When it was completed, he tells us, he finally began to inhabit his house. Plastering the walls came next, which he did with the help of his poet friend Ellery Channing.

In preparation for the onset of winter, Thoreau collected wood for his fireplace. "Every man looks at his wood-pile with a kind of affection," he writes. The logs warmed him twice, once while he was splitting them, and again when they were on the fire. His reveries before the fireplace evoke the symbolism of ascension and flight. He likens the smoke rising up the chimney to the flight of Icarus carrying a message to the gods. As we know, Icarus doesn't make it, owing to his hubris, suggesting perhaps that Thoreau himself fails to overcome the doubleness that precludes his total absorption in reality because he is trying to force the issue.

Henry Thoreau made Walden Pond famous, but before he went to live there, the area had been home to formerly enslaved African Americans, including Cato Ingraham, Zilpha White, and Brister Freeman and his wife, Fenda. Despite the town's reputation as a hotbed of antislavery agitation in the years leading up to the Civil War, Concord was formerly a slave town. A number of prominent families living there held slaves, even Emerson's grandfather the Reverend William Emerson, and his widow, Phoebe. Slavery was phased out following the Revolutionary War, but those freed from servitude continued to live in the area. In telling the story of "Black Walden," Elise Lemire writes: "Unable in most cases to purchase land, the abandoned slaves were permitted by their former owners to squat locally, but only on the most out-of-the-way, infertile places. Walden Woods was one of those sites."[31]

By the time Thoreau went to live in the woods, the only traces of those who had resided there were a few cellar dents marking where their shanties once stood. Within living memory, he writes, the area near his cabin site "resounded with the laugh and gossip of inhabitants, and the woods which border it were notched and dotted here and there with their little gardens and dwellings" (256). Brister Freeman figures most prominently in *Walden*. After he was relinquished by his former owner, he took the name Freeman to indicate his newfound status. One of the few former slaves to own land, Freeman tenaciously held on to it even as the town tried to wrest it from him. Along a path from the town to the pond are a hill and spring long named for him. In 1993 the Walden Woods Project purchased the property where he and his family had lived and dedicated it as a natural park in his memory.

Other former inhabitants Thoreau mentions are John Breed and Hugh Quoil, alcoholics who died in the woods; John Wyman, a potter, and his son; and four farming families attempting to scratch out an existence in the woods. The "blanched and accursed" soil surrounding the pond was symbolic of the plight of those who lived difficult lives on the margins of society (264). Aside from these imaginary neighbors, Thoreau had few visitors during the winter months. The deep snow may have kept them away, but it did not prevent him from tromping for miles through the drifts. Of the few who made the effort to see him were a woodchopper, a local farmer, and his friends Channing, Alcott, and Emerson. More frequently he kept company with the winter animals, especially the squirrels, hares, and foxes whose footprints dotted the snow.

In "The Pond in Winter," Thoreau awakens in the night troubled by a question put to him in his sleep: "What—how—when—where?" After this dark night of the soul, he is consoled, he writes, by "dawning Nature, in whom all creatures live, looking in at my broad windows with serene and satisfied face, and no question on *her* lips. I awoke to an answered question, to Nature and daylight" (282). As always in *Walden*, the dawn is symbolic of spiritual awakening. This awakening is the prelude to his rebirth with the coming of spring, announced in the following chapter.

Describing his morning work, he tells us that he goes in search of water with an axe and pail and a divining rod if need be. He cuts a hole in the ice, peers into "the quiet parlor of the fishes" below, and is moved to exclaim, "Heaven is under our feet as well as over our heads" (283). He was determined to discover how deep the pond was since many believed it to be bottomless. Using a line and stone to measure its depth, he then proceeded to map the dimensions of the pond. He drew two diameters which bisected where the pond was deepest. What he observed to be true of the pond was true in ethics also: "Such a rule of the two diameters not only guides us toward the sun in the system and the heart in man, but draw lines through the length and breadth of the aggregate of a man's particular daily behaviors and waves of life into his coves and inlets, and where they intersect will be the height and depth of his character" (291). Recalling what he wrote in "The Ponds"—"I am its stony shore, / And the breeze that passes o'er; / In the hollow of my hand / Are its water and its sand" (193)—we realize that he is taking measure not only of the pond but of himself also.

Thoreau watches as a crew of men descend on the pond to cut ice for transport to distant lands, including India. As he does so often in his mythologizing, he identifies something that is local and present with something distant and ancient, in this case Walden's water and that of the Ganges River in the time of the Vedas:

> In the morning I bathe my intellect in the stupendous and cosmogonical philosophy of the Bhagvat-Gita, since whose composition years of the gods have elapsed, and in comparison with which our modern world and its literature seem puny and trivial; and I doubt if that philosophy is not to be referred to a previous state of existence, so remote is its sublimity from our conceptions. I lay down the book and go to my well for water, and lo! there I meet the servant of the Bramin, priest of Brahma and Vishnu and Indra, who sits in his temple on the Ganges reading the Vedas, or dwells at the root of a tree with crust and water jug. I meet his servant come to draw water for his master, and our buckets as it were grate together in the same well. The pure Walden water is mingled with the sacred water of the Ganges. (298)

This regression to the origins is a common pattern in his writing. In equating Walden's water with that of the Ganges, his bathing in the pond—a daily spiritual practice, as we have seen—is the same as bathing in "the sacred water of the Ganges." In performing such rituals, Eliade points out, the adept "dies symbolically with immersion, and is reborn, purified, renewed."[32] One imagines it is the same with Thoreau.

The breakup of the ice on the pond in spring announces the return of life to the Walden woods, including the strange phenomenon of "sand foliage." One advantage the coming of the railroad to Concord offered was that, when a hillside was excavated to make way for the train, it afforded him the most direct route into town. On the way, he was struck by the sudden appearance of "sand foliage" on the embankment. As the frost thawed, the sand flowed down the slope like lava, taking the form of vegetation such as leaves or vines. In this phenomenon he sees the pattern for all of life, including human life. The hillside seems to illustrate "the principle of all the operations of Nature," symbolizing the resurrection of life that occurs every spring (308). "The earth is not a mere fragment of dead history," he concludes, "but living poetry like the leaves of a tree, which precede flowers and fruit,—not a fossil earth, but a living earth" (309).

In a nod to Jesus' parable of the Prodigal Son (Luke 15:24), Thoreau writes: "Such is the contrast between winter and spring. Walden was dead and is alive again" (311). The coming of spring reminds him of "the creation of the Cosmos out of Chaos and the realization of the Golden Age" (313). It is an invitation to live in the present rather than regretting lost opportunities. "We loiter in winter while it is already spring. In a pleasant spring morning all men's sins are forgiven. Such a day is a truce to vice" (314). We recover our lost innocence. All our faults are forgotten. "Why the jailer does not leave open his prison doors,— why the judge does not dismiss his case,—why the preacher does not dismiss his congregation! It is because they do not obey the hint which God gives them, nor accept the pardon which he freely offers to all" (315).

The sight of a hawk tumbling in the air and of golden and silver fishes gleaming "like a string of jewels" in the water attests to the importance of the natural world for our spiritual well-being:

> Our village life would stagnate if it were not for the unexplored forests and meadows which surround it. We need the tonic of wildness—to wade sometimes in marshes where the bittern and the meadow-hen lurk, and hear the booming of the snipe; to smell the whispering sedge where only

some wilder and more solitary fowl builds her nest, and the mink crawls with its belly close to the ground. At the same time that we are earnest to explore and learn all things, we require that all things be mysterious and unexplorable, that land and sea be infinitely wild, unsurveyed and unfathomed by us because unfathomable. We can never have enough of nature. We must be refreshed by the sight of inexhaustible vigor, vast and titanic features, the sea-coast with its wrecks, the wilderness with its living and its decaying trees, the thunder-cloud, and the rain which lasts three weeks and produces freshets. We need to witness our own limits transgressed, and some life pasturing freely where we never wander. (317–18)

This chapter comes as close to expressing Thoreau's religious credo as anything else he wrote. By religion he does not mean anything codified or organized; rather, it is a form of spirituality, a sense that nature is something sacred and with which he feels intimately connected.[33] Nature religion takes many forms, including paganism, animism, and pantheism. By his own admission, he was a pantheist. As we saw in the "Sunday" chapter of *A Week*, he identified with the god Pan. And in a letter to Horace Greeley he avowed, "I was born to be a pantheist."[34] Pantheism is the belief that the universe is a self-sufficient, interconnected whole that is rightly considered sacred. Despite allusions to "the Artist who made the world and me," Thoreau's God is neither personal nor transcendent but rather immanent in, if not identical with, the operations of nature.[35] His nature-based spirituality is best described as a form of ecstatic naturalism.

The phenomenon of the sand foliage illustrates the method of nature. He describes it as "excrementitious," an unusual way of saying that the world is self-creating (308). Nature is extruded from the bowels of the earth like the frost coming out of the ground or the leaves put forth from the tree. Baruch Spinoza, a seventeenth-century pantheist, made a distinction between *nature naturing* and *nature natured* in describing the method of nature. Nature natured implied that nature was created, while nature naturing indicated that it was perpetually creating itself out of itself alone. Thoreau would seem to agree with Spinoza that nature naturing is the more apt description of the operations of the natural world.

Thoreau's ecstatic naturalism is rooted in his intimate communion with nature, but his expression of it owes much to the Romantic nature mysticism of the nineteenth century. For the Romantics, Friedrich Schelling and Coleridge in particular, nature was organic, dynamic, and holistic, perfectly illustrated by Thoreau's description of the foliage of the sand bank.[36] This viewpoint is at odds not only with Christian teachings but also with philosophical naturalism. Christianity regards pantheism as heretical, while philosophical naturalism denies a spiritual element in nature. Yet, as Alan Hodder notes, Thoreau's form of nature religion has gained increasing acceptance: "Americans at the start of the twenty-first century are better able than those of earlier times to grant some credence to this religious premise, since 'nature religion' has come to be widely recognized at least as an intelligible form of American religiosity (in part through Thoreau's own influence), however suspect it remains in the eyes of much mainstream culture."[37]

With the return of spring the year has come full circle. It is time for a summing up. Thoreau tells us he went to the woods to learn what the experience had to teach him. In "Conclusion" he shares the fruits of his discovery. He was a notorious stay-at-home. Although he relished the literature of travel and exploration, he never ventured far from his birthplace. He made excursions to Quebec, the Maine woods, and Cape Cod. For a brief period, he tutored Emerson's nephews on Staten Island and, late in life, made a trip to Minnesota for his health. For the most part, however, he was content to bloom where he was planted. Or as he put it, "I have travelled a great deal in Concord" (4).

Here Thoreau employs metaphors of travel and exploration to suggest that we should view our lives as an adventure or a quest, and that the undiscovered territory we seek is not so much elsewhere, in some remote corner of the globe, but actually within ourselves. He begins, however, with a bit of indirection. He says that what we see around us is not all that there is. The tendency is to settle down, set bounds to our life, and act as though our fate has been decided. But, he declares, "the universe is wider than our views of it" (320).

We should look beyond our current situation, like curious passengers at the railing of their ship, and not like the sailors who merely toil at their tasks, missing out on the view. Taking the metaphor of travel further, Thoreau asserts that it is not really the game in Africa we seek; the real quarry is ourselves. Quoting a bit of poetry, he declares:

> Direct your eye right inward, and you'll find
> A thousand regions in your mind
> Yet undiscovered. Travel them, and be
> Expert in home-cosmography. (320)

In Thoreau's day the interior of Africa was as yet undiscovered by European explorers. Is not our own interior also a mystery? he asks. And is it really the source of the Nile that we seek or rather the headwaters of our spiritual life? In reference to other famous explorers, he says: "Be rather the Mungo Park, the Lewis and Clark and Frobisher of your own streams and oceans; explore your own higher latitudes.... Nay, be a Columbus to whole new continents and worlds within you, opening new channels, not of trade, but of thought." He sees in these exploring expeditions "an indirect recognition of the fact that there are continents and seas in the moral world to which every man is an isthmus or an inlet, as yet unexplored by him," that is, the private sea of one's solitude (321). If you fancy yourself well traveled, then "obey the precept of the old philosopher, and Explore thyself. Herein are demanded the eye and the nerve" (321–22).

Thoreau left the woods feeling that he had "several more lives to live, and could not spare any more time for that one." His life there had become routine. How predictable were the "ruts of tradition and conformity!" He needed a change. But he learned this at least from his experiment:

> If one advances confidently in the direction of his dreams, and endeavors to live the life which he has imagined, he will meet with a success unexpected in common hours. He will put some things behind, will pass an invisible boundary; new, universal, and more liberal laws will begin to establish themselves around and within him; or the old laws be expanded, and interpreted in his favor in a more liberal sense, and he will live with the license of a higher order of beings. In proportion as he simplifies his life, the laws of the universe will appear less complex, and solitude will not be solitude, nor poverty poverty, nor weakness weakness. If you have built castles in the air, your work need not be lost; that is where they should be. Now put the foundations under them. (323–24)

Thoreau is aware that others might think his philosophy and mode of living extreme but feels that he must exaggerate in order to get his point across. Indeed, he fears he is not "*extra- vagant*" enough, employing the term in the sense of wandering beyond the "narrow limits" of common experience. "I desire to speak somewhere without bounds," he writes, "for I am convinced that I cannot exaggerate enough even to lay the foundation of a true expression" (324). Sometimes one must shout in order to be heard.

The problem is, we settle for too little. We prize our dullest perceptions as common sense when, in fact, what passes for common sense is really the sense of people who are asleep. We wouldn't recognize a wise person if we saw one. We seem desperate to succeed in such desperate enterprises. Rather, we should do what is right for us. As Thoreau says in a well-known passage: "If a man does not keep pace with his companions, perhaps it is because he hears a different drummer. Let him step to the music which he hears, however measured or far away" (326). We should not settle for anything less than the truth.

Thoreau tells a fable of an artist in the city of Kouroo who sought perfection in his art. He thought that time was a factor only in relation to an imperfect work, whereas to achieve perfection would put him beyond time's reach. He proceeded to carve a staff and worked at it with such concentration and attention to detail that, without realizing it, he entered the realm of the eternal now. While he was engaged with his task, going with the flow, whole eons of time passed, but he remained perennially young. In making the staff he created a new world "with full and fair proportions; in which, though the old cities and dynasties had passed away, fairer and more glorious ones had taken their places" (327). When finished with his task, he realized that the apparent lapse of time had been an illusion. Only an instant had passed.

No doubt inspired by his reading of the Vedas, and in particular the Bhagavad Gita, this is a fable of Thoreau's own creation. Hodder indicates that it was added to *Walden* in Thoreau's last revision of the manuscript, sometime between 1853 and 1854. During this time, he was also carrying on correspondence with a younger friend, H. G. O. Blake. In one of these letters he wrote: "How admirably the artist is made to accomplish his self-culture by devotion to his art! The wood-sawyer through his effort to do his work well becomes not merely a better wood-sawyer, but measurably a better *man*."[38] The parable is also a reflection of the Gita's teaching of disinterested action, the importance of focusing on the work at hand, without consideration for the fruits thereof. Hodder adds that "the story may also be interpreted as an allegory of the creation of *Walden* itself, one which showcases Thoreau's own artistic credo."[39]

Thoreau admonishes us to love our life, no matter how poor it seems. Poverty is only relative after all. "Cultivate poverty like a garden herb, like sage," he writes. "Do not trouble yourself much to get new things, whether clothes or friends. Turn the old; return to them. Things do not change; we change. Sell your clothes and keep your thoughts" (328). We may not be able to afford some things, but voluntary poverty has the advantage at least that we are compelled to deal with the material that yields the most reward—our own selves. "It is life near the bone where it is sweetest." Wealth can purchase superfluities only. "Money is not required to purchase one necessary of the soul" (329). Here we see another latent Epicurean influence. As Lucretius observes in *The Way Things Are*:

> The human race
> Forever toils in vain, forever wastes
> Time over empty worries, never knows
> The limits of possessiveness, the brief
> Capacity of pleasure for increase.[40]

As we have seen, the Epicureans believed in maximizing pleasure by minimizing wants. Voluntary poverty is an important discipline in Thoreau's spiritual practice of simple living.

Thoreau is not interested in hearing about the lifestyles of the rich and famous. Talk of celebrities is trivial: "A goose is a goose still, dress it how you will." He desires only "to weigh, to settle, to gravitate toward that which most strongly and rightfully attracts" him; to accept life as it is; "to travel the only path that I can, and that on which no power can resist me." He seeks a solid bottom on which to stand, illustrated by the parable of the boy who is asked by a traveler on horseback if the swamp ahead of him has a hard bottom. The boy informs him that it does, whereupon the traveler enters the swamp and sinks to the horse's girth. "I thought you said this bog had a hard bottom," the rider says. "So it has," the boy replies. "But you have not got half way to it yet" (330).

Throughout *Walden*, Thoreau is seeking a hard bottom, a solid foundation for a philosophy at odds with convention. Recall what he wrote in the second chapter: "Let us settle ourselves, and work and wedge our feet downward . . . till we come to a hard bottom and rocks in place, which we can call reality" (97–98). In "The Pond in Winter" he was determined to measure the depth of what some believed was a bottomless pond. In each case he is searching for reality, for something beneath or beyond appearance. For him, as for the Romantics in general, that solid bottom is the Self, not the ego, which is up to its neck in "the bogs and quicksands of society" (330).

In this quest he is not satisfied with halfway measures. We have barely scratched the surface of the globe on which we live. "Most have not delved six feet beneath the surface, nor leaped as many above it." All too often we are sound asleep. "There is an incessant influx of novelty into the world, and yet we tolerate incredible dullness" (332). He relates the story of a bug which crawled out of a table that stood in a farmer's home for sixty years, hatched from an egg deposited in the living tree many years earlier. The incident teaches an extraordinary lesson:

> Who does not feel his faith in a resurrection and immortality strength-
> ened by the hearing of this? Who knows what beautiful and winged life,
> whose egg has been buried for ages under many concentric layers of wood-
> enness in the dead dry life of society, deposited at first in the laburnum
> of the green and living tree, which has been gradually converted into the
> semblance of a well-seasoned tomb,—heard perchance gnawing out now
> for years by the astonished family of man as they sat round the festive
> board,—may unexpectedly come forth from amidst society's most trivial
> and handselled furniture, to enjoy its perfect summer life at last. (333)

Only those who are prepared to listen will hear or heed Thoreau's message. As he says in the memorable closing lines of *Walden*: "Only that day dawns to which we are awake. There is more day to dawn. The sun is but a morning star" (333).

A Village Diogenes

"Conclusion" is both a summation of Thoreau's teaching in the book and a challenge to his readers. Once our basic needs are met, we are encouraged to "adventure on life now." Leading discussions on *Walden* with adult audiences over the years, I have discovered that many people find his message exhil-arating, while others think it impractical and unrealistic, something only a man without a family or a steady job could seriously propose. Many of his Concord neighbors considered Thoreau an eccentric. He was likened to the Greek philosopher and gadfly Diogenes, who made a virtue of poverty and used the example of his lifestyle to criticize society and corrupt institutions. He panhandled for a living and often slept in a large ceramic jar in the mar-ketplace. He was noted for carrying a lamp during the day, claiming to be looking for an honest man.

As I mentioned, Thoreau is often criticized for failing to do his own laun-dry and for dining with friends and family, as if to suggest that his pursuit of self-reliance was at someone else's expense; that, in other words, he was a hypocrite. This particular criticism is apparently of recent vintage, but it is indicative of a reaction to what many take to be a moralistic tone in Thoreau's writing and of a certain defensiveness on the part of some of his readers. Most consider it a reproach to the way they have chosen to live their own life. Yet on some level, many of us know that he has a point in criticizing the shallowness of American life and culture. We also know, as he did, that many people, especially the enslaved, the poor, and the marginalized in society, have suffered from prejudice and exploitation. Above all, we know that there is a better life to be had through simple living and awakening to the beauty and wonder of the natural world around us. He was at pains to point out that his way of life might not be for everyone, only for those who were dissatisfied with their lot in life and wished to improve it.

Thoreau left his cabin at the pond on September 6, 1847, having lived there for two years, two months, and two days. He might have stayed longer except for an appeal from Lidian Emerson to move back into the Emerson home while Waldo was away on a nine-month lecture tour of Britain and Europe. As for the cabin, Emerson bought it from Thoreau and then sold it to a farmer for use as a shed. Later on, it was sold to another farmer to be used for grain storage. After that, it collapsed and its wood was used to patch up a barn, which, as fate would have it, was eventually owned by Emerson's grandson.[41]

Did he regret leaving the pond? Looking back several years later, he noted in his journal: "Why I left the woods? I do not think that I can tell. I have often wished myself back. . . . Perhaps if I lived there much longer, I might live there forever. One would think twice before he accepted Heaven on such terms."[42]

CHAPTER 5

AFTER WALDEN

⌣

Lidian was relieved to have Thoreau back at Bush, the Emerson family home. She was not well, and the children needed looking after. No doubt she was glad to have a handy man around the house, since her husband was all thumbs when it came to necessary chores and repairs. By all accounts she had a great deal of affection for young Henry, and the feeling was mutual. The Emerson children, Ellen, Edith, and Edward, were also delighted. He would carry three-year-old Eddy around on his shoulders, make panpipes for the girls from willow shoots, gather them all around the fireplace and tell stories of the adventures of his childhood, or of a duel between turtles he had observed in the river, or the battle of the ants he witnessed near his Walden cabin.[1]

After Waldo returned from his trip abroad nine months later, Thoreau went back to living at his family's home, eager to complete his manuscript of *A Week*. The book was finally published in May 1849, to mixed reviews. Because he was as yet a little-known author, he needed to turn to a printer to get it published, with the provision that he was responsible for the cost of unsold copies. Unfortunately, sales were dismal; a little more than two hundred books were sold. (Four years later he was forced to take back—at considerable expense—706 copies, remarking, "I have now a library of nearly nine hundred volumes, over seven hundred of which I wrote myself.")[2] An unsigned review on the front page of Horace Greeley's *New-York Tribune* criticized the book's pantheistic tendencies and found Thoreau's favorable comparison of Eastern scriptures with the Christian Bible blasphemous: "Mr. Thoreau's treatment of this subject seems revolting alike to good sense and good taste."[3]

"Says I to my-self"

As much as possible, he kept to a certain routine: reading and writing in the morning and going on long walks in the afternoon. For income during this period, he took up surveying, did odd jobs around the town, and delivered lectures at various lyceums in the area. Discouraged by the poor reception his first book received, he put off completing the *Walden* manuscript, turning instead to his journal, which he had been keeping since 1837 at Emerson's suggestion.

Journal writing was a common practice among his acquaintances. Emerson and Alcott kept journals also and often allowed others to read them. While a student at Harvard, Thoreau wrote a class paper on the benefits of keeping a journal, which he said were three in number: "the preservation of our scattered thoughts," "reckoning up [one's] daily gains," and "to improve ourselves by reflection."[4] Emerson had advised keeping a journal in his 1837–38 "Human Culture" lecture series in Boston. This practice was in fact an important spiritual discipline for the Transcendentalists in their pursuit of self-culture. As Thoreau scholar William Rossi observes, "In the early 1850s, at least, the Journal served Thoreau as a means of self-culture in several ways," one of which is that "it preserved the records of particular moments of intuitive perception."[5] On July 13, 1852, Henry wrote, "*A Journal*—a book that shall contain all your joy, your extacy [*sic*]."[6]

Who was he writing for? His lectures and published writings were addressed to his listeners and readers. These were, as literary historian Lawrence Buell points out, rhetorically scriptural in tone. Scripture, Buell says, "is not the formulation of accepted truth but (in the opinion of the Transcendentalists, anyhow) the record of the scribe's spiritual experience, of the Word speaking through him. . . . The only crucial requisite of the prophet or poet is that he speak from direct experience, from 'within.'"[7] This description applies as much to Thoreau's writing as it does to that of other Transcendentalists, such as Emerson, who had clerical backgrounds. They all conceived of their writing as a form of scripture.

Thoreau's tone in the journal is less scriptural than his writing and speaking for the general public. As Lowell had said, he sometimes sounded a bit preachy. Here the tenor is intimate and confessional, but it is not a diary of his everyday affairs and does not reveal, for example, his love life. To be sure, he writes about his walks and what he has seen and heard along the way. He names a great many plants and birds and charts the course of the seasons. He tells us about his travels here and there. He describes experiences of both joy and disappointment. Most of all, he shares his thoughts about a good many things. Still, we wonder, who is he talking to? It's highly unlikely that he ever thought his journals would be published for us to read. Perhaps he gave us the answer in the journal itself: "Says I to my-self should be the motto of my Journal."[8]

Scholars have raised similar questions about the *Meditations* of Marcus Aurelius. Even while on his military campaigns in Germany, he continued to make entries in his journal. After his death of unknown causes in 180 CE while stationed in the provinces, those close to him recognized the worth of his writing and preserved it. Eventually it was given the title of *Meditations* or *Pensées*, thoughts. Hadot tells us that the *Meditations* belong to a type of writing called *hypomnemata* in antiquity, "which we could define as 'personal notes taken on a day-to-day basis.'" Evidently, it was quite common back then to keep such a journal. "It is important to emphasize, however," Hadot continues, "that in his case, most of these notes were exhortations to himself, or a dialogue with himself, usually composed with the utmost care."[9] While Thoreau's journal catalogues his observations on natural phenomena, some-times at great length, it also charts an internal dialogue on his mental states, and, in this sense, it is a spiritual journal.

In his book *The Spiritual Journal of Henry David Thoreau*, Malcolm Clem-ens Young outlines the characteristics of a spiritual journal: "First, it includes explicit references to religious life and experience. Second, the author regards the spiritual journal as a tool for religious formation. Third, it assumes that God is in part revealed through ordinary experience. Finally, it serves as testimony for seekers."[10] While I would substitute self-culture for religious formation, I think the first three traits listed are helpful in understanding the spiritual nature of Thoreau's journal. The fourth is questionable, however, since there is no evidence that he was writing it for an audience. Nevertheless, as was the case of Marcus Aurelius' *Meditations*, the value of Thoreau's jour-nal was recognized by those who knew of it and had reason to believe that it might be of benefit to future generations of religious seekers.

In his younger years, the journal was largely organized according to topics, such as "Sphere Music," "Creeds," "Rivers," "Homer," and so on. It also con-tains poetry, quotations from his reading, and notes useful for future pub-lication. Here and there, however, it gives evidence of its primary purpose, that of his spiritual self-culture. "Let the daily tide leave some deposit on these pages, as it leaves sand and shells on the shore," he wrote in July 1840. "So much increase of *terra firma*. This may be a calendar of the ebbs and flows of the soul; and on these sheets as a beach, the waves may cast up pearls and seaweed."[11] Emerson insisted in his "Human Culture" lectures that self-reliance is essential to one's self-culture. Thoreau adds that the experience of nature is essential to developing self-reliance. "When most at one with nature I feel supported and propped up on all sides by a myriad influences, as trees in the plain and on the hill side are equally perpendicular. The most upright man is he that most entirely reclines. . . . By his entire reliance he is made erect. Men of little faith stand only by their feet, or recline on the ground, having lost their reliance on the soul."[12]

Many of his early journal entries are also found in his subsequent writing. *A Week on the Concord and Merrimack Rivers* is a virtual scrapbook of material taken from his journal. They also show up in *Walden*. In fact, he seems to have torn pages from the journal as he used what was on them in his early writings. But beginning in 1849, after the publication of *A Week*, the journal becomes a work of its own, which many scholars consider his best writing, though of course it was not published until after his death. His friends recognized its worth and published it piecemeal at first in volumes organized around the passage of the seasons. A more complete version of the journal, arranged chronologically, was published in 1906 and again, in an annotated edition, in 1927. Even then there were entries omitted and some not recovered until the publication of the scholarly Princeton edition, ongoing since 1981.

What changed after 1849? Most notably, the entries became much longer and more polished, worked up from notes he had taken on his walks. Some go on for several pages, but long or short, they are not organized in a coherent fashion. Rather they are improvisations on familiar themes. To a considerable extent, both *A Week* and *Walden* are works of the imagination. Neither one is a factual account, not of his trip on the Concord and Merrimack Rivers nor of his life at Walden Pond. Both are mythic in the sense described by Mircea Eliade: "'Myth' means a 'true story' and beyond that a story that is a most precious possession because it is sacred, exemplary, significant."[13] Myths deal with the real world, as opposed to the actual one. This is a familiar theme in Thoreau's journal. For example, in an entry written sometime in the summer of 1850 he writes: "I find the actual to be far less real to me than the imagined. Why this singular prominence and importance is given to the former I do not know. In proportion as that which possesses my thoughts is removed from the actual it impresses me."[14] The facts of his life furnished the material to the mythology that he is writing. Myth tells the true story.

His journal is the record of the hero's quest in search of the Holy Grail, or the real world, hidden but not entirely obscured behind the actual one. This is where he hoped that facts—the sights, sounds, and objects of the natural world—would, like breadcrumbs dropped on the ground, lead him. Thoreau's comments on the real versus the actual are part of an entry several pages long. It seems to have been occasioned by the discovery of a button from the coat of Margaret Fuller's husband, the marquis Giovanni Ossoli, found on the beach where he, his wife, and their young son were killed in a shipwreck off the coast of Long Island on July 19, 1850.[15] Emerson sent Thoreau to the site of the wreck in hopes of finding some trace of the family's remains, including a manuscript Fuller had been working on describing the failed attempt at Italian independence.

It is typical in Thoreau's writing that some sensuous fact will prompt a reflection on its deeper meaning for him, in this case the fleeting nature of human existence. "This stream of events which we consent to call actual, and the mightier stream which alone carries us with it—what makes the difference? On the one our bodies float—and we have sympathy with it through them—on the other our spirits." *Memento mori*, "remember that you die," is a reminder of the inevitability of death, often symbolized by a skull or hourglass, or, in this instance, the button from a dead man's coat. So little remains once we have gone, "simply some bones lying on the beach."[16]

What matters now is what we are making of the one life that we have. "Our thoughts are the epochs of our life," he says, "all else is but as a journal of the winds that blew while we were here."[17] Do what you know you ought to do, namely, "cultivate the tree which you have found to bear fruit in your soul." Strive "to live a *super* natural life."[18] Note that the italics are his, and the two words "super" and "natural" are separated. He doesn't mean *other* worldly; he means *this* worldly, as when he says, in *A Week*, "a *natural* life," or a "*purely* sensuous life." The reality he seeks transcends the senses, but it is not unnatural. Heaven is not somewhere else, Thoreau argues. "Here or nowhere is our heaven."[19] Achieving a *purely* sensuous life is not easy to do, he admits. He's not sure he is up to the task. What he seeks often seems out of reach. "From time to time I overlook the promised land, but I do not feel that I am travelling toward it."[20] Thoreau's journal is the best record we have of his elusive quest for such a life.

The journal immediately following his Walden years, especially from 1849 to the middle of 1853, is largely devoted to describing the conditions and practices conducive to achieving a "*super* natural life." The first and most important of these conditions is nature. The journal is replete with paeans to nature, too numerous to count. On August 17, 1851, Thoreau writes:

> My heart leaps into my mouth at the sound of the wind in the woods. I whose life was but yesterday so desultory and shallow, suddenly recover my spirits, my spirituality, through my hearing. . . . Ah, I would walk, I would sit and sleep with natural piety. What if I could pray aloud or to myself as I went along by the brooksides a cheerful prayer like the birds! For joy I could embrace the earth. I shall delight to be buried in it.[21]

For good reason, many of his readers consider him to be a nature mystic. Mysticism is usually defined as an experience of transcendent reality, beyond the boundaries of our material world, and a sense of oneness or union with that reality, often considered divine. In Thoreau's case, that transcendent reality is not beyond nature but within it; his mysticism is this-worldly. The mystical quality of his writing, especially in his journal, is unmistakable. Consider this journal entry of July 16 the same year, which is worth quoting at length:

> Methinks my present experience is nothing; my past experience is all in all. I think that no experience which I have today comes up to, or is comparable with, the experience of my boyhood. And not only this is true, but as far back as I can remember, I have unconsciously referred to the experience of a previous state of existence. "Our life is a forgetting," etc. . . .
>
> My life was ecstasy. In youth, before I lost any of my senses, I can remember that I was all alive, and inhabited my body with inexpressible satisfaction; both its weariness and its refreshment were sweet to me. This earth was the most glorious musical instrument, and I was audience to its strains. To have such sweet impressions made on us—such ecstasies begotten of the breezes! I can remember how I was astonished. I said to myself—I said to others—There comes into my mind or soul an indescrib-able, infinite, all-absorbing, divine heavenly pleasure, a sense of elevation and expansion and [I] have had naught to do with it. I perceive that I am dealt with by superior powers. This is a pleasure, a joy, an existence which I have not procured myself. I speak as a witness on the stand and tell what I have perceived. The morning and the evening were sweet to me, and I led a life aloof from society of men. I wondered if a mortal ever knew what I knew. I looked in books for some recognition of a kindred experience but, strange to say, I found none. Indeed, I was slow to discover that other men had this experience, for it had been possible to read books and to associate with men on other grounds.
>
> The maker of me was improving me. When I detected this interference, I was profoundly moved. For years I marched as to a music in comparison with which the music of the streets is noise and discord.[22]

There is a note of Wordsworthian lament in the picture Thoreau paints here for lost intimacy with the natural world. "'Our life is a forgetting' etc.," he writes, referring, of course, to the poet's "Ode" on the intimations of immortality. And as Thoreau admits, such experiences become fewer in number and less intense with the passing years.

This journal entry also exhibits a central paradox of the spiritual life. He concludes his meditation, saying: "I was daily intoxicated and yet no man could call me intemperate. With all your science can you tell how it is, and whence it is, that light comes into the soul?"[23] Such experiences are both profound and fleeting. They are noetic, William James tells us. They give knowledge of hidden truths and of life lived on a higher plane. As the vision fades, the mystic is left to wonder if and how they might be summoned and sustained. There seems to be a contradiction here between surrendering and willing. Thoreau's dilemma, as David Robinson points out, is that "an act of complete merger required an extinction of consciousness and a life lived wholly in the body and the senses—a goal that the mind might paradoxically set for itself but that it could hardly achieve through planning or calculation."[24]

If such experiences cannot be summoned at will, mystics have nonetheless developed techniques and practices intended to increase the odds of their recurrence. Fasting, meditation, withdrawal, drugs, and various forms of asceticism have been employed in the effort. For Thoreau, as it was for others in the Transcendentalist circle, self-culture, or the cultivation of the soul, was the stated means for achieving this end. Many of the practices of self-culture that Thoreau engaged in are described in *Walden*, including reading, contemplation, solitude, walking in nature, and simple living. These are evident in the journal as well. The distinguishing feature of Thoreau's spiritual practice has to do with the role of the senses. Emerson's approach to self-culture is largely cerebral, whereas Thoreau's is markedly sensuous, by means of heightened perceptions.

This is especially apparent when, for instance, the chirping of birds, dogs barking in the distance, someone strumming a guitar, or simply "the sound of the wind in the woods" occasions a meditation on some weighty topic. In another journal entry he says, "The question is not what you look at, but how you look and whether you see."[25] Sharpening his perceptions was an essential means of Thoreau's cultivation of the soul. A vivid example of his heightened perceptions is described in an entry in September 1851:

As I was entering the Deep Cut, the wind, which was conveying a message to me from heaven, dropped it on the wire of the telegraph, which it vibrated as it passed. I instantly sat down on a stone at the foot of the telegraph-pole and attended to the communication. It merely said: "Bear in mind, Child, and never for an instant forget, that there are higher planes, infinitely higher planes of life than this thou art now travelling on. Know that the goal is distant, and is upward, and is worthy all your life's efforts to attain to." And then it ceased, and though I sat some minutes longer I heard nothing more.[26]

Altering one's perspective was another useful means of enhancing one's perceptions. Elevation was one way of doing this, whether climbing a mountain or a tree, as Thoreau was wont to do. His numerous moonlight walks taken during the summer of 1851 are another example. On June 11 he noted in his journal: "The woodland paths are never seen to such an advantage as in a moonlight night so embowered—still opening before you almost against expectation as you walk—you are so completely in the woods and yet your feet meet no obstacles. It is as if it were not a path but an open winding passage through the bushes which your feet find."[27] While he sees objects less clearly, his other senses are heightened. "After walking by night several times, I now walk by day," he writes, "but I am not aware of any crowning advantage in it. I see small objects better, but it does not enlighten me any. The day is more trivial."[28] On one of these walks he hears young partridges drumming as late as nine o'clock. "What singularly, space penetrating, and filling sound!" he says. "Why am I never nearer to its source!" This is a lead-in to another of his insightful observations:

> We do not commonly live our lives out and full; we do not fill all our pores with our blood; we do not inspire and expire fully and entirely enough, so that the wave, the comber, of each inspiration shall break upon our extremest shores, rolling till it meets the sand which bounds us, and the sound of the surf come back to us. Might not a bellows assist us to breathe? That our breathing should create a wind in a calm day! We do not live but a quarter part of our life. Why do we not let on the flood, raise the gates, and set all our wheels in motion? He that hath ears to hear, let him hear. Employ your senses.[29]

So-called fluvial excursions, or walks in water, were yet another method of altering his perceptions. On his birthday, July 12, 1852, he wrote: "Divesting yourself of all clothing but your shirt and hat, which are to protect your exposed parts from the sun, you are prepared for the fluvial excursion. You choose whatever depths you like, tucking your toga higher or lower, as you take the deep middle of the road or the shallow sidewalks."[30] He vividly describes the sensation of his bare feet walking on the muddy bottom, observing the fish darting out of his path, and turtles sunning themselves on the shore. Swamps offered him a similar opportunity to alter his perceptions. In an 1840 journal entry he asks, "Would it not be a luxury to stand up to one's chin in some retired swamp for a whole summer's day, scenting the sweet fern and bilberry blows, and lulled by the minstrelsy of gnats and mosquitoes?" Better the company of "decayed cranberry vines," he says, than the society of Greek sages at a banquet![31]

Refining one's perceptions is a pervasive theme in Thoreau's journal. Solitude and silence also play important roles in his cultivation of the soul. Sometime in 1844 he wrote:

> As the truest society approaches always nearer to solitude, so the most excellent speech finally falls into Silence. We go about to find Solitude and Silence, as though they dwelt only in distant glens and the depth of the wood, venturing out from these fortresses at midnight, and do not dream that she is then imported into them when we wend thither.... Silence is the communing of a conscious soul with itself. When we attend for a moment to our own infinity, then and there is silence, audible to all men at all times in all places. It is when we hear inwardly; sound when we hear outwardly.[32]

Because of passages like this in the journal and *Walden*, Thoreau is sometimes taken to be a misanthrope. It is hardly enough to say that he had many friends, which he did. To be considered antisocial is the risk one runs when attempting to cultivate the soul. Nevertheless, it is in solitude and silence that we are able to commune with our inner self. It is when we are estranged from ourselves that we are estranged from others. Poet May Sarton felt similarly. In her book *Journal of a Solitude* she wrote: "Here I am alone for the first time in weeks, to take up my 'real' life again at last. That is what is strange—that friends, even passionate love, are not my real life unless there is time alone in which to explore and discover what is happening or has happened. Without the interruptions, nourishing and maddening, this life would become arid. Yet I taste it fully only when I am alone."[33]

Closely related to the need for silence and solitude in the cultivation of the soul is the importance of simplicity. Thoreau found that by eliminating distractions and keeping his needs few, he was able to concentrate his mind and focus his energies on advancing his spiritual growth. "By simplicity, commonly called poverty, my life is concentrated and so becomes organized, or a κόσμος (cosmos), which before was inorganic and lumpish," he wrote in February 1857.[34] "There are two kinds of Simplicity," he noted in September 1853, "one that is akin to foolishness, the other to wisdom." The first is both outwardly and inwardly simple; the other, that of the philosopher, is only outwardly simple but inwardly more complicated. "A man who has equally limited views with respect to the end of living will not be helped by the most complex and refined style of living. It is not the tub that makes Diogenes the Jove-born, but Diogenes the tub."[35] This is a notion summed up in a phrase attributed to Wordsworth but frequently mentioned by the Transcendentalists: "simple living and high thinking." The one enables the other.

Of all the spiritual practices Thoreau engaged in, walking is undoubtedly the one he is best noted for. His friend Bronson Alcott called him "a peripatetic philosopher."[36] Emerson said in his eulogy for his friend, "The length of his walk, uniformly made the length of his writing."[37] If he did not walk, he did not write. Walking, or sauntering as Thoreau called it, was a form of meditation. It steadied his nerves, sharpened his senses, and brought him into nature, the source of his inspiration. "There is nothing so sanative, so poetic, as a walk in the woods and fields," he wrote in his journal. "Nothing so inspires me and excites such serene and profitable thought." His neighbors found it hard to believe that he spent so much time walking in nature, but he considered it necessary for his health and peace of mind to get Concord out of his head. A mile or two from the village, in the solitude of nature, he felt as though he met "some grand, serene, immortal, infinitely encouraging, though invisible companion and walked with him."[38]

By means of such practices, Thoreau sought to hone his perceptions and elevate himself. He is forever urging himself on. "There is elevation in every hour," he writes. "No part of the earth is so low and withdrawn, that the heavens cannot be seen from it, but every part supports the sky. We have only to stand on the eminence of the hour, and look out thence into the empyrean, allowing no pinnacle above us, to command an uninterrupted horizon."[39] Take advantage of every opportunity to improve yourself. "Cultivate the tree which you have found to bear fruit in your soil." Work yourself into a frenzy:

> Does not the stream still rise to its fountainhead in you? Go to the Devil and come back again. Dispose of evil. Get punished once for all. Die if you can. Depart. Exchange your salvation for a glass of water. If you know of any risk to run, run it. If you don't know of any, enjoy confidence. Do not

trouble yourself to be religious, you will never get a thank you for it. If you can drive a nail and have any nails to drive, drive them. If you have any experiments you would like to try, try them—now's your chance. Do not entertain doubts if they are not agreeable to you. Send them to the tavern. Do not eat unless you are hungry. There's no need of it. Do not read the newspapers. Improve every opportunity to be melancholy.[40]

It's hard to know what to make of this passage. Coming in the middle of his extended meditation on Ossoli's coat button, he seems to be spurring himself on, mindful of the precariousness of life and the need to get on with it. In contrast to this almost manic sense of urgency is the realization that the doors of perception cannot be forced. He counsels himself to slow down, to "observe the hours of the universe, not of the cars." Rather than the dictates of the will, we should heed our genius, which requires discipline and patience. "One moment of life costs many hours, hours not of business but of preparation and invitation. . . . That aim in life is highest which requires the highest and finest discipline. How much, what infinite, leisure it requires, as of a lifetime, to appreciate a single phenomenon! You must camp down beside it as for life, having reached your land of promise, and give yourself wholly to it."[41]

Moreover, the reality we seek cannot be approached directly. "Go not to the object, let it come to you," he writes. "What I need is not to look at all, but a true sauntering of the eye."[42] In a similar vein, he tells us that the naturalist cannot look at nature directly, "but only with the side of his eye. He must look through and beyond her. To look at her is as fatal as to look at the head of Medusa. It turns the man of science to a stone."[43] On another occasion, "sauntering far from home," he remarks that we are able to see "rare sights with the unconscious side of the eye, which you could not see by a direct gaze before."[44]

Thoreau was keenly aware of the paradox of the spiritual life—the seeming contradiction between passive reception and active engagement. This is apparent in the distinction just made between seeing and looking. On a Sunday morning in December 1841, the sound of the church bell brings to mind thoughts of time and eternity. Sin, he said, has to do not with our actions but with the extent to which we have allowed the temporal to eclipse the eternal. How to wrest eternity from the passage of time? "The whole duty of life is contained in the question how to respire and aspire both at once."[45] His spiritual practice embraced both poles of this dilemma. Revelations cannot be compelled, but they may be beseeched. Cultivating the soul by means of refining the senses and sauntering in nature increased the likelihood of their recurrence.

Another issue Thoreau faced was what Emerson called the problem of double consciousness. As Emerson described it in his essay "The Transcendentalist," the *actualities* of daily life stand in contrast to the *realities* of the ideal world. Coleridge, a major influence on Emerson, Thoreau, and the other Transcendentalists, made a distinction, mentioned earlier, between the Reason and the Understanding. By Reason he meant an intuitive apprehension of the true nature of the world, of reality. As Emerson expressed it in his essay "The Over-Soul," "We see the world piece by piece, as the sun, the moon, the animal, the tree, but the whole, of which these are the shining parts, is the soul."[46] The Understanding, by contrast, is empirical. Whereas the Reason is holistic, the Understanding is atomistic. It divides the world into parts, weighing, measuring, and counting everything. They represent two different ways of knowing. Each views the world differently. The intuitions of the Reason show us how our lives might be enriched and the world made fair. Though fleeting, they are compelling. They refuse to be dismissed by the Understanding and the measures of everyday experience. Unfortunately, the Understanding tends to predominate over the Reason, with the result that facts count for more than values.

For the European Romantics, a major influence on the American Transcendentalists, the image of the divine marriage represented the reconciliation of these two modes of consciousness. Literary scholar M. H. Abrams states that the Romantic writers sought "radically to recast, into terms appropriate to the historical and intellectual circumstances of their own age, the Christian pattern of the fall, the redemption, and the emergence of a new earth which will constitute a restored paradise."[47] In his book *Nature*, Emerson wrote: "The problem of restoring to the world original and eternal beauty, is solved by the redemption of the soul. The ruin or the blank that we see when we look at nature, is in our own eye. The axis of vision is not coincident with the axis of things, and so they appear not transparent but opake [*sic*]. The reason why the world lacks unity, and lies broken and in heaps, is, because man is disunited with himself." The marriage of matter and spirit is not celebrated.[48]

For Thoreau the imbalance between matter and spirit, or the Understanding and the Reason, is remedied by the marriage of the soul with Nature, as he noted in his journal: "It is the marriage of the soul with Nature that makes the imagination fruitful, that gives birth to imagination. When we were dead and dry as the highway, some sense which has been healthily fed will put us in relation with Nature, in sympathy with her; some grains of fertilizing pollen, floating in the air, fall on us, and suddenly the sky is all one rainbow, is full of music and fragrance and flavor."[49] This entry, dated August 21, 1851, comes two days after he had expressed a waning of his powers and the frequency of his ecstasies. "I fear that the character of my knowledge is from year to year becoming more distinct and scientific; that in exchange for views as wide as heaven's cope, I am being narrowed down to the field of the microscope. I see details, not wholes nor the shadow of the whole."[50] And yet those ecstasies remained the high-water mark of his spiritual life. Less than a month later he affirmed their enduring importance:

> Our ecstatic states, which appear to yield so little fruit, have this value at least: though in the seasons when our genius reigns we may be powerless for expression, yet, in calmer seasons, when our talent is active, the memory of those rarer moods comes to color our picture and is the permanent paint-pot, as it were, into which we dip our brush. . . .
> Our moments of inspiration are not lost though we have no particular poem to show for them. For those experiences have left an indelible impression, and we are ever and anon reminded of them.[51]

Following this passage, and going on for pages, is an extraordinary expression of Thoreau's philosophy, a bit of which was quoted in chapter 2. "We are receiving our portion of the Infinite," he writes. "The *Art of life!* Was there ever anything memorable written upon it? By what disciplines to secure the most life, with what care to watch our thoughts." How to live? he asks; how to get the most out of life? "If it is possible that we may be addressed, it behoves us to be attentive. If by watching all day and all night, I may detect some trace of the Ineffable, then will it not be worth the while to watch?"[52] Patience and perception are required. If by watching we may feel ourselves elevated and the world become living and divine, shall we not be watchmen? "To watch for, describe all the divine features which I detect in Nature," he writes. "My profession is to be always on the alert to find God in nature, to know his lurking places. To attend all the oratorios, the operas in nature."[53]

Starting in the summer of 1851, after studying Asa Gray's *Manual of Botany*, Thoreau began to catalogue the flowers he saw on his walks, noting when they blossomed. His phenological studies continued for many years afterwards and have since proved useful in gauging the onset of global warming.[54]

The lists and charts he made in his journal were also part of a larger project he envisioned but did not complete, a "Kalendar," as he put it, of all the natural phenomena he observed during the course of a year.[55] The later journal also reveals the increasing amount of time he spent on the rivers surrounding Concord. So much of the early journal describes his walks in the hills, woods, and fields of Concord that it comes as something of a surprise that during the last ten years of his life he was often boating rather than hiking. His time on these rivers increased after he was engaged by local farmers to study the impact on farming caused by the erection of dams by downstream industrialists. This led to an extensive report Thoreau gave to the House and Senate of the Commonwealth of Massachusetts on the hydrology of these rivers.[56]

His observations on natural phenomena, seasonal changes, and the dispersion of seeds indicate a growing interest in science during the last decade of his life. Some readers of the journal have concluded that Thoreau abandoned Transcendentalism in favor of an empirical approach to understanding the natural world, although I would argue that his Transcendentalist viewpoint and his scientific studies were equally important to him. When he received a questionnaire from the secretary of the Association for the Advancement of Science in 1853 asking him to indicate which branch of science he was most interested in, he hesitated to respond:

> I felt that it would be to make myself the laughing-stock of the scientific community to describe or attempt to describe to them that branch of science which specially interests me, in as much as they do not believe in a science which deals with the higher law. So I was obliged to speak to their condition and describe to them that poor part of me which alone they can understand. The fact is I am a mystic, a transcendentalist, and a natural philosopher to boot. Now I think of it, I should have told them at once that I was a transcendentalist. That would have been the shortest way of telling them that they would not understand my explanations.[57]

Transcendentalism was his hedge against the desacralization of the natural world threatened by the advance of materialism and soulless empiricism. As much as he was drawn to science, he remained somewhat skeptical of its claims. From time to time, he expressed his ambivalence about science. "Science is inhuman," he wrote in an 1859 journal entry. "With our prying instruments we disturb the balance and harmony of nature."[58]

In spite of his misgivings, Thoreau's botanical studies, his observations of the natural world, and his reading of writers such as Alexander von Humboldt led him to embrace the notion of nature as an organic whole. In a journal entry that was also used in *Walden*, he wrote: "There is nothing inorganic. This earth is not then a mere fragment of dead history, strata upon strata, like the leaves of a book—an object for a museum and an Antiquarian but living poetry like the leaves of a tree—not a fossil earth—but a living specimen."[59] Such observations confirmed for him what Humboldt had written in his magnum opus, *Kosmos*, a five-volume survey of the material universe, in which Humboldt attempted, he said, to "represent nature as one great whole, moved and animated by internal forces."[60]

During Thoreau's lifetime the woods around Concord and Walden Pond became decimated as the trees were cut down for firewood, lumber, and railroad ties. According to Laurence Buell, "the percentage of woodland in the town of Concord had steadily declined during Thoreau's lifetime, reaching an all-time low of little more than ten percent."[61] His studies of the forest trees and the damming of the rivers demonstrated the negative impact humans were having on the environment. In 1861, a year before his death, he wrote:

> Most men it seems to me, do not care for Nature and would sell their share in all her beauty, as long as they may live, for a stated sum—many for a glass of rum. Thank God, men cannot as yet fly, and lay waste to the sky as well as the earth! We are safe on that side for the present. It is for the very reason that some do not care for those things that we need to continue to protect all from the vandalism of a few.[62]

In response to multiple threats to nature, Thoreau became an early advocate for preservation. Through the course of his writing, especially in the journal, we can trace a growing concern for the natural world from an aesthetic appreciation to a spiritual connection and, finally, to a call for preservation. As Buell expresses it, Thoreau demonstrates a pattern "of pastoral aesthetics and romanticist natural piety interacting with empirical study and scientific interests . . . to produce what we should now call an environmentalist commitment."[63] He credits Thoreau's spiritual connection with nature in providing the impetus not only to his own preservationist stance but also for that of his readers. His advocacy for preservation is eloquently stated in the last pages of his journal. "Does not the landscape deserve attention?" he asks.

> What are the natural features which make a township handsome? A river, with its waterfalls and meadows, a lake, a hill, a cliff or individual rocks, a forest, and ancient trees standing singly. Such things are beautiful; they have a high use which dollars and cents never represent. If the inhabitants of a

town were wise, they would seek to preserve these things, though at a considerable expense; for such things educate far more than any hired teachers or preachers, or any at present recognized system of school education. I do not think him fit to be the founder of a state or even of a town who does not foresee the use of these things, but legislates chiefly for oxen, as it were.[64]

"Speak to me in this hour"

In March 1848 Thoreau received a letter from Harrison Gray Otis Blake, at the time a widowed ex–Unitarian minister living in Worcester, Massachusetts. Blake was a younger classmate of his at Harvard, and their paths had crossed a number of times since graduating. They were formally introduced to each other by Emerson, but Blake quickly latched onto Thoreau and soon became a devoted disciple. Having read some of Thoreau's writing in *The Dial*, Blake was moved to write him a letter." If I understand rightly the significance of your life, this is it," he wrote. "You would sunder yourself from society, from the spell of institutions, customs, conventionalities that you may lead a fresh, simple life with God. Instead of breathing a new life into the old forms, you would have a new life without and within. There is something sublime to me in this attitude,—as far as I may be from it myself. . . . Speak to me in this hour as you are prompted."[65] Incidentally, Blake had been one of the students at Harvard Divinity School who invited Emerson to deliver an address to the graduating seniors in 1838. In his infamous Divinity School address, Emerson encouraged the students to breathe "a new life into the old forms." In this letter, he sensed that Thoreau had moved beyond Emerson's position, into uncharted religious territory.

What followed was an extraordinary exchange of letters between the two men over a period of thirteen years. In truth, it was more of a one-sided correspondence between a master, Thoreau, and his disciple dealing with spirituality and the art of living, similar to that between the Roman Stoic philosopher Seneca and his younger disciple Lucilius, a Roman soldier and statesman. Seneca's letters cover a variety of topics, ranging from the love of nature and the charm of simple living to the degeneracy of drunkenness and the debasing effects of slavery. In the course of this correspondence, he tutored his disciple in the benefits of the Stoic philosophy. Thoreau's letters to Blake are similar. He is tutoring his disciple in the Transcendentalist philosophy as he has practiced it himself. His letters also covered a variety of topics, from simple living and self-culture to chastity and yoga.

Recognizing the wisdom conveyed in these letters, Blake invited a group of his friends, including Unitarian ministers Thomas Wentworth Higginson, David Atwood Wasson, and Edward Everett Hale, to hear them recited at his home. The letters—forty-nine in all—constitute a succinct expression of Thoreau's spiritual philosophy.

In his reply to Blake's invitation, Thoreau got to the point right away. To set about living a higher life, he said, "is to go [on] a journey to a distant country, gradually to find ourselves surrounded by new scenes and men; and as long as the old are around me, I know that I am not in any true sense living a new or better life."[66] We think that we might build a divine life on the foundations of the present one, like a thrush making her nest and laying her egg over one laid there by a cuckoo. This will not do; the cuckoo's egg will hatch first and crowd the young thrush out of the nest. "No," he says. "Destroy the cuckoo's egg, or build a new nest."[67] For change to happen, we must leave the old behind.

Thoreau prescribes simplicity, not for economic reasons, but as a way of reducing the problems of life to their simplest terms, distinguishing the necessary and the real. Examine yourself, he tells Blake, "see where your main roots run." What most people call common sense "is in fact the verist illusion." But there is a "faint glimmer of reality which sometimes illuminates the darkness of daylight," revealing "something more solid and enduring than adamant, which is in fact the corner-stone of the world." Though seemingly elusive and ethereal, such visions can be attained. "If a man constantly aspires, is he not elevated?"[68]

Thoreau assures Blake that he speaks from experience and says what he knows to be true. "I have no designs on society or nature or God," he writes. "I *live* in the *present*. I only remember the past—and anticipate the future. I love to live."[69] He urges his disciple to do the same. "Know your own bone," he says; "gnaw at it, bury it, unearth it, and gnaw it still." But don't be too moral, he cautions; you may cheat yourself out of life if you do. "Aim above morality. Be not *simply* good—be good for something."[70] Don't let anything come between you and the light.

In response to Blake's next query—how shall we earn our bread?—Thoreau rhetorically asks what kind of bread are we talking about; the bread that feeds our body only? The brain and heart also need nourishment but get scarcely any. We are more concerned about meeting our physical needs than we are about enabling our higher faculties. As for getting our bread, "a very few crumbs are enough, if it be of the right quality," that is to say, if it is earned honestly. Bread is meant to feed the soul and fortify our self-reliance.

"The heavens are as deep as our aspirations are high. So high as a tree aspires to grow, so high it will find an atmosphere suited to it. Every man should stand for a force which is perfectly irresistible."[71]

Blake asks if there is no sorrow in his philosophy. Although Thoreau admits to having transient regrets, he is stoically indifferent to sadness or misery. "I am of kin to the sod, and partake largely of its dull patience," he says. "I am too easily contented with a slight and almost animal happiness. My happiness is a good deal like that of the woodchucks."[72]

By the time he wrote his sixth letter to Blake on November 20, 1849, Thoreau had become quite busy. In addition to his regular routine of reading and writing in the morning and evening, in addition to taking long walks in the afternoon, he was working to pay off his debt, equal to about a year's wages, for the publication of *A Week*. This entailed tiresome hours making and peddling pencils and taking surveying jobs in and around Concord.

Hard-pressed for time though he was, he felt grateful for whatever leisure he had to enjoy his woodland walks. He was reminded of a passage from Harivansa, an ancient Sanskrit text: "Free in this world, as the birds in the air, disengaged from every kind of chains, those who have practiced the yoga gather in Brahma the certain fruit of their works." Though he confesses to being "rude and careless," he aspires to practice it faithfully.[73] While this passage is indicative of the profound influence Indian philosophy had on his own spiritual growth, we shouldn't take it too literally. Thoreau is advising his friend to transcend the superficial affairs of daily life, exemplified by the gossip of newspapers. "We want the inevitable news, be it sad or cheering," he says. "I think newspapers are a great improvement on a bad invention. Do not suffer your life to be taken by newspapers."[74] It is by means of yoga, or contemplation, that we can achieve the kind of detachment he advocates.

In Thoreau's next letter to Blake, dated April 3, 1850, he returns to the topic of appearance versus reality, a perennial theme in his writing. He says we are daily seduced by appearances when it is reality we should seek. Our resolve to do so is worn down by falsehoods. Why not lay them down and recline instead on the over-soul? "Let things alone; let them weigh what they will; let them soar or fall. . . . Let God alone if need be." If he loved God more, he would keep him—or rather himself—at a more respectful distance. "It is not when I am going to meet him, but when I am just turning away and leaving him alone, that I discover that God is. I say, God. I am not sure that that is his name. You will know whom I mean."[75]

If we could transcend our petty selves for just a moment, the universe would "appear crystallized and radiant around us." Likening the understanding to blindness in turning a biblical phrase, Thoreau declares, "Let the understanding lead the understanding," referring here to Coleridge's distinction between Reason and Understanding.[76] The Understanding, or the empirical mode of consciousness, will get us nowhere. The Reason, meaning the intuitive mode of consciousness, should not accompany the understanding, he says, but lead it like a far-off star.

"Will you live? or will you be embalmed?" Thoreau wants to know. People think it foolish to demand too much of life. But not Henry:

> I am not afraid that I shall exaggerate the value and significance of life, but that I shall not be up to the occasion which it is. I shall be sorry to remember that I was there, but noticed nothing remarkable, not so much as a prince in disguise, lived in the Golden Age a hired man, visited Olympus even, but fell asleep after dinner, and did not hear the conversation of the Gods. I lived in Judea eighteen hundred years ago, but I never knew that there was such a one as Christ among my contemporaries![77]

So often it is only in retrospect that we realize our missed opportunities. This would be less likely to happen if we were more attentive to the fleeting moment.

Thoreau's next letter to Blake, on May 28, deals with finding contentment in life—not as commonly lived, but as it might be. "We who walk the streets and hold time together, are but the refuse of ourselves," Thoreau tells him. "It is coffee made of coffee-grounds the twentieth time, which was only coffee the first time—while the living water leaps and sparkles by our doors." Drawing on agrarian metaphors, he urges Blake to cultivate his soul. "Some absorbing employment on your higher ground—your upland farm, whither no cart-path leads—but where you mount alone with your hoe—where the life ever-lasting grows—you raise a crop which needs not to be brought down into the valley to the market, which you barter for heavenly products."[78]

Referring again to the living water, Thoreau, quoting Alexander Pope, tells Blake, "Drink deep or taste not of the Pierian Spring. Be not deterred by melancholy on the path which leads to immortal health and joy."[79] This spring is a fountain sacred to the Muses, granting wisdom to all who drink from it. It was said to be slightly bitter to the taste, suggesting perhaps that wisdom contains a bit of melancholy.

The ninth letter was written in August 1850, shortly after Thoreau had gone to Long Island at Emerson's behest to search for remains of Margaret Fuller and her family, drowned in a shipwreck off Fire Island. Given the uncertainties of life, he urges Blake to do more of the work he knows he ought to do. "Do what nobody else can do for you," he writes. "Omit to do anything else." It's not easy to improve our lives. "We have repeatedly to withdraw into our shells of thought, like the tortoise." But there is no point in conforming outwardly while living your own life inwardly. "It will prove a failure. Just as successfully can you walk against a sharp steel edge which divides you right and left."[80]

There was a two-year hiatus between the ninth letter and the next one. Thoreau spent a great deal of that time surveying and studying botany. Shortly after their correspondence resumed, Blake became engaged, having been a widower and single parent for six years. In response to the news, Thoreau sends Blake essays on love and chastity affirming the moral high purpose of matrimony. "The object of love expands and grows before us to eternity," he writes, "until it includes all that is lovely, and we become all that can love."[81]

In a letter written February 27, 1853, Thoreau laments that, while his surveying pays the bills, he has been unable to follow his aspirations. "The one is the way of death," he says, "the other of life everlasting."[82] Likewise, the direction of the nation is not upward but westward. Such may be the nation's manifest destiny, but it is not his. He has had but one *"spiritual* birth," and it doesn't matter who is elected president, "not a new scintillation of light flashes on me." He has nothing more to learn "but something to practice," namely, his own self-culture.[83] Repeating a familiar image, he tells us that we are the proprietors of "an Upland farm, upland in the sense that it will produce nobler crops and better repay cultivation in the long run" and we ought to cultivate it. "How prompt we are to satisfy the hunger and thirst of our bodies; how slow to satisfy the hunger and thirst of our *souls.*"[84]

Self-culture is also the theme of letter fourteen, written in December 1853. Thoreau tells Blake that we cannot lift ourselves by our own waistbands because we can never get out of ourselves. But we can expand ourselves through discipline. "We must heap up a great pile of doing, for a small diameter of being," he says. We must do our work, as "the artist is made to accomplish his self-culture by devotion to his art!"[85] The sawyer, in doing his work, becomes not merely a better sawyer but a better person. "It is the art of mankind to polish the world, and everyone who works is scrubbing in some part."[86] Whether we spend the day in an ecstasy or despondency, we must have some work to show for it.

Subsequent letters dealt with more mundane matters, including Thoreau's visits to Cape Cod, his recent lectures, and progress on the *Walden* manuscript. In a letter to Blake in June 1855, he confesses, "I have been sick and good for nothing but to lie on my back and wait for something to turn up, for two or three months."[87] By September he felt well enough to resume their correspondence. Returning to the topic of simple living, he says it is not his purpose to tell others how to live but rather to live such a life himself. "As a preacher I should be prompted to tell men not so much how to get their wheat-bread cheaper—as of the bread of life compared with which *that* is bran. Let a man only taste these loaves and he becomes a skillful economist at once."[88] In Thoreau's time, economics was a branch of moral philosophy and not what we think of it today.[89] Thus, the aim of life is not to attain riches but to live better.

In letter twenty-eight, written May 21, 1856, Thoreau comments on the tension between solitude and society. By this time, *Walden* had been published. While the reviews were generally positive, he was often portrayed as a misanthropic hermit who prized solitude over society. In this letter he argues that they are equally important. Society "is an idling down on the plain at the base of a mountain." In climbing the mountain we are glad to have company, but very few people are so inclined. It is not that he wishes to be alone, "but that we love to soar, and when we do soar, the company grows thinner and thinner till there is none at all. It is either Tribune on the plain, a sermon on the mount, or a very private ecstasy still higher up."[90] We should aim at the summit even if others do not.

On a surveying trip to New Jersey at the invitation of Marcus Spring, who wished to establish a cooperative community near Perth Amboy, Thoreau met Walt Whitman for the first time. His encounter with the poet appears to have energized him, stirring up his desire for spiritual awakening, which seems to have flagged. In a letter written on December 6, he addresses Blake, having himself in mind also: "Blake! Blake! Are you awake? Are you aware what an ever-glorious morning this is? What long expected never to be repeated opportunity is now offered to get life and knowledge? For my part I am trying to wake up,—to wring slumber out of my pores. For, generally, I take events as unconcernedly as a fence post." He is reminded of his many blessings: "I am grateful for what I am and have. My thanksgiving is perpetual. It is surprising how contented one can be with nothing definite—only a sense of existence. . . . My breath is sweet to me. O how I laugh when I think of my vague indefinite riches. No run on my bank can drain it—for my wealth is not possession but enjoyment." What do you have to show for your years? he asks his friend. "Of what use a great fire on the hearth and a confounded little fire in the heart?"[91] Time is swiftly passing us by.

In September 1857 the failure of several large New York banks precipitated a financial panic not seen since the depression of 1837. In Thoreau's letter to Blake two months later, he expresses no sympathy for the banks, which have reaped what they had sown. They "have long laughed at transcendentalism, higher laws, etc., crying, 'None of your moonshine,' as if they were anchored to something not only definite, but sure and permanent." Now they find themselves "to be mere reeds shaken by the wind."[92]

This picture of financial collapse is juxtaposed with news of Blake's recent walk to the White Mountains. "I suppose that I feel the same awe when on their summits that many do on entering a church," Thoreau writes. He encourages Blake to consider what ascending Mount Washington, the highest of the peaks, meant to him. What did he find there? "It is after we get home that we really go over the mountain, if ever. What did the mountain say? What did the mountain do?"[93] In his essay "A Walk to Wachusett" he had written, "Now that we have returned to the desultory life of the plain, let us endeavor to import a little of that mountain grandeur into it."[94] No doubt this is what he is hoping Blake will do also.

Thoreau is often uncannily prophetic, calling attention to developments more alarming in our day than in his. In his forty-sixth letter to Blake, dated May 20, 1860, he asks, "What is the use of a house if you haven't got a tolerable planet to put it on?" This question is put to Blake in the context of a discourse about self-reliance. He is asking, What is your foundation? How are you grounded? Whether we use a microscope, a telescope, or our naked eye, we only discover ourselves. We make our own fate. If we rely simply on what the church teaches, "then all your joy and serenity is reduced to grinning and bearing it." But if you practice self-reliance, "your success will be in proportion to your devotion" to the effort. "Where is the 'Unexplored land' but in our own untried enterprises?" he asks. "To an adventurous spirit any place,—London, New York, Worcester, or his own yard, is 'unexplored land.'" Though we are often tempted to give up trying, Thoreau will have none of it. "You must make tracks into the Unknown. That is what you have your board and clothes for. Why do you ever mend your clothes, unless that, wearing them, you may mend your ways. Let us sing."[95]

By the time Thoreau wrote his last letter to Blake, on May 3, 1861, seven southern states had seceded from the Union and Lincoln had been sworn in as the new president. Meanwhile, Thoreau was suffering from tuberculosis, preparing several of his lectures for publication, and planning a trip to Minnesota, hoping that inland air might improve his condition. Although he wished that Blake might have accompanied him, he traveled instead with Horace Mann Jr., son of the well-known educator. Almost a year to the day later, Thoreau succumbed to the disease, as had his father and one of his sisters before him.

As was the case with Thoreau's journal, these letters—which once inspired and enlightened a devoted follower and his friends over 150 years ago—were treasured as a valuable spiritual resource. Bradley P. Dean, who edited these letters for publication, writes, "If not inevitable, surely it is fitting that these letters are now available to a still-wider audience, to new generations of seekers who can enjoy and benefit from the masterful insights of a great spiritual teacher."[96]

CHAPTER 6

YEARS OF DECISION

In historian Bernard DeVoto's phrase, 1846 was "the Year of Decision." "Sometimes there are exceedingly brief periods which determine a long future," he wrote. "A moment of time holds in solution ingredients which might combine in any of several or many ways, and then another moment precipitates out of the possible the at last determined thing."[1] In his history of that fateful year, he chronicles the US invasion of Mexico, leading to the annexation of New Mexico, Arizona, and California; the settlement of the long-running dispute with Great Britain over the nation's northern boundary; the westward migration of the Mormons and the ill-fated Donner Party; and a little-noticed event in a small New England town. In July of that year, Henry Thoreau walked into Concord from his cabin in Walden Woods to fetch a shoe that had been repaired and ended up spending the night behind bars. DeVoto's portrayal of Thoreau's decision to go to jail rather than pay the poll tax he owed is rightfully set in the context of sweeping national events. "In those noon woods and beside those midnight waters," he wrote, "hour by hour of patient thought slowly pulled Henry Thoreau nearer causes. And nearer decision."[2] It is proof of the "butterfly effect," which holds that a minor event in one place can have major consequences elsewhere.

As the story is recounted by Emerson's son Edward, Sam Staples, Concord's tax collector, deputy sheriff, and jailer, stopped Thoreau in the street and asked him to pay his delinquent tax, offering to advance the money himself. "Thoreau explained that he did not mean to pay. Staples said, 'Then I shall have to shut you up.' 'One time is as good as another.' 'Come along, then.'"[3] The money was delivered to the jailer's door later that evening by an anonymous veiled woman, perhaps one of Thoreau's aunts. By then it was late; Staples had decided to turn in for the night. The next morning, Henry

was released and picked up his mended shoe. Soon thereafter, he found himself in a huckleberry field, where "the State was nowhere to be seen."[4] When
he heard about Thoreau's action, Emerson didn't approve. According to
Bronson Alcott, Emerson "thought it mean and skulking, and in bad taste."[5]

In truth, Thoreau was not the first person in Concord to be arrested for
refusing to pay the poll tax as a form of political protest. In January 1843,
Staples had arrested Bronson Alcott for the same offense. And later that
year, Alcott's friend Charles Lane also refused to pay his tax. Neither of them
spent a night in jail, however; Samuel Hoar, one of Concord's leading citizens, paid their taxes to save the town from embarrassment.

Although the cause of abolition was not popular in the North, Concord
became a hotbed of antislavery activism. A week after his release from jail,
Thoreau hosted a meeting of the Concord Female Anti-Slavery Society at
his cabin in Walden Woods. The organization had been founded in 1837
by Prudence Ward, Mary Merrick Brooks, and other women in the town.
Importantly, their membership included Cynthia Thoreau and Lidian Emerson, both of whom exerted influence on other members of their respective
families, including Henry Thoreau and Waldo Emerson. Henry's famous
night in jail was not a one-off event. It needs to be viewed in the context of
ongoing organized opposition to slavery in Concord.

"Civil Disobedience"

Feeling that he ought to explain his action to the local townspeople, Thoreau
delivered a lecture at the Concord Lyceum, "On the Rights and Duties of the
Individual in Relation to Government," in January 1848. A year later, Elizabeth Palmer Peabody asked him for permission to publish the essay in her
short-lived journal *Aesthetic Papers*. There it was titled "Resistance to Civil
Government." It was republished in 1866 under the more familiar title "Civil
Disobedience."

While he accepts the motto "That government is best which governs least,"
what Thoreau really wants is a better government, one that is ruled by conscience rather than expediency (63). Instead of respect for the law, the state
should cultivate respect for what is right. Failing that, citizens are prone to
becoming agents of injustice. In the essay he is primarily concerned about the
US invasion of Mexico, the extension of slavery, and the removal of Native
Americans, all of which he considers unjust actions. Further, he examines the

extent to which the nation's commerce, dependent on slave labor, makes citizens complicit in these egregious violations of morality. He advocates passive resistance as the means by which we may be absolved of complicity and rid ourselves of these evils.

"All men recognize the right of revolution," Thoreau argues; "that is, the right to refuse allegiance to and resist the government, when its tyranny or its inefficiency are great and unendurable" (67). They did so in 1775. Why not now, when a sixth of the population is enslaved and when the United States has invaded and conquered a foreign country? "If I have unjustly wrested a plank from a drowning man, I must restore it to him though I drown myself," he says. "This people must cease to hold slaves, and to make war in Mexico, though it cost them their existence as a people" (68).

In the state of Massachusetts, opponents of abolition are not politicians from the South, Thoreau says, "but a hundred thousand merchants and farmers here, who are more interested in commerce and agriculture than they are in humanity, and are not prepared to do justice to the slave and to Mexico, *cost what it may.*" Although there are many "who are *in opinion* opposed to slavery and to the [Mexican] war," they do little to put an end to them. Moreover, "even voting for the right is *doing* nothing for it" (68–69). It is only expressing a feeble desire that something should be done about it.

Over the years, many of Thoreau's critics have faulted him for retreating to Walden Pond while the evil of slavery continued unabated, insinuating that his decision to remain there was selfish and that spending one night in jail was an ineffectual form of protest. No doubt he wished he could write in peace and uninterrupted, but, as he confesses in the essay: "If I devote myself to other pursuits and contemplations, I must first see, at least, that I do not pursue them sitting upon another man's shoulders. I must get off him first, that he may pursue his contemplations too" (71). As we will see, from this point on he became increasingly outspoken in his opposition to slavery, even as he continued to write and take his daily walks in the woods.

Returning to his previous point, Thoreau insists that it is not enough merely to entertain an opinion; one must take steps to enact it. "Action from principle,—the perception and the performance of right—changes things and relations; it is essentially revolutionary, and does not consist wholly with anything that was. It not only divides states and churches, it divides families; aye, it divides the *individual,* separating the diabolical in him from the divine" (72). There is no contradiction between action from principle and his advocacy of simple living or the importance of contemplation in nature. None of these is sacrificed to another. All three are integral to his Transcendentalist outlook.

"Unjust laws exist," Thoreau declares. "Shall we be content to obey them, or shall we endeavor to amend them, and obey them until we have succeeded, or shall we transgress them at once?" (73–74). This is a familiar dilemma. Most people seem to think we should obey them until we can alter or repeal them and, further, that to resist or break them will only make matters worse. "But it is the fault of the government itself that the remedy *is* worse than the evil," he argues. Why does the state always persecute those who point out its flaws rather than make necessary reforms? Rather than be an agent of injustice, one should break the laws. "Let your life be a counter friction to stop the machine. What I have to do is see, at any rate, that I do not lend myself to the wrong which I condemn." Addressing the abolitionists directly, he says they should withdraw their support, "both in person and property," from the state (73–74).

Thoreau asserts that it is better to go to jail than to obey unjust laws. Those jailed for their principles will find themselves in good company: "It is there that the fugitive slave, and the Mexican prisoner on parole, and the Indian come to plead the wrongs of his race, should find them; on that separate, but more free and honorable ground, where the State places those who are not with her but against her,—the only house in a slave-state in which a free man can abide with honor" (76). In what is perhaps a rebuke to Emerson, he argues that what might seem to be an ineffectual action is, on the contrary, a powerful one. "Cast your whole vote, not a strip of paper merely, but your whole influence. A minority is powerless while it conforms to the majority, . . . but it is irresistible when it clogs by its whole weight" (76). If an agent of the state asks what may be done, the answer is, resign. "When the subject has refused allegiance, and the officer has resigned his office, then the revolution is accomplished." Although Thoreau advocates nonviolent resistance, he is not a pacifist, as his subsequent antislavery addresses make clear. Even if blood should flow from acts of disobedience, "is there not a sort of blood shed when the conscience is wounded?" he asks. "I see this blood flowing now" (77).

Thoreau makes it clear that the tax he refused to pay was, at least indirectly, in support of government-sanctioned aggression in Mexico and the extension of slavery to Texas and the West. He did so on the basis of a "Higher Law," expressed in the Declaration of Independence, that superseded the

US Constitution, which validated slavery by virtue of the so-called three-fifths clause in Article I, Section 2. Of this Higher Law he declares, "They who know of no purer sources of truth, who have traced up its stream no higher, stand, and wisely stand, by the Bible and the Constitution, and drink at it there with reverence and humility; but they who behold where it comes trickling into this lake or that pool, gird up their loins once more, and continue their pilgrimage toward its fountain-head" (88). Conscience, not God's law or the Constitution, is the basis of morality.

Tracing the long march from monarchy to democracy, Thoreau allows that "progress toward a true respect for the individual" has been slow. But he believes it is always possible to take further steps in recognizing human rights. He imagines "a State at last which can afford to be just to all men, and to treat the individual with respect as a neighbor; which even would not think it inconsistent with its own repose, if a few were allowed to live aloof from it, not meddling with it, nor embraced by it, who fulfilled all the duties of neighbors and fellow-men" (89–90).

Though little noticed when it first appeared in Peabody's magazine, "Civil Disobedience" has become one of the most quoted and influential of all of Thoreau's writings, having inspired such authors and activists as Leo Tolstoy, Martin Buber, Mohandas Gandhi, and Martin Luther King Jr. The essay was subsequently included, posthumously, in *A Yankee in Canada, with Anti-Slavery and Reform Papers* in 1866. In 1906 it came to the attention of Gandhi, then living in South Africa and fighting the "Black Act" requiring Asians to register with the government and have their fingerprints recorded. A few years later he wrote: "I actually took the name of my movement from Thoreau's essay, 'On the Duty of Civil Disobedience.' . . . Until I read that essay I never found a suitable English translation for my Indian word, *Satyagraha*."[6] In 1962, Martin Luther King Jr. acknowledged the importance of Thoreau's essay for the American civil rights movement:

> During my early college days I read Thoreau's essay on civil disobedience for the first time. Fascinated by the idea of refusing to cooperate with an evil system, I was so deeply moved that I reread the work several times. I became convinced then that non-cooperation with evil is as much a moral obligation as is cooperation with good. . . . As a result of his writings and personal witness we are the heirs of a legacy of creative protest. It goes without saying that the teachings of Thoreau are alive today, indeed, more alive than ever before. Whether expressed in a sit-in at lunch counters, a freedom ride into Mississippi, a peaceful protest in Montgomery, Alabama,

it is the outgrowth of Thoreau's insistence that evil must be resisted and no moral man can patiently adjust to injustice.[7]

Thoreau's essay has been read by generations of high school students, although I suspect it may be too controversial in many schools today. Yet it continues to inspire those who have read it in their pursuit of antiwar and social justice aims. It represents one person's effort to divest himself of complicity in the injustice of slavery. Perhaps if he had remained at Walden Pond and gone entirely off the grid, so to speak, he might have thought he could succeed in doing so. But deep down he knew this was not possible and that more would need to be done. In succeeding addresses on the topic of slavery he came to realize that individual passive, nonviolent resistance would not be sufficient to end the evil institution. He was not a pacifist like Adin Ballou, nor a passive non-resistant like William Lloyd Garrison.[8] He was open to the possibility of more forceful action should that become necessary. Although Gandhi, King, and others have taken "Civil Disobedience" to advocate nonviolence, Thoreau allows that blood might need to be shed before slavery is finally abolished.

"Slavery in Massachusetts"

"Civil Disobedience" was Thoreau's response to those, like Emerson, who thought it a foolish gesture to go to jail rather than pay a paltry tax. Initially given as a lecture at the Concord Lyceum, it might have been forgotten had not Elizabeth Peabody printed it in her magazine. While he spoke to Concord townspeople in his 1848 lecture, Thoreau's next address, given on July 4, 1854, was addressed to the citizens of Massachusetts. By this time he was actively involved in assisting runaway slaves en route to Canada. His family had sheltered numerous fugitives in their home, while Henry got them onto trains headed north. Another pivotal development was the passage in 1850 of the Fugitive Slave Act, which required northern states to return those who escaped from servitude to their southern "owners." This law infuriated the abolitionists, including Thoreau, Emerson, Alcott, and many others who vowed to disobey it.

The address "Slavery in Massachusetts" was given before a large audience at an antislavery celebration held in Framingham. It was hastily written in response to the capture and rendition of Anthony Burns, an escaped slave. The Boston Vigilance Committee, organized to defend such fugitives and abolitionist speakers, quickly devised a plan to free Burns from the federal courthouse where he was being held. According to Thomas Wentworth Higginson, one of the organizers, a meeting was to be held in Boston's Faneuil Hall to whip up the crowd to storm the courthouse. Meanwhile, a smaller group, including Higginson, was to break into the building during the ensuing melee. The plot did not go according to plan. The crowd that stormed out of Faneuil Hall was disorganized because its leaders were caught at the back of the procession, not at the head of it.

Realizing what had happened, Higginson and his group attacked the building anyway, using a heavy timber to batter in the door. Higginson, joined by two Black men, squeezed their way inside. In the furious fight that ensued, a deputy marshal was killed and Higginson was left bleeding from a gash in the chin. Forced from the building, they regrouped for another assault. Seeing that the deputy marshals were heavily armed, the group hesitated. Higginson described what came next: "In the silent pause that ensued there came quietly forth from the crowd the well-known form of Mr. Amos Bronson Alcott, the Transcendental philosopher. Ascending the lighted steps alone, he said tranquilly, turning to me and pointing forward, 'Why are we not within?'" Seeing none willing to join him, "he said not a word, but calmly walked up the steps,—he and his familiar cane."[9] When he heard the sound of a gun going off inside the courthouse, he retreated as calmly as he had advanced. In the aftermath of the events of May 26, Higginson, Wendell Phillips, and Theodore Parker were arrested for their involvement.

Thoreau praised the heroism of Higginson in his journal and prepared a speech for the crowd gathered in Framingham. He arrived unannounced and was not included in the roster of speakers. While he was outspoken in his opposition to slavery, he was not perceived as a leader in the abolitionist effort. Evidently he did not read the entire address at the time. It was later published, in full, in William Lloyd Garrison's magazine *The Liberator*. While "Civil Disobedience" focused on the US invasion of Mexico, the extension of slavery, and the removal of Native tribes, his address on slavery in Massachusetts was directed squarely at the hated Fugitive Slave Law.

He began by expressing outrage at the capture and remission of Anthony Burns to his southern enslavers. Fugitives like Burns were considered the property of their owners and as such had no recourse to habeas corpus. It was only necessary to prove ownership for them to be sent back to the South. Thoreau singled out the governor of Massachusetts and the trial judge, both of whom, he said, had shirked their moral responsibility to free

Burns. Having failed to do that, they should have resigned their office. "I wish my countrymen to consider," he said, "that whatever the human law may be, neither an individual nor a nation can ever commit the least act of injustice against the obscurest individual, without having to pay the penalty for it. A government which deliberately enacts injustice, and persists in it, will at length ever become the laughing-stock of the world" (96).

In contrasting human law with moral law, Thoreau is again claiming that the Higher Law nullifies the Fugitive Slave Act. Peter Wirzbicki describes the Higher Law ethos as "a distinctive orientation toward radical politics: nonconformist, rooted in a critical and idealist philosophy, privileging the sanctity of conscience over expediency." The notion was a response to the moral indignation the Transcendentalists felt at enslaving Black people and treating them as property. The Higher Law ethos has had an enormous impact on American political theory. As Wirzbicki contends: "Born in antebellum America, the Higher Law was a political and intellectual orientation that would have lasting influence on American and global radical traditions. Echoes of it would reappear everywhere from American labor organizers to Gandhi's India to King's civil rights movement."[10]

When Thoreau declares, "Whoever has discerned truth, has received his commission from a higher source than the chiefest justice in the world, who can discern only law," one might ask, how can we be so sure? (98). The Transcendentalists grounded their appeal to the Higher Law in Kantian moral philosophy, as interpreted by Coleridge. According to this view, we gain our knowledge of the world by means of the Understanding, through the senses. But the senses deal only with empirical facts. Morality, our sense of what is right and wrong, comes to us intuitively, by way of the Reason. Thus the Reason enables us to discern truth, while the Understanding can "discern only law," or expediency. For Thoreau, "action from principle" was his response to what he felt was a moral imperative, deeply rooted in his religious views.

Setting aside his criticism of the churches on the issue of abolition, he believes the press has had a more pernicious influence on the slavery question, siding with the slaveholders, commercial interests, and corrupt politicians. He concludes that "the majority of the men of the North, and of the South, East, and West, are not men of principle. If they vote, they do not send men to Congress on errands of humanity, but while their brothers and sisters are being scourged and hung for loving liberty. . . . [I]t is the mismanagement of wood and iron and stone which concerns them" (102).

In a marked departure from the passive resistance he advocated in "Civil Disobedience," Thoreau now becomes more militant and adversarial. "I need not say what match I should touch, what system endeavor to blow up,—but as I love my life, I would side with the light, and let the dark earth roll from under me" (102). He had foolishly believed that he might conduct his private affairs without interference from the state. But the rendition of Anthony Burns changed all that. Now he recognizes that a private peace is not possible. "I dwelt before, perhaps, in the illusion that my life passed somewhere only *between* heaven and hell, but now I cannot persuade myself that I do not dwell *wholly within* hell" (106).

As he envisions visiting one of his favorite ponds, he wonders what the beauty of nature signifies when people are base. "We walk to lakes to see our serenity reflected in them; when we are not serene, we go not to them. Who can be serene in a country where both the rulers and the ruled are without principle? The remembrance of my country spoils my walk. My thoughts are murder to the State, and involuntarily go plotting against her" (108). He concludes the essay with the arresting image of a white water lily growing in "the slime and muck of earth" (108). It is a symbol of hope. "The foul slime stands for the sloth and vice of man, the decay of humanity; the fragrant flower that springs from it, for purity and courage which are immortal" (109).

Captain John Brown

Under the terms of the Kansas–Nebraska Act of 1854, settlers in these new territories would vote whether to be slave or free states. Citizens of New England were encouraged to settle in Kansas, nearer to the South than Nebraska, in order to work toward prohibiting slavery there. They were met with fierce opposition from proslavery forces from neighboring Missouri who terrorized the "Free-Staters," as the newcomers were called. Among these settlers were John Brown and his sons, who were caught up in the fight for "Bleeding Kansas." Brown, a militant abolitionist, was not a pacifist. Incensed at the sack of Lawrence, Kansas, by the so-called border ruffians and the near-fatal caning of abolitionist senator Charles Sumner in the nation's Capitol, Brown and his sons attacked and killed five proslavery men who had threatened them. Subsequently Brown plotted a raid on the federal arsenal at Harpers Ferry, Virginia, in hopes of instigating a slave insurrection in the South. The raid, which occurred on October 16, 1859, was a failure.

Brown was captured and tried for murder, treason, and conspiracy. Following a guilty verdict, he was sentenced to be hanged.

Brown was no stranger to Emerson and Thoreau, both of whom met the man when he first came to Concord in March 1857. Upon his arrival, he dined with the Thoreau family. Later, Emerson dropped by to invite Brown to spend the night at his home. Brown had come to Concord at the invitation of Franklin Sanborn in hopes of raising money. Although he collected very little, he did manage to fire the imagination of Thoreau and Emerson with his tales of events back in Kansas. Brown returned to Concord in May 1859 to raise additional funds.

On October 19, Thoreau heard the news of Brown's raid at Harpers Ferry while visiting with Bronson Alcott at Emerson's house. Fearing that Brown had been killed, he was livid with anger. That evening he wrote in his journal: "When a government puts forth its strength on the side of injustice, as ours (especially today) to maintain slavery and kill the liberators of the slave, what a merely brute, or worse than brute, force it is seen to be! A demoniacal force! It is more manifest than ever that tyranny rules."[11] Throughout the North, Brown was condemned as a madman for his raid at Harpers Ferry. But among his fiercest defenders was Thoreau, who, along with Emerson, did much to rescue Brown's reputation and confirm his martyrdom. As historian David S. Reynolds writes in his book *John Brown, Abolitionist*, "Among the Transcendentalists it was Thoreau who made the earliest and boldest moves on behalf of Brown."[12]

Working feverishly, he composed a speech which he delivered in the vestry of First Parish Church on October 30, "A Plea for Captain John Brown."[13] When Sanborn and others advised him not to appear, he replied, "I did not send to you for advice but to announce that I am to speak." Instead of condemning Brown's action, Thoreau defended his character. He described him as "a man of rare common sense and directness of speech, as of action; a transcendentalist above all, a man of ideas and principles,—that was what distinguished him" (115). While it might seem odd that Thoreau would call Brown a "transcendentalist," we should recall that the Transcendentalists embraced virtue ethics, which placed the cultivation of moral character above obedience to laws—especially if those laws were considered to be unjust.

Some had argued that Brown was a fool, others that he had thrown his life away; still others asked what he thought to gain by his action. Thoreau replied, "Such do not know that like the seed is the fruit, and that, in the moral world, when good seed is planted, good fruit is inevitable, and does not depend on our watering and cultivating; that when you plant, or bury, a hero in his field, a crop of heroes is sure to spring up" (119). Reading all the newspapers he could get his hands on, Thoreau found in them not a single expression of admiration for the fact that Brown had risked his life for the cause of the oppressed. "No man in America has ever stood up so persistently and effectively for the dignity of human nature, knowing himself for a man, and the equal of any and all governments," he declared. "In that sense he was the most American of us all" (125).

It does not matter that the government is a representative one, nor that its leaders are elected, Thoreau said. "What shall we think of a government to which all the truly brave and just men in the land are enemies, standing between it and those whom it oppresses? A government that pretends to be Christian and crucifies a million Christs every day!" (129–30). Brown believed he had "a perfect right to interfere by force with the slaveholder, in order to rescue the slave," and Thoreau agreed with him (132). His stance was becoming increasingly militant, even more so than indicated in his "Slavery in Massachusetts" speech: "I do not wish to kill nor to be killed, but I can foresee circumstances in which both these things would be by me unavoidable." Defending Brown's use of armed force, Thoreau says, "I think that for once the Sharps' rifles and the revolvers were employed in a righteous cause. The tools were in the hands of one who could use them" (133).

In the closing paragraphs of the speech, Thoreau elevates Brown to sainthood, even likening his martyrdom to that of Christ: "I am here to plead his cause with you. I plead not for his life, but for his character—his immortal life; and so it becomes your cause wholly, and is not his in the least. Some eighteen hundred years ago Christ was crucified; this morning, perchance, Captain Brown was hung. These are the two ends of a chain which is not without its links. He is not Old Brown any longer; he is an Angel of Light" (137). John Brown has written a new testament, he says. Like Christ, he has championed the poor, the weak, the enslaved, and the oppressed. Thoreau envisions a time when slavery is abolished. "We shall then be at liberty to weep for Captain Brown. Then, and not till then, we will take our revenge" (138).

Those attending the speech were not sure what to expect. Doubtless many thought Brown a lunatic. Perhaps young Edward Emerson summed up the reaction best when he said, "Many of those who came to scoff remained to pray."[14] Thoreau repeated the address in quick succession to audiences elsewhere. On November 1 he addressed a crowd of 2,500 people at Boston's

Tremont Temple. The speech was also reported or summarized in numerous publications, including William Lloyd Garrison's newspaper *The Liberator*, and was included in a commemorative volume of writings, *Echoes of Harpers Ferry*, which was widely circulated. The tide was beginning to turn.

Brown's trial opened in Virginia on October 27. He was charged with murder in the deaths of five people, inciting a slave insurrection, and treason against the state of Virginia. The jury found him guilty of all three charges on November 2, and he was sentenced to be hanged one month later. On December 2, the day of Brown's execution, a memorial service commemorating the "Martyrdom of John Brown"—planned largely by Thoreau—was held in the Concord town hall. On July 4, 1860, a celebration of Brown's life was held in North Elba, New York, where he had been buried. Thoreau composed a speech for that occasion but was not there to deliver it himself.

In this speech, afterwards titled "The Last Days of John Brown," Thoreau noted that Brown's career during the last six weeks of his life was like a meteor streaking through the sky. For one who preferred communing with nature to tending to human affairs, the raid and its aftermath had gripped Thoreau's attention, not only for the forcefulness of Brown's action but also for the calmness and humility he had demonstrated during his trial and in awaiting his execution. Brown showed that he "was above them all. The man this country was about to hang appeared the greatest and best in it" (145). Those who adhered to the spirit of Christ's teachings as opposed to the strictures of the Christian church were most likely to appreciate what Brown had done. By now it had become apparent that many in the North and even a few in the South were stirred by his behavior. Editors who had once called Brown crazy were now saying only that his was "a crazy scheme" (149).

Brown had given an impassioned speech at his trial.[15] It was a blunder, Thoreau said, that the authorities "did not hang him at once, but reserved him to preach to them" (151). He also thought it a mistake that they did not hang Brown with his accomplices since that put the spotlight solely on him. The scene could not have been better stage-managed. "Who placed the slave woman, and her child, whom he stooped to kiss for a symbol, between his prison and the gallows?" (152), Thoreau asked.[16] When he heard that Brown was dead,. Thoreau wasn't sure what that meant. "Of all the men who were said to be my contemporaries, it seemed to me that John Brown was the only one who *had not died*. . . . I meet him at every turn. He is more alive than ever he was. He has earned immortality. He is not confined to North Alba nor to Kansas. He is no longer working in secret. He works in public, and in the clearest light that shines on this land" (153). In the words of the most popular song of the Civil War, "His truth goes marching on!"

Many readers of Thoreau's speeches about John Brown are surprised, if not shocked, that he should have defended Brown's actions. Since he advocated passive resistance in "Civil Disobedience," he is often taken to be a pacifist. But with every step the government took to appease southern enslavers—the gag rule which forbade the raising, consideration, or discussion of slavery in Congress; the annexation of Texas; the Kansas–Nebraska Act; the Fugitive Slave Law; the trial of Anthony Burns; and, finally, the *Dred Scott* case denying the personhood of Black people—Thoreau, like many others, grew more outspoken, militant, and desperate.

Until recently, it was alleged that, compared with other reformers in their era, the Transcendentalists were "like a band of monks sitting cross-legged on the floor," as one critic put it.[17] Admittedly, thoughts of the state ruined his walks, and he preferred the serenity of nature to the turmoil of politics. But he could not remain indifferent to the injustice of slavery. As he had said in "Civil Disobedience": "If I devote myself to other pursuits and contemplations, I must first see, at least, that I do not pursue them sitting upon another man's shoulders. I must get off him first, that he may pursue his contemplations, too" (71).

It could also be argued that making a few impassioned speeches hardly counts as radical action. And yet, as Reynolds states in his biography of Brown, Thoreau and Emerson, both of whom likened the execution of Brown to the crucifixion of Christ, not only rescued Brown's reputation but also opened the way for the election of Abraham Lincoln and the abolition of slavery. In Reynolds's opinion, "had the Transcendentalists not sanctified the arch-Abolitionist John Brown, he may have very well remained an obscure, tangential figure—a forgettable oddball. And had that not happened, the suddenly intense polarization between the North and the South that followed Harpers Ferry might not have occurred."[18] They had hoped that Brown would succeed where they had failed. While they theorized, Brown acted. And they defended him even knowing what he had done in Kansas.

On November 8, 1859, a few days after the trial, Emerson joined Thoreau in defense of Brown. In a speech titled "Courage," delivered before a large audience in Boston, Emerson spoke of Brown as "that new saint whom none purer or more brave was ever led by love of men into conflict and death,—that new saint awaiting his martyrdom, and who, if he shall suffer, will make the gallows glorious like the cross."[19] Emerson's words, like Thoreau's, were widely reported in newspapers north and south, sharply dividing opinion about Brown. The controversy they stirred up resulted in splitting the Democratic Party, which fielded both northern and southern slates in the presidential election of 1860, thereby helping Abraham Lincoln eke out a win in a four-way race.[20]

Neither Thoreau nor Emerson was a professing Christian. Both had criticized the Christian churches for their hypocrisy, especially on the slavery issue. Like others in the Transcendentalist circle, Thoreau drew a distinction between the religion *about* Jesus and the religion *of* Jesus. It was the religion about Jesus that he rejected. He admired the religion of Jesus, as expressed in the Sermon on the Mount. In *A Week* he wrote, "Let but one of these sentences be rightly read from any pulpit in the land, and there would not be left one stone of the meeting-house upon another."[21] In Thoreau's view, Jesus was a prophetic figure who was crucified for his moral righteousness; and so was Brown. This is what he meant when he called Brown "a transcendentalist above all." Likening him to Christ was not merely a provocative statement; for many it was also a persuasive one.

As mentioned earlier, Thoreau's essay "Civil Disobedience" inspired Mohandas Gandhi, Martin Luther King Jr., and many others in their efforts to achieve civil rights and social justice. But Thoreau has had critics as well who have found fault with his political methods. One of them is the political philosopher Hannah Arendt, who argued that his notion of civil disobedience is too individualistic and subjective to be effective. He based his argument on the ground of individual moral conscience. But, she insisted, conscience is non-political. "It is not primarily interested in the world where the wrong is committed or in the consequences that the wrong will have for the future course of the world."[22] Moreover, his rules of conscience are negative. "They do not say what to do; they say what not to do."[23] To be effective, civil disobedience must be a collective action. It "arises when a significant number of citizens have become convinced either that the normal channels of change no longer function, and grievances will not be heard or acted upon, or that, on the contrary, the government is about to change and has embarked upon and persists in modes of action whose legality and constitutionality are open to grave doubt" (74).

While Arendt's critique of Thoreau's political philosophy might have some validity with reference to "Civil Disobedience," where he argues for passive resistance and washing one's hands of complicity with slaveholding, it loses force as his stance becomes more public, activist, and radical in confronting an increasingly proslavery political climate. In "Civil Disobedience," Thoreau spoke to Concord townspeople at the local lyceum. In "Slavery in

Massachusetts," he addressed his state's complicity in returning fugitive slaves to southern enslavers. "A Plea for Captain John Brown" was a public performance intended for a national audience in defense of Brown's character and actions. In this way he is seeking to convince his fellow citizens "that the normal channels of change no longer function, and grievances will not be heard or acted upon" unless militant action is taken to abolish slavery.

In Arendt's critique of Thoreau there is also the implication that changing laws is more important than changing minds. While it may be true that moral suasion alone is insufficient to remedy injustice, it is also true that laws alone are ineffective. In *Walden,* Thoreau says, "Moral reform is the effort to throw off sleep."[24] What political scientist Jack Turner writes about Emerson applies to Thoreau as well: "True opposition to slavery, for Emerson, requires intellectual and moral wakefulness. Social reform begins with self-reform, and self-reform begins with critical self-awareness."[25] Their emphasis on the importance of awakening had profound implications not only for their opposition to slavery then but also, just as importantly, for our own reckoning with racism today. Both focused their attention on the extent to which people were ignorant of their complicity in the maintenance of slavery. "Complicity is collaboration with wrongdoing," Turner argues. "One becomes complicit in injustice by either explicitly authorizing it or tacitly supporting it through one's civic, social, and economic actions (or inactions)."[26] The effort to throw off sleep is the first and most important step to take in addressing the issue in our day as it was in theirs. While it may not have been sufficient, it was necessary.

If Thoreau had merely refused to pay his tax and spent a night in jail on that account without publicly defending his actions, Arendt would be correct in saying that they were strictly negative, private, and individualistic. Turner, however, insists that Thoreau has a positive politics. He writes: "The performance of conscience before an audience transforms the invocation of conscience from a personally political act into a publicly political one. The aim of the performance is to provoke one's neighbors into a process of individual self-reform that will make them capable of properly vigilant democratic citizenship and conscientious political agitation."[27] In truth, Thoreau came forward when he felt called. He showed up when it mattered most.

Thoreau's abolitionist activities were not limited to giving speeches. The Thoreau family home was a trusted station on the Underground Railway and Henry was an active conductor. Following the enactment of the Fugitive Slave Law, it became increasingly risky to assist runaway slaves on their way to Canada and freedom. Details are scant because anything written down could have been incriminating. But southern abolitionist Moncure Conway describes one such incident. Visiting the Thoreau home, he chanced upon a fugitive from Virginia who was being ministered to by Henry and his sister Sophia. In Conway's words: "I observed the tender and lowly devotion of Thoreau to the African. He now and then drew near to the trembling man, and with a cheerful voice bade him feel at home, and have no fear that any power should again wrong him. That whole day he mounted guard over the fugitive, for it was a slave-hunting time. But the guard had no weapon, and probably there was no such thing in the house."[28] Henry usually accompanied the fugitives to the Concord railroad station but sometimes took them by wagon nearly thirty miles to the station in West Fitchburg. On another occasion he assisted one of John Brown's accomplices on his escape to Canada.

In truth, Thoreau was ambivalent about reform for the reason that it did not go far enough if it didn't result in personal and social transformation. In an early essay called "Reform and the Reformers," he argues that reformers of his day deal with evil's effects, not its causes. Moreover, "they give us their theory and wisdom only," having nothing to show for their efforts except some resolutions. Finally, he finds them too negative, lacking an affirmative spirit. His views on reform can easily be dismissed as a form of naïve moral perfectionism. To be sure, he expected a lot from his fellow citizens. But his critique of reform and reformers needs to be understood in the context of democratic self-cultivation. In the decades leading up to the Civil War, there was widespread exploration of what it meant to be democratic citizens. In a nation freed from notions of aristocracy yet lacking a system of universal public education, self-culture played an important role in shaping expectations of common citizens for participation in democratic decision-making. "Our education is sadly neglected," we saw him declare in *Walden*. "It is time that we had uncommon schools, that we did not leave off our education when we begin to be men and women. . . . Instead of noblemen, let us have noble villages of men."[29] He considered it vital that citizens, freed from the dominance of an aristocracy, develop a sense of moral principle and act on that basis.

CHAPTER 7

EXCURSIONS

As we have seen, Thoreau went to Walden Pond to write *A Week* and while there also completed a first draft of *Walden*. At the same time, he wrote an essay on Thomas Carlyle and began giving lectures. In addition, he made his first trip to Maine, which he described in an article for *Union Magazine*, "Ktaadn and the Maine Woods." As he was completing *A Week*, he continued to revise *Walden*, making additional trips to Maine and to Cape Cod and Canada. *Walden* was finally published in 1854, the same year that Anthony Burns was arrested in Boston for fleeing enslavement, prompting Thoreau to deliver his "Slavery in Massachusetts" address.

Most of his major writing after *Walden*, including *The Maine Woods* and *Cape Cod*, wasn't published until after his death in 1862. The same is true for many of his well-known essays, which began as lectures given during the 1850s. Thus it is difficult to examine Thoreau's writings in a linear fashion, as scholars often try to do. It is also a bit misleading to characterize books and essays that appeared posthumously as later works. For example, "Life without Principle," one of his most popular lectures, was first delivered in 1854 but wasn't published until 1863. Although this chapter deals with many of these writings, we should bear in mind that there is a considerable foreground to their publication. For the same reason, it is hard to trace the arc of his spiritual development. But we do know that during the last years of his life Thoreau's spirituality broadened and deepened, embracing a cosmic consciousness. We are not alone in the universe; we are embedded in it. As he once said, are we not a part of the Milky Way?

Following the publication of *Walden*, Thoreau sought other topics that might appeal to his growing audience. Travel literature was quite popular in his day, including accounts of adventure and exploration. Judging by references to

133

such literature in his own writing, *Walden* especially, he was a fan as well. No doubt he thought his excursions to the Maine woods, as well as his subsequent visits to Canada and Cape Cod, would provide material for lectures, which they did. In addition, he lectured on a variety of topics, including "Walking, or the Wild," "Autumnal Tints," and "The Succession of Forest Trees," among others. He revised these lectures for publication during the last months of his life. Many of these so-called later essays were published as *Excursions*, part of a multivolume collection of his works, the first of which appeared in 1893.

Aside from these trips and lectures, Thoreau continued his pattern of journal-keeping and walks in the Concord area. He also began to spend more time boating on the Concord, Assabet, and Sudbury Rivers, mapping their contours and currents; collecting data for what he called his "Kalendar," charting natural phenomena annually for each month of the year; and amassing nearly three thousand pages of information about Native Americans in twelve large notebooks.

The Maine Woods

Thoreau made three trips to the state of Maine, the first in 1846 while he was still living at the pond. These excursions were the subject of a series of popular lectures, later compiled and published posthumously as *The Maine Woods*. The most memorable of the three narratives was the first, published as "Ktaadn, and the Maine Woods" in 1848. He was excited at the prospect of ascending the mysterious Mount Ktaadn (better known as Mount Katahdin), the second-highest peak in New England, which had been climbed by white explorers only four times previously. He was accompanied in this adventure by a cousin who lived in Maine and several others, including a local guide—a party of six men in all. There were signs everywhere of the impact logging was having on the primal forests, cutting and removing upwards of two hundred million board feet of lumber annually. Most people who lived there were either Native Americans or lumbermen.

The party eventually came to the end of the trail, still some distance from the mountain, beyond which they were forced to travel on rivers and lakes solely by batteau, a flat-bottomed boat adapted for the purpose. Travel was arduous, involving numerous rapids and portages with their batteau weighing upwards of six hundred pounds including gear and provisions. "At Ambejijis Falls," Thoreau tells us, "there was the roughest path imaginable cut through the woods; at first up hill at an angle of nearly forty-five degrees, over rocks and logs without end."[1] Signs of moose and bears were everywhere, adding a touch of danger to the trek. At one point he was forced to pull himself up twenty or thirty feet by the roots of trees next to a waterfall, meeting with a torrent of water at the top.

The woods were damp and mossy, giving the impression of a swamp. They were darker and thicker than any he had ever seen. His slog through the forest was "scarcely less arduous than Satan's anciently through Chaos."[2] It was the most treacherous country he had ever encountered. Nearing the mountain, he left his companions behind as he navigated huge rocks and ravines. The scene conjured up visions of ancient Greek mythological figures:

> Occasionally, when the windy columns broke in to me, I caught sight of a dark, damp crag to the right or left; the mist driving ceaselessly between it and me. It reminded me of the creations of the old epic and dramatic poets, of Atlas, Vulcan, the Cyclops, and Prometheus. Such was Caucasus and the rock where Prometheus was bound. . . . It was vast, Titanic, and such as man never inhabits. Some part of the beholder, even some vital part, seems to escape through the loose grating of his ribs as he ascends. He is more lone than you can imagine.

The thin air of the mountain deranged his mind.

> Vast, Titanic, inhuman Nature has got him at a disadvantage, caught him alone, and pilfers him of some of his divine faculty. Nature does not smile on him as in the plains. She seems to say sternly, why came ye here before your time? This ground is not prepared for you. Is it not enough that I smile in the valleys? I have never made this soil for thy feet, this air for thy breathing, these rocks for thy neighbors.[3]

He turned back short of reaching the summit and rejoined his party, disappointed that he hadn't achieved his goal. Passing through the dank purgatory of the aptly named Burnt Lands, Thoreau realized that he had experienced "primeval, untamed, and forever untameable *Nature*," unlike anything he had witnessed before. Confined to our cities, we have not seen pure Nature, "thus vast, and drear, and inhuman." Here Nature was "something savage and awful, though beautiful":

> This was that Earth of which we have heard, made out of Chaos and Old Night. Here was no man's garden, but the unhandselled globe. It was not lawn, nor pasture, nor mead, nor woodland, nor lea, nor arable, nor wasteland. It was the fresh and natural surface of the planet Earth, as it was

made forever and ever,—to be the dwelling of man, we say,—so Nature
made it, and man may use it if he can. Man was not to be associated with
it. It was Matter, vast, terrific,—not his Mother Earth that we have heard
of, not for him to tread on, or be buried in,—no, it were being too familiar
even to let his bones lie there—the home this of Necessity and Fate. There
was there felt the presence of a force not bound to be kind to man.[4]

This was perhaps the most unsettling experience Thoreau ever had—the
realization that nature played no favorites. The idea that nature was benefi-
cent had been a comforting illusion to someone living in a village like Concord, with its tame woods and slow-flowing river. In an essay, "Wordsworth
in the Tropics," Aldous Huxley comments on the disparity between visions
of nature tame and nature wild:

> In the neighborhood of latitude fifty north, and for the last hundred years or
> thereabouts, it has been an axiom that Nature is divine and morally uplift-
> ing. For good Wordsworthians—and most serious-minded people are now
> Wordsworthians, either by direct inspiration or at second hand—a walk in
> the country is the equivalent of going to church....
> The Wordsworthian who exports this pantheistic worship of Nature to
> the tropics is liable to have his religious convictions somewhat rudely dis-
> turbed. Nature, under a vertical sun, and nourished by the equatorial rains,
> is not at all like that chaste, mild deity who presides over the *Gemuthlichkeit*,
> the prettiness, the cozy sublimities of the Lake District.[5]

Huxley pokes fun at the sentimentality of Romantic writers concerning
nature. He argues that such adoration of nature has two defects. The first is
that it is possible only where nature has been totally subordinated to human
use; and second, that it is possible only for those who refuse to believe that
nature is always alien and inhuman.

Thoreau himself has been forced to come to this realization. Experiencing
nature is nothing like viewing it in an arboretum. He is shocked to realize
that it is completely other:

> I stand in awe of my body, this matter to which I am bound has become so
> strange to me. I fear not spirits, ghosts, of which I am one,—that my body
> might,—but I fear bodies, I tremble to meet them. What is this Titan that
> has possession of me? Talk of mysteries!—Think of our life in nature,—
> daily to be shown matter, to come in contact with it, rocks, trees, wind on
> our cheeks! the *solid* earth! The *actual* world! The *common sense*! Contact!
> Contact! *Who are we? where are we?*[6]

This is a vision of the sublime, not in the customary sense of inspiring, glorious, or blissful, but in its original meaning: awful, terrifying, or mysterious. As a Harvard student, Thoreau wrote a senior essay on the sublime as defined by Edmund Burke in *A Philosophical Enquiry into the Origin of Our Ideas of the Sublime and Beautiful*. In this paper he concluded that "the emotion excited by the sublime is the most unearthly and godlike we mortals experience. . . . [T]hat principle which prompts us to pay an involuntary homage to the infinite, the incomprehensible, the sublime, forms the very basis of our religion."[7]

Thoreau's experience on Mount Katahdin is a perfect case in point. In his book *The Idea of the Holy*, German theologian and philosopher Rudolf Otto coined the term "numinous," by which he meant a non-rational, non-sensory experience or feeling whose primary and immediate object is outside the self. Rather than dealing with religious concepts and categories, Otto takes a phenomenological approach to religion. In his view, the "numinous" is the primary datum of religious experience, characterized either by the feeling of *mysterium tremendum*, something "singularly *daunting* and awe-inspiring," or by that of *mysterium fascinans*, something "uniquely attractive and *fascinating*."[8] Drawing upon Otto's work, Mircea Eliade states that "in each case we are confronted by the same mysterious act—the manifestation of something of a wholly different order, a realty that does not belong to our world, in objects that are an integral part of our natural 'profane' world."[9] Thoreau's description of his disorienting experience on Mount Katahdin would seem to be an example of the *mysterium tremendum* sort, a departure from his more common *mysterium fascinans* type of experiences, both of which are sacred, albeit differing in essence. His regression to the origins in the encounter on Mount Katahdin was not a revelation of paradise, as it had been in ascending Mount Wachusett and Saddleback Mountain, but rather, he says quoting poet John Milton, a revelation of "Chaos and ancient Night."[10]

Thoreau's subsequent trips to the Maine woods proved to be less dramatic. On the second outing, recounted in "Chesuncook," a Native guide named Joe Aitteon was hired to help the party search for moose in hopes of shooting one. Thoreau himself had qualms about hunting. He approved of killing animals for food but not for sport. "I trust I shall have a better excuse for killing a moose, than that I may hang a hat on its horns," he wrote.[11] He observed the guide closely, hoping to learn more about Native customs and folkways. Having worked as a lumberman, the guide had grown accustomed to white society, but he still proved quite capable of finding and killing a moose, which he did. Thoreau made detailed measurements of the animal before Aitteon skinned it with his knife. He laments the fact that people enjoy killing as many moose and other wild animals as possible and never consider appreciating them for what they are in their natural habitat.

Thoreau marveled at the magnificent trees of the Maine woods. "My eyes were all the while on the trees, distinguishing between the black and white spruce and the fir," he writes. "I was struck by this universal spiring upward of the forest evergreens."[12] They shudder and heave a sigh when the lumberman sets foot on the forest floor. He has been to the lumberyard and woodworker's shop and has witnessed the turpentine being harvested. "I saw the tops of the pines waving and reflecting the light at a distance high over the rest of the forest," he writes. "I realized that the former were not the highest use of the pine. It is not their bones or hide or tallow that I love most. It is the living spirit of the tree, not its spirit of turpentine, with which I sympathize, and which heals my cuts. It is as immortal as I am, and will perchance go to as high a heaven, there to tower over me still."[13]

As he has done previously, Thoreau calls for the preservation of nature and the wilderness. The kings of England had their forests and used them for food and sport, sometimes destroying villages to expand the woodlands. "Why should not we," he asks, "who have renounced the king's authority, have our national preserves, where no villages need be destroyed, in which the bear and panther, and some even of the hunter race, may still exist, and not be 'civilized off the face of the earth.'" The forests should be preserved "not for idle sport or food, but for inspiration and our own true recreation."[14]

Native guide Joe Polis was hired on Thoreau's third trip to the Maine woods, recounted in "The Allegash and East Branch," the longest and most detailed essay of the three. Polis was described by a local as "one of the aristocracy" and "the best man we could have" (158). He was a leader of the Penobscot nation, owned a house and land in Oldtown, sent his son to a white school, visited New York, Philadelphia, and Washington, observed the Sabbath, and once paid a visit to Daniel Webster, but he retained his Native customs. He was a font of "Indian wisdom," and Thoreau pumped him for information about his language and traditional crafts and lore. Polis was not very forthcoming, however. "'How do you do that?'" Thoreau once asked. "'O, I can't tell you,' he replied. 'Great difference between me and white man.'"[15]

The party slogged their way through one dismal swamp after another. Once, at Mud Pond Carry, Thoreau and his companion lost their way. "We sank a foot deep in water and mud at every step, and sometimes up to our knees, and the trail was almost obliterated," he wrote. "It would have been amusing to behold the dogged and deliberate pace at which we entered that swamp, without interchanging a word, as if determined to go through it, though it should come up to our necks."[16] On another occasion, one companion got lost and Thoreau feared the worst. Fortunately, he was found the next morning, comfortably smoking his pipe. Altogether, the experience was not a pleasant one and Thoreau was aware of his vulnerability in the wilderness. He preferred the light and open spaces that the lakes afforded. Returning to Oldtown, he asked Polis if he was glad to be home again. "It makes no difference to me where I am," Polis replied.[17] Given his fondness for Concord, it is unlikely that Thoreau would have said the same.

Thoreau's writing in *The Maine Woods*, especially his account of the Kta-adn experience, sets him apart from other Transcendentalist nature writers of the period, not only Emerson but also Thomas Wentworth Higginson and Thomas Starr King, for whom nature was never dark or inhuman. His descriptions of nature are reverential and often poetic but never sentimental.

"Life without Principle"

"Life without Principle" was first published in the *Atlantic Monthly* in 1863, over a year after Thoreau's death. It had been one of his most frequently delivered lectures, given under several different titles, including "Getting a Living," "The Connection between Man's Employment and His Higher Life," "Life Misspent," "The Higher Law," and "What Shall It Profit a Man?" As literary historian Lawrence Buell observed, Transcendentalist writing was often scriptural in nature, owing perhaps to the fact that almost all of the Transcendentalists were or had been Unitarian ministers, accustomed to reading and writing in a prophetic or moralistic vein.[18] Thoreau was no exception. Although he said his religion was very laic, or non-clerical, and had "signed off" from the Unitarian Church, his writing was every bit as religious as that of his fellow Transcendentalists.[19] If *A Week* and *Walden* are scriptures—which I believe they are—then I would suggest that "Life without Principle" is a sermon.

The alternative titles of this "sermon" suggest as much. Protestant preaching was an elaboration on a theme, often a verse or sentence taken from the Bible. Thoreau's theme has a scriptural ring to it, even if it is not strictly biblical:

"Let us consider the way in which we spend our lives." Contrary to endorsing
the symbiosis between what sociologist Max Weber called the Protestant
ethic and the spirit of capitalism, the essay is an attack on that very notion.
"I think that there is nothing, not even crime, more opposed to poetry, to
philosophy, ay, to life itself, than this incessant business," he wrote. "The ways
by which you may get money almost without exception lead downward."[20]
The emphasis on work robs us of the leisure necessary for cultivating the
soul, which alone makes life worth living. If we walk in the woods for the love
of them, we are considered a loafer, but if we cut down those very woods, we
are considered an enterprising citizen for having done so. This observation
is especially prophetic in light of the role trees play today in safeguarding
humanity from the adverse effects of overdevelopment and climate change.

We should aim to get our living by loving—to find work that is not only
financially rewarding but also personally fulfilling. Anything less is drudgery.
Sadly, he says, most people seem willing to sell their birthright for a mess
of pottage, a reference to Esau in the book of Genesis. There seems to be
little advice given on "how to make getting a living not merely honest and
honorable, but altogether inviting and glorious; for if getting a living is not so,
then living is not."[21] It would appear that most people merely make shift to
live, not knowing any better.

In offering his own advice on the subject, Thoreau points to the California Gold Rush, insisting that it would be better to "sink a shaft down to the
gold within" oneself and work that mine than to be lured by the idea of easy
riches.[22] But instead of living an inward and thoughtful life, we settle for a
superficial one. "In proportion as our inward life fails, we go more constantly
and desperately to the post-office," he observes. "You may depend on it, that
the poor fellow who walks away with the greatest number of letters, proud of
his extensive correspondence, has not heard from himself this long while."[23]
No doubt the same can be said in our day of emails, texts, and social media.

As is so often the case with Thoreau, the remedy for our fallen condition is self-culture, the prerequisites of which are self-reliance, leisure, and
nature. We need to free ourselves from the pressure to conform to destructive
social norms, to seek a "path, however solitary and narrow and crooked," in
which we might "walk with love and reverence," he writes. "Wherever a man
separates from the multitude, and goes his own way in this mood, there is
indeed a fork in the road, though ordinary travellers may see only a gap in the
paling. His solitary path across-lots will turn out to be the *higher way* of the

two."[24] In order to accomplish this, we require such leisure as will provide an opportunity for cultivating awareness and self-reflection, both of which are hard to come by in an economy that prioritizes work over everything else. "I cannot easily buy a blank-book to write thoughts in," he complains; "they are commonly ruled for dollars and cents."[25]

In cultivating awareness, we must guard against conventional wisdom. "Read not the Times," Thoreau says. "Read the Eternities." By "the Times" he means not just the triviality of everyday life, as reported in the daily papers, but, more importantly, the tendency to view everything through a materialistic lens. True knowledge is intuitive, not empirical. "Knowledge does not come to us by details, but in flashes of light from heaven," he argues. "Even the facts of science may dust the mind by their dryness, unless they are in a sense effaced each morning, or rather rendered fertile by the dews of fresh and living truth."[26]

Thoreau admits that such matters as "politics and the daily routine" are necessary social functions but believes they "should be unconsciously performed, like the corresponding functions of the physical body."[27] Even so, many of his readers think he is excessively polemical and negative in his critique of the impact of society on the individual, believing that it implicates them in their own complicity. Some think he is uncaring of those who are struggling to make ends meet. It is the same criticism leveled against the argument of the "Economy" chapter in *Walden*. It is easy to say, "You must get your living by loving." For quite a few people then and now, this aspiration seems to be out of reach.

For others, however, the situation is different. Having bought into the notion that wealth and success are necessary for happiness and self-esteem, many people today are finding themselves unfulfilled. They have chosen paths, in many cases laid out for them by the expectations of others, that have led not to a *"higher way"* but to a dead end. The COVID pandemic and the ensuing lockdown, which significantly disrupted the customary work–life balance, have provided a valuable opportunity for reflection and reassessment. In an essay appearing in *Fast Company* in 2021, authors Jonathan van Belle and John Kaag cite an article in Harvard Business School's *Working Knowledge*: "We're in the middle of a Great Resignation. Employees have had the time and space to think about what really matters to them and there are plenty of options, so it's no surprise resignation rates are through the roof." Commenting on the article, the authors offer this thought: "As we tender our mass resignation, many of us might wonder: Is there a roadmap for what comes next? There is a map, but it leads into a forest, and to a man named Henry David Thoreau."[28]

For those pondering the difference between "getting a living" and "making a life," Thoreau offers valuable advice. To be sure, he is provocative. As he once said, one must speak loudly to the hard of hearing. Increasingly, his message is getting through. More and more people are questioning the choices they have made and prioritizing personal fulfillment over corporate advancement. They are trying to get their living by loving. In doing so, they have scaled back on consumerism and wasteful habits, preferring a simpler and more sustainable lifestyle. Not only are they the better for it, but so also are the planet and the commons. To "live deep and suck out all the marrow of life," as Thoreau urges us to do, is not simply an individual act; it has social and political implications too. It is no accident that when his essays were anthologized, "Life without Principle" was included in the volume *Reform Papers*.

"A Succession of Forest Trees"

In 1860 Thoreau was invited to give an address at the Middlesex County Cattle Show, an annual agricultural fair in Concord. He chose as his topic a theory of tree succession that he had been working on for some time. He had often been asked "how it happened, that when a pine wood was cut down an oak one commonly sprang up, and *vice versa*." Quite simply, he said, the new trees came from a seed, transported from one place to another, carried by birds, animals, or the wind. It had long been assumed that if a tree grew where none of its kind had been before, either its seed must have been planted there or it must have generated spontaneously. He marshals ample evidence gleaned from detailed observations to advance his own theory. Rather than settling for other explanations, he asks, why not consult nature at the outset? "Though I do not believe that a plant will spring up where no seed has been, I have great faith in a seed—a, to me, equally mysterious origin for it. Convince me that you have a seed there, and I am prepared to expect wonders."[29]

Thoreau's argument is noteworthy for several reasons. If it seems obvious to us today, it is at least in part because he advanced it in defiance of powerful voices in the scientific community at the time, particularly that of Louis Agassiz, the foremost American scientist of his era, who held that species—including trees—were unchanging and spontaneously created. It is also notable for the fact that his theory requires no metaphysical explanation. The dissemination of seeds in the succession of forest trees is an entirely natural process. It is not guided by divine forces or intelligent design. As previously mentioned, Thoreau sought to avoid the disenchantment of the world, the pitfall of positivism. Even if the world is *objectively* devoid of meaning, it is *subjectively* saturated with wonder, magic, and mystery. This is why he insisted he was a mystic and a Transcendentalist, as well as a natural philosopher. In this respect, he was an early proponent of religious naturalism, yet another reason why his argument is so remarkable.

"The Succession of Forest Trees" is part of a much larger project Thoreau was working on but did not live long enough to complete. It wasn't until the last decade of the twentieth century that the scope of his work was fully understood. Although his papers were widely scattered after his death, Bradley B. Dean managed to track down and assemble several manuscripts, which he published as *Faith in a Seed: The Dispersion of Seeds and Other Late Natural History Writings* and *Wild Fruits: Thoreau's Rediscovered Last Manuscript.* Largely written during the last two years of Thoreau's life, they show how his research into seeds and forest trees prepared him for a positive reception of Darwin's controversial theory of evolution.

At a memorable dinner at Franklin Sanborn's home on New Year's Day 1860, attended by Alcott and Thoreau in addition to the host and a guest, the small group gathered around the table to discuss an advance copy of the latest book by Darwin, *On the Origin of Species*, brought to Concord by their dinner guest, Charles Loring Brace, nephew of renowned botanist Asa Gray, Agassiz's major rival in the debate over evolution.[30] "A man receives only what he is ready to receive, whether physically or intellectually or morally," Thoreau wrote in his journal a few days afterwards. "We hear and apprehend only what we already half know. If there is something which does not concern me, which is out of my line, which by experience or by genius my attention is not drawn to, however novel and remarkable it may be, if it is spoken, we hear it not, if it is written, we read it not, or if we read it, it does not detain us."[31] By this time Thoreau was fully prepared to receive and appreciate the momentous significance of what he called the development theory.

Reflecting on Darwin's book, Thoreau concluded that "the development theory implies a greater vital force in Nature, because it is more flexible and accommodating, and equivalent to a sort of constant new creation."[32] In typical fashion, he finds that the development theory has wider application than in biology alone. It also applies to human self-culture and spiritual growth. "The value of any experience is measured," he says, "not by the amount of money, but the amount of development we get out of it." We are better off for picking our own fruits locally than by purchasing exotic ones at the store. The highest use and enjoyment of fruits is the pleasure received by the one who plucks it. "Better for us is the wild strawberry than the pine-apple."[33]

Thoreau's study of trees, seeds, and wild fruits is not complete without factoring in the spiritual dimension, namely, the way in which nature elevates our lives. We "are lifted out of the slime and film of our habitual life" when we reverence the natural world, "to truly worship sticks and stones" even. "I would fain improve every opportunity to wonder and worship, as the sun-flower welcomes the light," he writes. "The more thrilling, wonderful, divine objects I behold in a day, the more expanded and immortal I become."[34]

His interest in science was never at the expense of his spirituality. To the contrary, the deeper his science penetrated the world of nature, the more miraculous nature was shown to be—not in a supernatural sense, but rather in a *super* natural or ecstatic one. The highest use of nature is not in its utility as raw material to be cut down, extracted, or dug out of the ground, but, as he says, in its ability to heal us and make us well:

> Live in each season as it passes; breathe the air, drink the drink, taste the fruit, and resign yourself to the influences of each. Let these be your only diet-drink and botanical medicines. . . . Be blown on by all the winds. Open all your pores and bathe in all the tides of Nature, in all her streams and oceans, at all seasons. Miasma and infection are from within, not without. . . . Grow green with the spring, yellow and ripe with autumn. Drink of each season's influence as a vial, a true panacea of all remedies mixed for your special use. . . . For all Nature is doing her best each moment to make us well. She exists for no other end. Do not resist her. With the least inclination to be well, we should not be sick. Men have discovered, or think that they have discovered, the salutariness of a few wild things only, and not all of Nature. Why, Nature is but another name for health.[35]

"Walking"

Many of Thoreau's readers consider "Walking" his greatest essay, a manifesto in celebration of nature and personal freedom, encapsulated in the term "wild-ness." When published in the *Atlantic Monthly* in June 1862, two months after his death, it combined two lectures previously given separately, "Walking" and "The Wild." As Alan Hodder points out, the essay "has been construed in the environmentalist community, not to say popular culture generally, as a tribute to wilderness and a foundational document in the century and a half–long movement to preserve and protect wild places."[36] A well-known line from the text, "in Wildness is the preservation of the world," was adopted as the motto of the Sierra Club, perhaps the nation's best-known and most influential environmental organization.

Thoreau announces his theme in these opening lines: "I wish to speak a word for Nature, for absolute Freedom and Wildness, as contrasted with a Freedom and Culture merely civil,—to regard man as an inhabitant, or a part and parcel of Nature, rather than a member of society. I wish to make an extreme statement, if so I may make an emphatic one, for there are enough champions of civilization; the minister, and the school-committee, and every one of you will take care of that."[37] While it is true that the essay has inspired a widespread movement to preserve the nation's wilderness areas and that in *The Maine Woods* and other writings he advocated establishing national forest preserves, it is important to note that the word he uses here is "wildness," not "wilderness." John Hanson Mitchell contrasts the two notions. Wilderness, he says, is an entity, a place, however fragile. "Wildness, by contrast, is more deeply rooted. It is an ancient, life-sustaining current, a force of nature that can be most easily experienced in wilderness, but also lurks in the wilder corners of suburbia, or even in cities, and exists as potential even in some of the most barren, devastated environments. In wildness is not only the preservation of the world, but also the restoration of the world."[38] We can justifiably argue that wilderness preservation is essential to combating climate change and overdevelopment and that it promotes human health, but readers of the essay are most often impressed not with the instrumental value of preservation but rather with the idea of the wild as a spiritual resource.

The first part of the essay addresses the notion of personal freedom, epitomized by the term "walking." As we have seen, Thoreau's spiritual practice included not only reading, solitude, contemplation, journal-writing, simple living, religious cosmopolitanism, and action from principle but also, and perhaps most importantly, sauntering in nature. He writes, "I think that I cannot preserve my health and spirits unless I spend four hours a day at least—and it is commonly more than that—sauntering through the woods and over the hills and fields absolutely free from all worldly engagements."[39] He explores the etymology of the word, proposing that it derives either from pilgrims to the holy land, *sante-terrer*, or from vagrants without a permanent home, *sans terre*. In either case, these are "Walkers Errant," compared to whom "we are but half-hearted crusaders." Nothing short of complete devotion to the cause will suffice:

> We should go forth on the shortest walk, perchance, in the spirit of undy-
> ing adventure, never to return; prepared to send back our embalmed hearts
> only, as relics to our desolate kingdoms. If you are prepared to leave father
> and mother, and brother and sister, and wife and child and friends, and
> never see them again; if you have paid your debts, and made your will, and
> settled all your affairs, and are a free man; then you are ready for a walk.[40]

Most of us are amateur walkers by comparison. We are often advised to get up and move about, told that even ten minutes of walking every day is good for our health. Often confined to sidewalks, our outings are but tours of the neighborhood. Thoreau will not hear of it: "The walking of which I speak has nothing to do with taking exercise as it is called, as the sick take medicine at stated hours—as the swinging of dumb-bells or chairs; but is itself the enterprise or adventure of the day. If you would get exercise go in search of the springs of life."[41] Even when we do go for a walk in the woods, we often take our worries with us. "I am alarmed when it happens that I have walked a mile into the woods bodily, without getting there in spirit," he admits. "I cannot easily shake off the village."[42]

The aim of our walks should be not to get somewhere but to let go of the need to be anywhere except where we are. Walks to the store, the tavern, or the depot are merely prosaic; the walks of which Thoreau speaks are the stuff of myth and poetry, admirably described in a poem he includes in the essay "The Old Marlboro Road." As David Robinson observes in his perceptive essay on the poem, to walk the Marlboro Road "was to be in the immediate present, but also in the era of myth."[43] The abandoned road no longer goes to the actual Marlboro but to the Marlboro of the imagination:

> When the spring stirs my blood
> With the instinct to travel,
> I can get enough gravel
> On the Old Marlboro Road.
> > Nobody repairs it,
> > For nobody wears it;
> > It is a living way,
> > As the Christians say,

Not many there be
Who enter therein,
Only the guests of the
Irishman Quin.[44]

The poem conjures up the spirit of Chaucer's *Canterbury Tales:* "Whan that
April with his shoures soote / The droghte of March hath perced to the
roote . . . / Thanne longen folk to goon on pilgrimages." It reinforces the
notion that our walks should be viewed as a pilgrimage, not to a particular
place but to no place in particular: "What is it, what is it / But a direction
out there, / And the bare possibility / Of going somewhere?"[45] In Robinson's
words, Thoreau brings "the road to life as the ideal place for the true saunterer, the walker whose walks become imaginative quests and deeply spiritual
pilgrimages."[46]

Where we walk is less important than how we walk, or rather in what
frame of mind we walk. "There is a right way; but we are very liable from
heedlessness and stupidity to take the wrong one," Thoreau declares. "We
would fain take that walk, never yet taken by us through this actual world,
which is perfectly symbolical of the path which we love to travel in the interior and ideal world; and sometimes, no doubt, we find it difficult to choose
our direction, because it does not yet exist distinctly in our idea."[47] This passage perfectly captures his prescription for walking as a spiritual practice.

There is an extensive literature on the phenomenon of walking, wonder-
fully chronicled by Rebecca Solnit in her book *Wanderlust: A History of
Walking.* Commenting on the nineteenth-century interest in walking, she
writes: "In many ways, walking culture was a reaction against the speed and
alienation of the industrial revolution. It may be countercultures and sub-
cultures that will continue to walk in resistance to the postindustrial, post-
modern loss of space, time, and embodiment. Most of these cultures draw
from ancient practices—of peripatetic philosophers, of poets composing
afoot, or pilgrims and practitioners of Buddhist walking meditation—or old
ones, such as hiking and flaneury."[48] Of all the walkers Solnit mentions—
Jean-Jacques Rousseau, William Wordsworth, Walt Whitman, and John
Muir, among others—Americans are most likely to consider Thoreau their
spiritual guide in the art of walking. In his book *Concord Days*, Bronson
Alcott pays tribute to Thoreau, calling him a quintessential "peripatetic philosopher."[49] If he couldn't walk, he couldn't think.

In my view, there is no writer with whom Thoreau shares a greater affinity than the Chinese Taoist philosopher Zhuangzi (ca. 369 BCE–ca. 286 BCE). As I noted in chapter 2, it is unlikely that Thoreau was aware of Zhuangzi. He may have gleaned a bit of information about Taoism from some of the books he read about neo-Confucianism, in particular that of the sinologist Guillaume Pauthier. The notion of Tao, or the Way of Heaven, is common to both philosophies, although it has somewhat different meanings. In Confucianism it means morality, truth, sincerity, or the proper way or method. It is a central term in Confucian virtue ethics. Thoreau quoted numerous passages concerning the Tao in his selections from the Chinese Four Books for the "Ethnical Scriptures" column in *The Dial*. For the Taoists it means eternal truth, the way of nature, the source and essence of all things. It is ultimate, all-pervasive, and dynamic.[50]

Zhuangzi would have appealed to Thoreau for his emphasis on what he called "free and easy wandering," the title of the first chapter of *The Book of Zhuangzi*. As translator Burton Watson explains, "Zhuangzi employs the metaphor of a totally free and purposeless journey, using the [Chinese] word *you* (to wander, or a wandering) to designate the way in which the enlightened man wanders through all of creation, enjoying its delights without ever becoming attached to any one part of it."[51] Like Thoreau, he often relies on enigmatic fables to convey his message since ordinary language is inadequate to describe the way of nature. The Perfect Man of ancient times, Zhuangzi says, "wandered in the free and easy wastes, ate in the plain and simple fields, and strolled in the garden of no bestowal. Free and easy, he rested in inaction; plain and simple, it was not hard for him to live; bestowing nothing, he did not have to hand things out. The men of old called this the wandering of the Truth-Picker."[52] Thoreau is our American Truth-Picker.

The notion of free and easy wandering expresses the Chinese principle of *wu-wei*, which is often taken to mean doing nothing, but should rather be understood as doing what is effortless or going with the natural flow of things. In his essay "Walking," Thoreau insists that "there is a subtle magnetism in Nature, which, if we unconsciously yield to it, will direct us aright." Conversely, resistance to the current will only result in frustration. Nature "is not indifferent to us which way we walk. There is a right way; but we are very liable from heedlessness and stupidity to take the wrong one."[53] Zhuangzi would emphatically agree.

Zhuangzi's teaching is therapeutic, as is Thoreau's, in response to our fruitless resistance. Describing the human condition, he writes: "Sweating and laboring to the end of his days and never seeing his accomplishment, utterly exhausting himself and never knowing where to look for rest—can you help pitying him? I'm not dead yet! he says, but what good is that? His body decays, his mind follows it—can you deny that this is a great sorrow? Man's life has always been a muddle like this."[54] For both writers, wandering represents the manner in which people should navigate the world, seeking solace from worry and emotional strife. As Carl J. Dull observes, "For both, the idea of wandering plays a critical role in therapeutic liberation from conformity, homogenization, and superimposed linguistic structures."[55]

Despite Thoreau's entreaties, few people today spend even a fraction of the time he did walking in the out-of-doors. Walking seems like a waste of time when cars can get us places so much faster. In *Walden*, Thoreau says a friend once told him that it would be faster to get to Fitchburg by train than by walking the distance. "But I am wiser than that," he says. "I have learned that the swiftest traveller is he that goes afoot. I say to my friend, suppose we try who will get there first. The distance is thirty miles; the fare ninety cents. That is almost a day's wages. . . . Well, I start now on foot, and get there before night. . . . You will in the meanwhile have earned your fare, and arrive there sometime tomorrow."[56] This story is recounted and beautifully illustrated in a popular children's book, *Henry Hikes to Fitchburg* by D. B. Johnson.[57] While his friend is doing odd jobs around the village to earn his fare, Henry hikes to Fitchburg. He is pictured crossing the Sudbury River, carving a walking stick, pressing ferns and flowers in a book, climbing a tree, finding a bird's nest in the grass, jumping into a pond to cool off, and picking blackberries to share with his friend. The point is that even if he didn't get there before his friend did, he had more fun along the way. What is more, as contemporary Norwegian writer and "Walker Errant" Erling Kagge reveals, "the secret held by all those who go by foot: life is prolonged when you walk. Walking expands time rather than collapses it."[58]

As previously mentioned, the essay combined two lectures, one on walking and the other on nature. Thoreau announces the second part with some of his best-known words: "The West of which I speak is but another name for the Wild; and what I have been preparing to say is, that in Wildness is the preservation of the world."[59] For him, the West was not merely the direction of American migration and manifest destiny; it represented the spirit of wildness, freedom, and spiritual vitality. It is this spirit that he wishes to preserve. "Life consists with Wildness. The most alive is the wildest. Not yet subdued to man, its presence refreshes him."[60]

Though often identified with wilderness areas, the wild can be found closer at hand than the forests of California or Alaska. Thoreau derives as much spiritual sustenance from the swamps surrounding his village. "I enter a swamp as a sacred place—a *sanctum sanctorum*," he writes. "There is the strength—the marrow of nature."[61] Such places are valuable and should be preserved not only for aesthetic reasons but also for the essence of wildness they embody and exude. In Zhuangzi's philosophy, humans possess an inborn nature which can be obscured through ignorance and misunderstanding. Knowledge of this inborn nature must be cultivated by means of self-culture, including experiences in nature.[62] In Thoreau's view, the wild is the essence of both nature and our inborn human nature, since both arise from the same source. It too must be cultivated. Society, including our child-rearing methods, are geared to training the wild out of us:

> Here is this vast, savage, howling Mother of ours, Nature lying all around, with such beauty, and such affection for her children, as the leopard,—and yet we are so early weaned from her breast to society—to that culture which is exclusively an interaction of man on man,—a sort of breeding in and in, which produces at most a merely English nobility, a civilization destined to have a speedy limit.
>
> In society, in the best institutions of men it is easy to detect a certain precocity. When we should still be growing children, we are already little men. Give me a culture which imparts much muck from the meadows, and deepens the soil, not that which trusts to heating manures, and improved implements and modes of culture only.[63]

It is this emphasis on the wild that gives Thoreau's nature spirituality its distinctive character. Romantic nature religion, typical of Wordsworth and Emerson, is tame by comparison. Edward Abbey, author of the essay "Down the River with Henry Thoreau," likens him to suburban coyotes in the American Southwest who torment domesticated household dogs:

> They yip, yap, yelp, howl, and holler, teasing the dogs, taunting, enticing them with the old-time call of the wild. And the dogs stand and tremble, shaking with indecision, furious, hating themselves, tempted to join the coyotes, run off with them into the hills, but—afraid. Afraid to give up the comfort, security, and safety of their household existence. Afraid of the unknown and dangerous.
>
> Thoreau was our suburban coyote. Town dwellers have always found him exasperating.[64]

Akin to these coyotes, Thoreau admits, "For my part, I feel that with regard to Nature, I live a sort of border life, on the confines of a world, into which I make occasional and transient forays only."[65] Although he was once tempted to eat a groundhog raw, hoping he might assimilate its wildness, he really means wildness in a spiritual sense, albeit a somewhat transgressive, antinomian one. It is this kind of spirituality that puts him at odds with his more orthodox or "urban" readers.

Thoreau's contrarian streak also applies to his use of language. There is a Society for the Diffusion of Useful Knowledge, he says, but argues that we have an "equal need for a Society for the Diffusion of Useful Ignorance, what we call Beautiful Knowledge, a knowledge useful in a higher sense; for what is our boasted so-called knowledge but a conceit that we know something, which robs us of our actual ignorance."[66] Empirical data may be useful, but they are a poor substitute for knowledge of the way things truly are. It is the difference, he says, between feeding cattle hay and grass. To those who know only "myriad facts," higher wisdom seems like ignorance. But such ignorance "is not only useful, but beautiful, while [our] knowledge, so called, is oftentimes worse than useless beside being ugly."[67]

Whether we call Thoreau a mystic or not, it is nevertheless true that, like the Transcendentalists generally, he possessed a mystical epistemology, that is, an awareness of knowledge beyond reason and sense perception. The numerous ecstatic experiences described in his journal attest to this. Likewise this passage in "Walking":

> My desire for knowledge is intermittent; but my desire to bathe my head in atmospheres unknown to my feet is perennial and constant. The highest that we can attain to is not Knowledge, but Sympathy with Intelligence. I do not know that this higher knowledge amounts to anything more than a novel and grand surprise on a sudden revelation of the insufficiency of all that we called Knowledge before—a discovery that there are more things in heaven and earth than are dreamed of in our philosophy. It is the lighting up of the mist by the sun. Man cannot *know* in any higher sense than this, any more than he can look serenely and with impunity in the face of the sun.[68]

This knowledge cannot be communicated in prosaic, discursive language. "The science of Humboldt is one thing, poetry is another thing," Thoreau says. It takes a poet to speak for Nature. But he does not know any poetry that adequately expresses his yearning for the wild. Even the best he finds too tame. "Mythology," he concludes, "comes nearer to it than anything." Myth, as Eliade has said, narrates a return to the primordial beginning of things before nature was desacralized. In Thoreau's words, myth is "the crop which the old world bore before its soil was exhausted, before the fancy and imagination were afflicted with blight;—and which it still bears wherever its pristine vigor is unabated."[69] In this respect the essay exhibits a nostalgia for paradise, a time when all things were still wild and free. With the passage of time, the wild has become domesticated, in response to which, as R. W. B. Lewis writes in his book *The American Adam*, "Thoreau prescribes the following cure: the total renunciation of the traditional, the conventional, the socially acceptable, the well-worn paths of conduct, and the total immersion in nature."[70]

Thoreau laments the fact that so few people are drawn to nature, preferring the comfort of society instead. "Nature is a personality so vast and universal that we have never seen one of her features," he writes. "The walker in the familiar fields which stretch around my native town, sometimes finds himself in another land than is described in their owners' deeds, as it were in some far away field on the confines of the actual Concord." To illustrate what he means by this, he offers another fable, this one of an encounter on Spaulding's farm. In the woods there he comes across a "noble hall" inhabited by "an ancient and altogether admirable and shining family." In this mythic place, far removed from "the land called Concord," he sees "their park, their pleasure ground, in a meadow beyond the wood." He thinks he hears "the sounds of a suppressed hilarity." It seems "they recline on sunbeams." They know nothing of Spaulding even though he drives his wagon through their realm. "Nothing can equal the serenity of their lives. Their coat of arms is simply a lichen."[71] They have no politics and they do not labor. Away from Spaulding's farm, the memory fades. But if not for such families, he thinks he might move from Concord.

This is a vision of the natural life that Thoreau aspires to—serene and in harmony with nature. Such visions are fleeting; they flit across the landscape of the imagination like the faint shadow of birds' wings. "Our winged thoughts are turned to poultry. They no longer soar," he writes. "We hug the earth—how rarely we mount! Methinks we might elevate ourselves a little more." He describes climbing a tall white pine tree once, at the top of which were delicate white blossoms that the villagers had never witnessed before, having seen only the flowers that grow at their feet. Harking back to chanticleer in *Walden*, he announces the rooster's philosophy:

> Above all, we cannot afford not to live in the present. He is blessed over all mortals who loses no moment of the passing life in remembering the

past. Unless our philosophy hears the cock crow in every barn-yard within our horizon, it is belated. That sound commonly reminds us that we are growing rusty and antique in our employments and habits of thought. His philosophy comes down to a more recent time than ours. There is something suggested by it not in Plato or the New Testament. It is a newer testament—the Gospel according to this moment.[72]

Thoreau concludes the essay recounting a November walk during which he views the slanting rays of the setting sun light up a meadow, gilding the grass with a warm autumnal glow, a sight reminiscent of Elysium: "So we saunter toward the Holy Land; till one day the sun shall shine more brightly than he has done, shall perchance shine into our minds and hearts, light up our whole lives with a great awakening light, so warm and serene and golden as on a bank-side in Autumn."[73]

Early on, Thoreau was pegged as a nature writer. His friend and frequent walking partner Ellery Channing wrote the first Thoreau biography, titled *Thoreau, the Poet-Naturalist*. Another close friend, H. G. O. Blake, edited several volumes of excerpts from Thoreau's journal emphasizing his observations of nature through the seasons. With the publication of his complete writings, including the journal, a fuller picture of Thoreau emerged, bringing to light his importance as a social critic, political theorist, and advocate of simple living. More recently he has become an icon of the environmental movement. In Lawrence Buell's words, "Thoreau is the patron saint of American environmental writing."[74]

He advocated setting aside nature preserves, but he was not an environmental purist. John Burroughs gave him mixed reviews as a naturalist.[75] What distinguishes him as a nature writer and elevates him to sainthood are passages like this one from his journal: "Ah, I would walk, I would sit and sleep with natural piety. What if I could pray aloud or to myself as I went along by the brooksides a cheerful prayer like the birds! For joy I could embrace the earth. I shall delight to be buried in it."[76] Readers then and since have been captivated and inspired by Thoreau's natural piety, perhaps best described by Robert Richardson: "The nature-friendly outlook we Thoreauvians share is not some mere personal preference, some vaguely recreational feeling for the outdoors, but is instead a powerful, basic, *religious* conviction—fully worthy to be called a *belief*—in the sanctity of Nature, a belief that will help us in the fight against the destroyers, the despoilers, and the deniers. It is a religious conviction that we will be *saved, redeemed, delivered, born again—through Nature*."[77]

"Autumnal Tints"

"Autumnal Tints" was the last lecture Thoreau delivered, given December 11, 1860, in Waterbury, Connecticut. That same month he came down with a bad cold that turned into bronchitis, precipitating the flare-up of tuberculosis that ended his life less than a year and a half later. In hopes of remission, he traveled to Minnesota in May 1861, but his health continued to worsen. The essay was published in the *Atlantic Monthly* in October 1862, five months after his death.

Though unintentional, it is fitting that this was his last lecture, since the essay deals with death. Annually in New England, timetables are given for the advance of the brilliant coloring of leaves in autumn, from Maine to New York and beyond. Millions of "leaf peepers" troop to see the foliage change from green to yellow and red. Thoreau describes this process in vivid detail, beginning with the red maples which start to turn color in late September, standing out from the other types of trees. Next he describes the ripening of the elm trees, starting in October, followed by the sugar maples later in the month. Last come the scarlet oaks, which reach their prime as the leaves of other trees are falling.

Thoreau beckons his village neighbors to venture outside to view the beauty of the forest. But they will not *see* it if they do not *look* for it. "Objects are concealed from our view," he says, "not so much because they are out of the course of our visual ray as because we do not bring our minds and eyes to bear on them; for there is no power to see in the eye itself, any more than in any other jelly. . . . There is just as much beauty visible to us in the landscape as we are prepared to appreciate,—not a grain more."[78] He sees what most of us miss. Leaves do not simply turn brown, wither up, and fall off; rather they acquire a brilliant tint, a last flush of life. Our appetites are largely confined to the ripeness of the fruits we eat, he says. "But round about and within our towns there is annually another show of fruits, on an infinitely grander scale, fruits which address our taste for beauty alone."[79]

These leaves also convey a profound message: they teach us how to die. When they fall, the whole earth becomes a vast cemetery:

> It is pleasant to walk over the beds of these fresh, crisp, and rustling leaves. How beautifully they go to their graves! how gently lay themselves down and turn to mould!—painted of a thousand hues, and fit to make the beds of us living. . . . How many flutterings before they rest quietly in their graves! They that soared so loftily, how contentedly they return to dust again, and are laid low, resigned to lie and decay at the foot of the tree, and

afford nourishment to new generations of their kind, as well as to flutter on high! They teach us how to die. One wonders if the time will ever come when men, with their boasted faith in immortality, will lie down as gracefully and as ripe,—with such an Indian-summer serenity will shed their bodies as they do their hair and nails.[80]

We are accustomed to the idea that old age entails a diminution of our powers, a loss of our faculties, a process of gradual senescence and decline. But Thoreau will not have it so. "I believe that all leaves, even grasses and mosses, acquire brighter colors just before their fall," he writes.[81] And by implication, so may we.

Thoreau's own death teaches us a profound lesson. In September 1859 he wrote in his journal:

> I have many affairs to attend to, and feel hurried these days. . . . It is not by a compromise, it is not by a timid and feeble repentance, that a man will save his soul and *live*, at last. He has got to *conquer* a clear field, letting Repentance & Co. go. That's a well-meaning but weak firm that has assumed the debts of an old and worthless one. You are to fight in a field where no allowances will be made, no courteous bowing to one-handed knights. You are expected to do your duty, not in spite of everything but *one*, but in spite of *everything*.[82]

Such, undoubtedly, was his frame of mind as he contemplated his own demise. He put aside his ambitious project of creating a Kalendar chronicling the natural history of Concord and turned instead to preparing for publication writings that would secure his reputation as one of America's foremost authors.

Thoreau was no stranger to death. Two rather dramatic confrontations with death were the result of shipwrecks, that of the *St. John* off the coast of Cape Cod in 1849, and the other of the *Elizabeth* off the coast of Long Island in 1850 which took the life of Margaret Fuller, Giovanni Ossoli, and their son. In both cases the images of death he witnessed were stark reminders of the precariousness of life. His brother John had died from tetanus, and he experienced the deaths of his grandfather, father, and one of his sisters from tuberculosis, a leading cause of adult mortality in his day. At the time there was little that could be done for consumption, as it was then called, aside from recommending a change of climate.

Even as his health continued to decline, he seemed to enjoy life as much as ever. In a letter to one of his friends who had inquired about his final days

Sophia Thoreau wrote: "During his long illness I never heard a murmur escape him, or the slightest wish expressed to remain with us, his perfect contentment was truly wonderful. None of his friends seemed to realize how very ill he was, so full of life, and good cheer did he seem."[83] One visitor was Parker Pillsbury, a reformer and family friend who asked him what he could see, so near was he to the other side. "One world at a time," was Henry's characteristic reply. He passed away a few days later.

Spiritual pilgrims visiting Authors Ridge in Concord's Sleepy Hollow Cemetery are struck by the difference between the headstones of Emerson and Thoreau, both of whom are buried there. Emerson's is a huge piece of rose quartz, a fitting tribute to America's favorite philosopher. By contrast, Thoreau's modest headstone, barely a foot high, marked only with his first name, and often surrounded by leaves, pine cones, and notes left by admirers, is more in keeping with the simplicity he advocated and lived in his own life.

CHAPTER 8

PILGRIMAGE

⌒

Thoreau's funeral was held at Concord's First Parish Church. Since he had "signed off" from the church many years before, it was held in the vestry rather than the sanctuary. Nevertheless, the current minister, the Reverend Grindall Reynolds, participated, along with Bronson Alcott, Emerson, and others. Alcott not only planned the service but also arranged to have children dismissed from school so that they could attend. The bell tolled forty-four times as mourners entered the building. Emerson delivered a moving eulogy, concluding:

> The scale on which his studies proceeded was so large as to require longevity, and we were the less prepared for his sudden disappearance. The country knows not yet, or in the least part, how great a son it has lost. It seems an injury that he should leave in the midst of his broken task, which none else can finish,—a kind of indignity to so noble a soul, that it should depart out of nature before yet he has been really shown to his peers for what he is. But he, at least, is content. His soul was made for the noblest society; he had in a short life exhausted the capabilities of this world; wherever there is knowledge, wherever there is virtue, wherever there is beauty, he will find a home.[1]

His coffin, accompanied by a procession of more than three hundred schoolchildren, was carried to the New Burying Ground across the street from the church.[2] It was later moved to Authors Ridge in Sleepy Hollow Cemetery to rest near those of his friends Alcott, Emerson, and Hawthorne.

Thoreau's reputation began to grow shortly after his death as pilgrims and curiosity seekers alike beat a path to Concord and Walden Pond. On June 12, 1872, Alcott accompanied Mary Adams, a visitor from Dubuque, Iowa, to a Unitarian picnic at Walden Pond. Along the way, he pointed out the location of Thoreau's cabin. She suggested placing stones at the site since there was nothing else to indicate where the cabin had been. She laid the first stone and some of the other picnickers followed suit. "The rude stones were a monument more fitting than the costliest carving of the artist," Alcott noted in his journal. "Henry's fame is surely to brighten with years, and this spot be visited by admiring readers of his works."[3] This cairn has grown steadily over the years as visitors continue to add their stones to it, many of them inscribed with a favorite Thoreau quote or something more personal. Following the reunification of Germany in 1990, pieces of the Berlin Wall were brought by pilgrims from the former German Democratic Republic.

I have visited the site many times, and I am seldom alone. For many people the experience is a deeply spiritual one. In my book *Transcendentalism and the Cultivation of the Soul*, I described that on one occasion I met a man at the cairn who had been an addict and spent time in prison for dealing drugs. While in prison he had taken a class on American literature and read *Walden*, one of the books assigned. The class visited Walden Pond on an outing. He told me that the book and that visit had changed his life. Now he was off drugs, married, and a father. Later, I ran into a man with two young children. He said that he and his wife had brought their older child, now about nine years old, to Walden Pond when he was just an infant. Now he'd brought his two sons there to explain why they had named the older boy Walden. Such stories remind us of what Thoreau wrote in *Walden* about books and reading: "There are probably words addressed to our condition exactly, which, if we could really hear and understand, would be more salutary than the morning or the spring in our lives, and possibly put a new aspect on the face of things for us."[4]

The pond and cabin site attract well over half a million visitors per year. The visitors' center at the pond houses a Thoreau exhibit and a bookshop run by the Thoreau Society, the nation's oldest and largest literary organization. The society hosts an annual gathering in July, bringing together scholars and Thoreau fans from all over the world. Pilgrims who are drawn to the pond cannot fail to feel his presence there. As one notable visitor, Loren Eisley, described his experience: "I advanced upon the trail of the oak leaves. We were all the eye of the Visitor—the eye whose reason no physics could explain. Generation by generation the eye was among us. . . . I had emerged on the path as followed by the author of *Walden*. The eye was everywhere, and as for Walden it too was everywhere that the eye existed."[5]

Inspired by the mythic significance of the pond and the recognition that it is in reality part of a larger ecosystem, Walden Woods, Concord citizens, and members of the Thoreau Society mounted a concerted effort to rescue 2,680 acres of land surrounding the pond from proposed development. Rock musician Don Henley founded the Walden Woods Project, which raised money to purchase most of this threatened property. In addition, the project established a study center and the Thoreau Institute, a state-of-the-art library housing a significant collection of materials for scholarly research. It also offers a wide range of educational programs for local and global audiences of all ages.

In his eulogy of Thoreau, Emerson called attention to his friend's "broken task." Whatever else he might have meant by this, surely it included projects Thoreau didn't live long enough to complete. Foremost among them was the unfinished Kalendar, his phenological studies of the flora and fauna of Walden Woods. By noting the annual arrivals of migrating birds and the leaving and flowering of plants, these records have contributed to the effort to track the onset of climate change. Warming temperatures have altered many aspects of Concord's natural environment. Using Thoreau's detailed records, biologist Richard B. Primack has been able to determine that blueberries, for example, now begin flowering six weeks before they did in Thoreau's day.

Emerson could not have known the impact that Thoreau's life and teachings would have on subsequent generations. He enumerated Thoreau's many fine qualities and accomplishments and yet expressed disappointment that he hadn't lived up to his potential. But for many of Thoreau's friends and followers, what Emerson said was a low blow:

> With his energy and practical ability he seemed born for great enterprise and for command: and I so much regret the loss of his rare powers of action, that I cannot help counting it a fault in him that he had no ambition. Wanting this, instead of engineering for all America, he was the captain of a huckleberry party. Pounding beans is good to the end of pounding empires one of these days, but if, at the end of years, it is still only beans![6]

It would seem that Emerson either misunderstood or underestimated Thoreau. In either case, it is difficult to know why he felt the need to cast shade on his friend's reputation. Nevertheless, "the captain of a huckleberry party" seems to have had the last word. Thoreau's influence today extends far beyond the shores of Walden Pond. *Walden* has been translated into every major language, including Farsi and Icelandic. His writings have been the focus of international conferences held in France, Sweden, Iceland, Japan, and other countries. Studies of Thoreau's writings have been published by scholars in Britain, Germany, France, Sweden, Bulgaria, Japan, India, Russia, Iran, Iceland, and elsewhere.[7] Thoreau himself was a global thinker who drew on ancient and modern wisdom from the East and West.

Although he is widely known and appreciated today, Thoreau's reputation was slow to develop. Until late in the twentieth century, it rested primarily on *Walden*, his best-known book. As I mentioned previously, it fostered the popular myth of Thoreau as the hermit of Walden Pond. With the posthumous publication of essays in the *Atlantic Monthly* and his books *Excursions, The Maine Woods, Cape Cod, A Yankee in Canada, with Anti-Slavery and Reform Papers*, he began to attract greater attention. Late nineteenth-century nature writers John Muir and John Burroughs paid tribute to his influence. A succession of naturalists during the twentieth century, including Joseph Wood Krutch, Edwin Way Teale, and Annie Dillard, have also acknowledged his importance. As Teale, a past president of the Thoreau Society, wrote: "Running through all of Thoreau's writings, running all through his life, is the intensity of his feeling for nature, for wildness. To few people in the world has nature meant so much as it did to Thoreau."[8]

With the closing of the American frontier in 1890, the public perception of wilderness gradually changed. Where once wilderness needed to be tamed, now it needed to be preserved. Here, too, Thoreau's influence is apparent. He had called for the preservation of wild areas in several of his writings, most notably in *The Maine Woods* and "Walking." As the environmental movement gained strength during the twentieth century, it became clear that something more was called for. In the view of Roderick Nash, author of *Wilderness and the American Mind*, "what was new as the end of the twentieth century approached was the realization that the future of wilderness on earth depended as never before on the promulgation of a convincing philosophy."[9] Nash credits Thoreau and the Transcendentalists with providing the needed philosophical rationale. "Transcendentalism was one of the major factors conditioning Thoreau's ideas regarding nature," Nash writes. "The core of Transcendentalism was the belief that a correspondence or parallelism existed between the higher realm of spiritual truth and the lower one of material objects. For this reason natural objects assumed importance because, if rightly seen, they reflected universal spiritual truths. . . . As a way of thinking about man and nature, Transcendentalism had important implications for the meaning of the American wilderness."[10]

For Thoreau and the Transcendentalists, reverence for nature went hand in hand with living simply. Naturalist John Burroughs, an early champion of Thoreau's philosophy, drew the connection between the two:

> There can be little doubt, I think, but that intercourse with Nature and a knowledge of her ways tends to simplicity of life. We come more and more to see through the follies and vanities of the world and to appreciate the real values. We load ourselves up with so many false burdens, our complex civilization breeds in us so many false or artificial wants, that we become separated from the real sources of our strength and health as by a gulf.[11]

Today, Thoreau is as well known for his advocacy of simple living as he is for promoting the preservation of wild places. Writings such as *Walden* and "Life without Principle" have inspired a variety of social reforms resting on two interrelated assumptions: the life-enhancing panacea of nature and the soul-degrading influence of materialism. The first is the remedy for the second.

Thoreau was neither the first nor the only one to seek a way of living that reduced one's material and social needs to a minimum in order to pursue spiritual truths, moral ideals, and aesthetic impulses. What he and other Transcendentalists called plain living and high thinking encompassed a wide spectrum of practices. Some, like Thoreau, sought solitude living in the woods or by a pond. Others formed cooperative communities like Brook Farm and Fruitlands. Such experiments are even more prevalent today, as witnessed in widespread back-to-the-land, tiny house, and voluntary simplicity movements. If Thoreau was not the first to advocate simple living, he is nevertheless credited with persuading others to practice it in their own way.

Though he was not known as an activist in his own time, his radical environmentalism, combined with his antislavery activities and his critique of materialism, have since called attention to the contemporary relevance of his political views.[12] As previously noted, his essay "Civil Disobedience" inspired Gandhi, Martin Luther King Jr., and many others in passive resistance to social injustice and war. The essay also highlights the importance of active resistance to the complicity of individuals and society in racism and oppression. While it is often taken to mean that one should simply refuse to condone or participate in unjust actions, Thoreau's argument goes beyond that. As he wrote in *Walden*, "Moral reform is the effort to throw off sleep."[13]

One's responsibility is not simply to opt out. It also entails a commitment to awaken to one's complicity in injustice and a willingness to redress whatever complicity one finds. In awakening to his own responsibility, he realized that he had to act against slavery and unjust war even if it took him away from his treasured walks in the woods. His argument gains currency in light of questions today concerning restorative justice, reparations, and white privilege.

His influence is greater now in another respect as well. He is justly celebrated as an advocate for wilderness preservation, simple living, and action from principle. But the impetus for all three of these comes from his unconventional yet deeply felt spirituality, rooted in his experience of the natural world. As I have noted, early biographers and critics focused on his nature writings and social commentary primarily. Within the academic community this is largely true today. According to Alan Hodder, "Several critics duly noted certain 'mystical' tendencies in Thoreau's writings, but most found this ostensible mystical or spiritual dimension of his life and writing extraneous, unpalatable, or simply impossible to discuss in an academic context."[14] Even as scholars have begun to take a closer look at the religious views of the Transcendentalist writers, they mainly treat them either in the context of American intellectual and cultural history or in that of church or social reform. Less attention has been paid to their impact on the interior, affective life of his readers.

Thanks in part to the work of a few scholars, including Hodder and K. P. Van Anglen, it has become more respectable to focus on the spiritual dimension of Thoreau's writings.[15] Hodder attributes the growing popular and scholarly interest in the spiritual Thoreau to the fact that "he was among the first Americans to articulate and embody in a performative way an approach to being religious or 'spiritual' that has become increasingly recognizable and even appealing to a large swath of Americans, particularly since the 1960s." He continues: "A religiosity that once seemed eccentric, incredible, even perverse to many now seems enviable and even in some respects normative to a large cohort of unchurched but not spiritually uninterested Americans. Religiously, we might say, American culture has finally caught up with Henry Thoreau—so much so that we are beginning to see him occupy a central place in the story of religion in America as he has long occupied in American literary, scientific, and political history."[16]

Recent treatments of Thoreau's religious views have set them in the context of the breakup of Christian hegemony and growing unbelief as these played out in mid-nineteenth-century Concord, highlighting his disdain for formal religion and, alternately, emphasizing the fusion of his religious ascet-icism and his social justice activism.[17] While these are informative, they have tended to avoid any discussion of Thoreau's ecstatic spirituality. As Alda Balthrop-Lewis argues in her book *Thoreau's Religion: Walden Woods, Social Justice, and the Politics of Asceticism*, the focus "on practices of contemplation and individual mystical experiences, or what is sometimes called 'spiritual-ity' ... leads to [the] neglect of the social, political, and economic features of religious practices."[18]

In my view, it is precisely Thoreau's spiritual vision that so many of his readers find attractive. His ecstatic spirituality is the common denominator and motivating factor in all of his interests and commitments. And it is this which is of greatest interest to readers today. Studies continue to show that even as church membership and denominational affiliation have declined, Americans remain concerned with spiritual issues, preferring to pursue them outside the context of religious organizations. They are best described as spiritual but not religious. Many consider themselves seekers for whom per-sonal religious experience, often mystical in nature, occupies a central place in their spiritual life. Commonly dissatisfied with our materialistic culture, they seek a simpler way of life in harmony with nature.

Given the fact that Thoreau quit the church he was raised in and was scornful of formal religion, it might seem odd that anyone would consider him a spiritual guide. But many of today's seekers have followed a similar path, questioning religious dogmas, rejecting the hypocrisy of churches, and embracing a religious cosmopolitanism. And many would agree with what he wrote in 1850, which I quoted in the introduction: "I do not prefer one religion or philosophy to another. I have no sympathy with the bigotry and ignorance which make transient and partial and puerile distinctions between one man's faith or form of faith and another—as Christian and heathen. I pray to be delivered from narrowness, partiality, exaggeration—bigotry. To the philosopher all sects and all nations are alike. I like Brahma, Hare Bud-dha, the Great Spirit as well as God."[19] Like Thoreau, they have been drawn to other religious traditions and philosophies in search of wisdom, insights, and meaningful spiritual practices.

What his readers find most compelling—frequently overlooked in aca-demic treatments of his writing—is his "Gospel according to this moment." As he wrote in his journal, Thoreau went to Walden Pond hoping to leave his self behind and to delight in the contemplation of his soul:

> When I hear [the church] bell ring, I am carried back to years and sab-
> baths when I was newer and more innocent I fear than now, and it seems
> to me as if there were a world within a world. Sin, I am sure is not in overt
> acts, or indeed in acts of any kind, but is in proportion to the time which
> has come behind us and displaced eternity. . . . The whole duty of life is
> contained in this question: How to respire and aspire both at once.[20]

This is the dilemma of double consciousness. On the one hand, we are
caught up in the affairs of the everyday world, with all of its distractions and
demands. On the other hand, we are from time to time aware of a world
within this hectic outer world that remains detached and centered while
everything else goes spinning about. How to reconcile these two forms of
consciousness is one of the fundamental challenges of the spiritual life, contained in Thoreau's apt expression "how to respire and aspire both at once"—
that is, how to find *nirvana* in *samsara*, eternity in the fleeting moment. It
is to live fully in the present, or as Thoreau himself expressed it in another
journal passage:

> Nothing must be postponed. Take time by the forelock. Now or never!
> You must live in the present, launch yourself on every wave, find your eter-
> nity in each moment. Fools stand on their island opportunities and look
> toward another land. There is no other land; there is no other life but this,
> or the like of this. . . . Take any other course, and life will be a succession
> of regrets. Let us see vessels sailing prosperously before the wind, and not
> simply stranded barks. There is no world for the penitent and regretful.[21]

To live fully in the present we must leave our ego behind, Thoreau insisted.
We don't know how deeply he studied the Hindu texts he read, but he knew
well enough that there is a difference between the ego and the soul, and that
the soul in each person is an incarnation of the Over-soul, God, or the Great
Spirit. And he was quite aware of the extent to which the ego gets in the
way of our ability to find eternity in each moment. Following the advice of
the Bhagavad Gita, he withdrew from the petty affairs of daily life to find a
solitary place where he might live simply by himself in contemplation and
leisure. He left the village behind, but he knew he wouldn't succeed in cultivating his soul unless he left his petty self behind as well.

Thoreau's spiritual life was devoid of doctrines or formulas or philosophical propositions. It was oriented around intoxicating experiences of joy in
and oneness with the natural world. He often referred to these as ecstasies,
or what we might call mystic states. As recounted in the lengthy journal entry

I quoted in chapter 5, "such ecstasies begotten of the breezes" came spontaneously and were not procured by him in any way. These experiences assured him that he was dealt with by a superior power which sought to improve him and the quality of his life. At the same time, he was curious to know how it was that such "light comes into the soul."[22]

William James describes mystical states as transient but compelling. Though fleeting, they are nevertheless, in his words, "illuminations, revelations, full of significance and importance," and carry with them a "sense of authority."[23] In Thoreau's case—as I suspect is true for most of us—these ecstatic experiences arose more naturally and occurred more often in youth than they did in adulthood. His journal, which he faithfully kept for most of his life, is as much an account of the ebb and flow of his ecstasies as they are a record of the local flora and fauna.

Barely a month before the journal entry just quoted, Thoreau was lamenting the loss of such youthful ecstasies: "Ah, the life that I have known! How hard it is to remember what is most memorable! We remember how we itched, not how our hearts beat. I can sometimes recall to mind the quality, the immortality, of my youthful life, but in memory is the only relation to it."[24] How to recall to mind not just the feeling of euphoria but also the wisdom, the knowledge, the truth of "what is most memorable" in our lives—the "world within a world"—is the most crucial issue and critical task of our own spirituality, and it was the central preoccupation of Thoreau in his adult religious life.

During the early 1850s, following his sojourn at Walden Pond, he gave his most sustained attention to the fundamental paradoxes of the spiritual life. Foremost among these is this: How do we command what is essentially spontaneous? Granted that these experiences are fleeting and at the same time central to our religious life and spiritual well-being, how, if at all, do we recapture them? Given that they are most likely to occur when the will is in abeyance, how is it possible to summon them?

In his quest to discover how and whence it is that "light comes into the soul," Thoreau was led to develop a spiritual practice that would enable him to leave his ego behind and allow him to respire and aspire both at once. As the frequency of these mystic states diminished, he was drawn to the idea that he might, through a certain kind of regimen, put himself in a receptive frame of mind and thereby increase the odds that such experiences might recur. This regimen was in keeping with what was then termed self-culture, which the Transcendentalists took to mean the cultivation of the soul. If it was the self they intended to cultivate, it was the self in a larger, more spiritual sense—the self with a capital S—and not the limited, narrow self of the individual ego. It was this latter sense of self that Thoreau hoped to leave behind when he went to Walden Pond.

Thoreau wanted his readers to find and follow their own path in life, and not his or anyone else's. He insisted that people make hard choices, no doubt easier for him since he wasn't as enmeshed in relationships and commitments as most of us are. He never married, lived at home with his parents, and did odd jobs for a living. He could be difficult and exasperating, both for his friends and for his readers. Behind the curtain, all saints and sages have their blemishes and foibles; Henry Thoreau is no exception. The question for us is whether or not his message has relevance today.

Has society become so consumption-oriented, education so utilitarian, science so materialistic, and everyday life so consumed with social media and to-do lists that we ignore entirely the prompting of the spirit? Is seeking ecstasies in the woods a frivolous pursuit in light of the serious problems we face, including homelessness, poverty, discrimination, and racism? Was Thoreau's living at Walden Pond a selfish retreat from society, or did he have something to teach us about how we might enhance our lives and improve the lives of others with a due appreciation of the importance of solitude, nature, and self-reliance?

The issues Thoreau addressed in his writing and in his person are perennial and universal in human experience—anxiety, alienation, prejudice, and a lack of meaning and purpose in life. In response to these, he continues to challenge us to live a life that is deliberately chosen rather than one laid out for us by others, or simply fallen into and tolerated by force of habit. As he declares in the "Spring" chapter of *Walden,* it is possible that we might learn to live now instead of always postponing life and deferring to our duties, to atone for the sin of displacing eternity with the minutiae of everyday life, and to cease loitering "in winter when it is already spring."

By his own admission, Thoreau had no interest in recruiting followers, admonishing his readers to find and follow their own spiritual path instead. Many of them then and since have done so. While it may sound contradictory to suggest that he could be a spiritual guide for people today, I believe that he has much to offer spiritual seekers, especially during these difficult times. As I write, we are living in the aftermath of a worldwide pandemic which has taken the lives of millions of people. At the same time, climate change is contributing to a dangerous combination of rising sea levels, drought, wildfires, and weather-related disasters. The nation continues to struggle with economic and racial injustice. We are also faced with the depletion of natural resources, species extinction, and mountains of waste due to unconstrained growth.

In light of such challenges, it might seem that any advice from Thoreau is ineffectual, and that comparing our world to his is unwarranted. But in fact there has never been a period in our history without suffering, struggle, and hardship. During Thoreau's lifetime the nation experienced endemic poverty, two financial panics, wars of aggression against Mexico and Native nations, the enslavement of four million African people, polarized politics, and the incurable disease of tuberculosis. Hence, withdrawing to Walden Pond might seem more like an escape than an answer, an accusation often made by his critics.

In response to such criticism, Andreas Hess argues in a 2020 essay "Purposeful Solitude: Reading Thoreau in a Lockdown" that the dichotomy so often drawn between public engagement and private retreat is a false one:

> The two realms of public and private must not be seen as alternatives but as being co-existential. We cannot be engaged 24/7; we need to draw breath and recharge our batteries for the next struggle and the next public engagement. Critical reflection rarely happens when one is in the middle of a fight but only with a distance both in terms of time and space. What Thoreau did was exactly that—a successful and thus recommendable experiment in shifting involvements.[25]

Thoreau's retreat to Walden Pond was strategic. It was not simply to get away and absolve himself of responsibility for the nation's problems. It was to disengage from conformity and complicity, to break the hold of an unhealthful and unjust social order on its citizens, and to rethink his position. In the process, he discovered for himself—and demonstrated for others—the importance of action from principle, simple living, and environmental sustainability.

Nor was he simply chasing after rainbows and fleeting ecstasies. In moments of heightened awareness, he discerned the essential difference between the real world and the actual one, between what is truly important and what is merely superficial. What he learned from his experience—so eloquently expressed in *Walden*—was that "if one advances confidently in the direction of his dreams, and endeavors to live the life which he has imagined, he will meet with a success unexpected in common hours. . . . If you have built castles in the air, your work need not be lost; that is where they should be. Now put the foundations under them."[26] He encourages us not merely to dream of a better world but to create one.

Finally, Thoreau instructs us in the art of life. For him, philosophy was not a matter of subtle thoughts and abstract propositions; it was a way of living. As such, it had much in common with ancient philosophies in India, China, Greece, and elsewhere. These philosophies, as I have pointed out, were therapeutic in nature. They were developed in response to the problems of living, including heartache, anger, despair, and loss. They counseled adherents to seek solace in nature, balance in life, and harmony with the universe. By means of spiritual exercises, followers were taught to distinguish between what contributes to human flourishing and what inhibits it. In my view, Thoreau offers his readers a similar philosophy, "the Gospel according to this moment," no less worthwhile than those of more ancient vintage. The disciplines he recommends—reading, solitude, contemplation, sauntering in nature, simple living, action from principle, and so on—are not simply congenial to today's spiritual seekers but are also beneficial and rewarding.

Thoreau has never been more popular than he is today. For years he was dismissed as a loner, a misanthropist, and a shirker. To be sure, he had an aversion to small talk and could be standoffish. His criticism of his fellow citizens was sometimes caustic and, as we have seen, he was prone to exaggeration. In his eulogy of Thoreau, Emerson quoted one of his female friends who said, "I love Henry, but I cannot like him; and as for taking his arm, I should as soon think of taking the arm of an elm-tree."[27] While true enough, I suspect this criticism is intended to discredit his reputation and deflect attention from the imperative to live our lives more deliberately, as he has done and implores us to do. To be sure, he demands a great deal from his readers, including introspection, discipline, and perseverance. But he wants to assure us that we are not so stuck in our ways that we cannot change and that life is full of possibilities.

Like that beautiful bug he describes in *Walden* which emerged from the dry leaf of an old table that stood in a farmer's kitchen, hatched from an egg deposited in the living tree many years earlier, Thoreau's wisdom has been buried under the dead weight of a society that prioritizes social conformity, conservative politics, and the exploitation of people and the natural world. Perchance this will be the summer that brings forth his beautiful and winged thoughts at last.

NOTES

PREFACE

1. Henry David Thoreau, *Walden*, ed. L. Lyndon Shanley (Princeton: Princeton University Press, 1973), 326.
2. Henry David Thoreau, *Excursions*, ed. Joseph J. Moldenhauer (Princeton: Princeton University Press, 2007), 202.
3. Thoreau, *Walden*, 14.
4. Thoreau, *Walden*, 15.

INTRODUCTION

1. *The Correspondence of Henry David Thoreau*, ed. Robert N. Hudspeth, 2 vols. (Princeton: Princeton University Press, 2013), 1:308. Hereafter Thoreau, *Correspondence*, cited by volume and page.
2. Solnit writes, "This compartmentalizing of Thoreau is a microcosm of a larger partition in American thought, a fence built in the belief that places in the imagination can be contained." Rebecca Solnit, "The Thoreau Problem," *Orion Magazine*, https://orionmagazine.org/article/the-thoreau-problem/.
3. Henry David Thoreau, *Journal*, ed. John C. Broderick et al., 8 vols. to date (Princeton: Princeton University Press, 1981–2009), 5:469–70. Hereafter *PJ*, cited by volume and page. (I have added punctuation and made very slight changes to make these entries more readable.)
4. Laura Dassow Walls, *Henry David Thoreau: A Life* (Chicago: University of Chicago Press, 2017), 191–92.
5. *PJ*, 4:52.
6. *Journal of Henry David Thoreau*, ed. Bradford Torrey and Francis H. Allen, 14 vols. (1927; repr., Boston: Houghton Mifflin Company, 1949), 11:113. Hereafter *JHDT*, cited by volume and page.
7. See Jan Stievermann, "Emersonian Transcendentalism and the Invention of Religion(s) in the Nineteenth Century," *ESQ* 67 (2021): 533–70; and Leigh Eric Schmidt, *Restless Souls: The Making of American Spirituality* (San Francisco: HarperSanFrancisco, 2005).
8. *PJ*, 2:55.
9. *PJ*, 2:4.
10. *PJ*, 4:53–55.

11. Thoreau, *Correspondence*, 2:138.

12. David M. Robinson, "Unitarian History and the Transcendentalist Literary Consciousness," Henry Whitney Bellows Lecture, Unitarian Church of All Souls, New York, 1989.

CHAPTER 1: BECOMING HENRY DAVID THOREAU

1. The best biographies of Thoreau are Walter Harding, *The Days of Henry Thoreau* (New York: Alfred A. Knopf, 1965); Robert D. Richardson Jr., *Henry David Thoreau: A Life of the Mind* (Berkeley: University of California Press, 1986); and Laura Dassow Walls, *Henry David Thoreau: A Life* (Chicago: University of Chicago Press, 2017). On Concord, see Robert A. Gross, *The Transcendentalists and Their World* (New York: Farrar, Straus and Giroux, 2021).

2. On the Unitarian view of Arminianism, see Conrad Wright, *The Beginnings of Unitarianism in America* (Boston: Starr King Press, 1955), 3: "Arminianism asserted that men are born with the capacity both for sin and for righteousness; that they can respond to the impulse toward holiness as well as the temptation to do evil; and that life is a process of trial and discipline by which, with the assistance which God gives to all, the bondage to sin may be gradually overcome." Also see Daniel Walker Howe, *The Unitarian Conscience: Harvard Moral Philosophy, 1805–1861* (Cambridge: Harvard University Press, 1970), 67: "One of the distinguishing theological characteristics of the Boston Unitarians was their Arminianism, that is, their belief in the freedom of man to work out his own salvation." And further, Howe on Arminianism and self-culture: "The Unitarian moralists were continually exhorting themselves as well as others, to fill every moment not spent in work with careful self-improvement. . . . Self-cultivation was the essence of Massachusetts Arminianism" (110).

3. See Robert A. Gross, "'Doctor Ripley's Church': Congregational Life in Concord, Massachusetts, 1778–1841," *Journal of Unitarian Universalist History* 33 (2009–10): 10.

4. Robert A. Gross, "Faith in the Boardinghouse: New Views of Thoreau Family Religion," *Thoreau Society Bulletin*, no. 150 (Winter 2005): 3–4.

5. Howe, *Unitarian Conscience*, 3.

6. See Annie Decker, "Henry Thoreau, Harvard, and the Work of Reading," *Journal of Unitarian Universalist History* 27 (2000): 58–83.

7. Orestes A. Brownson, *New Views of Christianity, Society, and the Church*, in *The Transcendentalists: An Anthology*, ed. Perry Miller (Cambridge: Harvard University Press, 1960), 117.

8. In truth, the Unitarians' adherence to Locke's empiricism was not complete. It was hedged by Dugald Stewart, Thomas Reid, and others in the so-called Scottish common sense school who argued that moral truths are intuitively self-evident. See Howe, *Unitarian Conscience*, 45–49.

9. Thoreau, *Correspondence*, 1:30. *Lebenstag* means "life day," or a special day in one's life.

10. Henry David Thoreau, *Early Essays and Miscellanies*, ed. Joseph J. Moldenhauer and Edwin Moser (Princeton: Princeton University Press, 1975), 27.

11. Thoreau, *Early Essays*, 48.

12. Thoreau, *Early Essays* 114.

13. Thoreau, *Early Essays* 115–17.

14. *PJ*, 1:5.
15. The occasion is recounted in *The Letters of Ralph Waldo Emerson*, vol. 7, ed. Eleanor M. Tilton (New York: Columbia University Press, 1990), 22.
16. William Ellery Channing, *Selected Writings*, ed. David Robinson (New York: Paulist Press, 1985), 226.
17. Channing, *Selected Writings*, 228.
18. Channing, *Selected Writings*, 228–29.
19. Channing, *Selected Writings*, 146.
20. *The Early Lectures of Ralph Waldo Emerson*, vol. 2, ed. Stephen E. Whicher, Robert E. Spiller, and Wallace E. Williams (Cambridge: Harvard University Press, 1964), 215, 304.
21. Emerson, *Early Lectures*, 2:250, 252.
22. Emerson, *Early Lectures*, 2:364.
23. Emerson, *Early Lectures*, 2:221, 261.
24. Emerson, *Early Lectures*, 2:261, 275.
25. Emerson, *Early Lectures*, 2:292.
26. Richardson, *Thoreau*, 57.
27. *PJ*, 1:116.
28. Henry David Thoreau, *Excursions*, ed. Joseph J. Moldenhauer (Princeton: Princeton University Press, 2007), 4–5.
29. Thoreau, *Excursions*, 5, 7.
30. Robert D. Richardson, *Three Roads Back: How Emerson, Thoreau, and William James Responded to the Greatest Losses of Their Lives* (Princeton: Princeton University Press, 2023), 56.
31. Richardson, *Three Roads Back*, 23.
32. Richardson, *Three Roads Back*, 27–28. For Thoreau's early views of science, see Robert Kuhn McGregor, *A Wider View of the Universe: Henry Thoreau's Study of Nature* (Urbana: University of Illinois Press, 1997), 33–57.
33. *PJ*, 1:311.
34. Thoreau, *Excursions*, 37.
35. Thoreau, *Excursions*, 41, 43.
36. Thoreau, *Excursions*, 43–44, 45–46.
37. Robert Sattelmeyer, *Thoreau's Reading: A Study in Intellectual History* (Princeton: Princeton University Press, 1988), 39.
38. Thoreau, *Early Essays*, 265.
39. Thomas Carlyle, *Essays Critical and Miscellaneous*, vol. 1 (London: Chapman and Hall, 1887), 473–74, 479, 485.
40. Thomas Carlyle, *Sartor Resartus* (New York: Oxford University Press, 1999), 147, 195.
41. See Conrad Wright, *The Liberal Christians: Essays on American Unitarian History* (Boston: Beacon Press, 1970), 6–15; and Conrad Wright, "American Unitarianism in 1805," *Journal of Unitarian Universalist History* 30 (2005): 3–6.
42. *PJ*, 2:55.
43. Quoted in Henry David Thoreau, *Essays*, ed. Jeffrey S. Cramer (New Haven: Yale University Press, 2013), xv.
44. See Thoreau, *Correspondence*, 1:286.
45. *PJ*, 3:244; see also 233 and 246. Some scholars contend that Thoreau can't be considered a Transcendentalist before he made these entries. To the contrary, Sattelmeyer argues,

"If Thoreau was not confirmed in his Transcendental views by the time he left Harvard, his conversion would be complete within a relatively short time." Sattelmeyer, *Thoreau's Reading*, 23.

46. *PJ*, 1:50–51.

CHAPTER 2: THE ART OF LIFE

1. Robert Sattelmeyer, *Thoreau's Reading: A Study in Intellectual History* (Princeton: Princeton University Press, 1988), 31.
2. Caleb Smith, *Thoreau's Axe: Distraction and Discipline in American Culture* (Princeton: Princeton University Press, 2013), 9.
3. *PJ*, 1:311.
4. Henry David Thoreau, *Early Essays and Miscellanies*, ed. Joseph J. Moldenhauer and Edwin Moser (Princeton: Princeton University Press, 1975), 128–39.
5. Thoreau, *Early Essays*, 140.
6. Thoreau, *Early Essays*, 147.
7. Thoreau, *Early Essays*, 177.
8. Henry David Thoreau, *Walden*, ed. L. Lyndon Shanley (Princeton: Princeton University Press, 1973), 14–15.
9. Christopher W. Gowans, "Self-Cultivation Philosophies," paper presented to the Columbia Society for Comparative Philosophy, February 24, 2017, http://christophergowans.com/selfcultivation-philosophies.
10. Pierre Hadot, *Philosophy as a Way of Life*, trans. Michael Chase, ed. Arnold I. Davidson (Malden, MA: Blackwell Publishing, 1995), 102.
11. Quoted in Henry Dwight Sedgwick, *The Art of Happiness, or the Teachings of Epicurus* (North Stratford, NH: Ayer Company Publishers, 1999), 41.
12. Lucretius, *The Way Things Are*, trans. Rolfe Humphries (Bloomington: Indiana University Press, 1968), 81.
13. Seneca, *Moral Essays*, vol. 2, trans. John W. Basore (Cambridge: Harvard University Press, 2001), 107.
14. Seneca, *Moral Essays*, 2:283.
15. Marcus Aurelius, *Meditations*, trans. Robin Waterfield (New York: Basic Books, 2021), 58.
16. *PJ*, 4:52.
17. *PJ*, 1:26–27.
18. Thoreau, *Walden*, 8.
19. Thoreau, *Walden*, 15.
20. Thoreau, *Walden*, 129.
21. Thoreau, *Walden*, 90.
22. Thoreau, *Walden*, 98.
23. Pierre Hadot, "There Are Nowadays Professors of Philosophy, but Not Philosophers," *Journal of Speculative Philosophy* 19, no. 3 (2005): 230.
24. Hadot, "There Are Nowadays Professors of Philosophy," 232.
25. Hadot, *Philosophy*, 265, 266.
26. Epictetus, *Discourses*, vol. 2, trans. W. A. Oldfather (Cambridge: Harvard University Press, 2000), 125.
27. Seneca, *Epistles*, vol. 1, trans. Richard M. Gummere (Cambridge: Harvard University Press, 2002), 325.

28. Hadot, *Philosophy*, 272.

29. Stanley Cavell, *The Senses of Walden: An Expanded Edition* (Chicago: University of Chicago Press, 1981). See also David M. Robinson, "Thoreau, Stanley Cavell and American Philosophy," in *Henry David Thoreau in Context*, ed. James S. Finley (New York: Cambridge University Press, 2017); and Rick Anthony Furtak, Jonathan Ellsworth, and James D. Reid, eds., *Thoreau's Importance for Philosophy* (New York: Fordham University Press, 2012). In *Thoreau's Living Ethics: Walden and the Pursuit of Virtue* (Athens: University of Georgia Press, 2004), Philip Cafaro very helpfully examines Thoreau's philosophy in the context of virtue ethics.

30. Hadot, *Philosophy*, 274.

31. William Jones, trans., *Institutes of Hindu Law; or the ordinances of Menu, according to the gloss of Calluca*, 2 vols. (London: Rivingtons and Cochran, 1825); Rammohan Roy, *Translations of several principal books, passages, and texts of the Veds . . .* , 2nd ed. (London: Parbury, Allen, and Co., 1832); William Ward, *A View of the history, literature, and religion of the Hindoos . . .* (Hartford: Huntington, 1824); Isvara Krishna, *The Sankhya Karika*, trans. Henry Thomas Colebrooke (London: Valpy, 1837); Charles Wilkins, trans., *Bhagvat Geeta, or Dialogues of Kreeshna and Arjoon* (London: Nourse, 1785).

32. Thoreau, *Correspondence*, 2:43.

33. Thoreau, *Walden*, 298.

34. *The Bhagavad Gita*, trans. Barbara Stoler Miller (New York: Columbia University Press, 1986), 64. In drawing parallels between Walden and the Bhagavad Gita, Paul Friedrich, in *The Gita within Walden* (Albany: State University of New York Press, 2009), argues that the Gita may have been yet another influence in Thoreau's decision to move to Walden Pond. Consider, for example, the instruction given the adept in the passage just quoted. More importantly, both texts are essentially therapeutic in nature. According to Friedrich: "The protagonists in both texts, Arjuna and Thoreau, move from situations of despondency, despair, or desperation in the midst of battle, literal, literary, or metaphorical—the field of Kuru or the mortgaged farm fields of Concord—to a denial of this and an affirmation of the opposite pole of peace and harmony through an identification with Krishna or Nature. To move from one situation to its denial to the affirmation of its diametrical opposite in terms of absolute values is perhaps the most basic tension in both texts" (33).

35. Thoreau, *Walden*, 95–96.

36. *The Works of Confucius; containing the original text, with a translation*, trans. J. Marshman (Serampore: The Mission Press, 1809); David Collie, *The Chinese classical work, commonly called The Four Books* (Malacca: The Mission Press, 1828); Jean-Pierre-Guillaume Pauthier, *Confucius et Mencius ou les quatre livres de philosophie politique de la Chine* (Paris: Charpentier, 1841).

37. See Philip J. Ivanhoe, *Confucian Moral Self Cultivation* (Indianapolis: Hackett Publishing Company, 2000), ix.

38. Arthur Christy, *The Orient in American Transcendentalism* (New York: Columbia University Press, 1932), 195.

39. Thoreau, *Early Essays*, 140.

40. Thoreau, *Early Essays*, 151.

41. The concept of reclusion as both a personal and a political statement remained a powerful element in Chinese culture and politics until recent times. See Barry Andrews, "Thoreau as Moral Hero," *The Concord Saunterer: A Journal of Thoreau Studies*, n.s. 24 (2016): 1–12.

42. David T. Y. Ch'en argues that Thoreau may in fact have read the *Tao-te-king* in a French translation by Pauthier. See David T. Y. Ch'en, "Thoreau and Taoism," in *Asian Response*

to *American Literature* (Delhi: Vikas Publications, 1972), 407–10. Also see Lin Yutang, *The Wisdom of Laotse* (New York: Modern Library, 1948), 7.

43. In Lin Yutang, *The Wisdom of China and India* (New York: Random House, 1942), 635.

44. Lin Yutang (1895–1976) was a popular interpreter of Chinese philosophy and culture for Western readers. An avowed fan of Thoreau's writing, he tells us that Confucianism and Taoism represent two sides of the Chinese outlook on life. In his view, Taoism and Confucianism are essentially complementary: "For Taoism is the playing mood of the Chinese people, as Confucianism is their working mood." Lin Yutang, *My Country and My People* (New York: Reynal and Hitchcock, 1935), 117.

45. Catherine L. Albanese, *A Republic of Mind and Spirit: A Cultural History of American Metaphysical Religion* (New Haven: Yale University Press, 2007), 26.

46. See Arthur Versluis, *The Esoteric Origins of the American Renaissance* (New York: Oxford University Press, 2001), 137.

47. *The Journals and Miscellaneous Notebooks of Ralph Waldo Emerson*, vol. 7, ed. A. W. Plumstead and Harrison Hayford (Cambridge: Harvard University Press, 1969), 413.

48. Thoreau, *Early Essays*, 177.

49. *The Collected Works of Ralph Waldo Emerson*, vol. 8, ed. Joel Myerson (Cambridge: Harvard University Press, 2010), 129.

50. Emerson, *Collected Works*, 8:149.

51. Quoted in Robert D. Richardson, *Nearer the Heart's Desire: The Poets of the Rubaiyat* (New York: Bloomsbury, 2016), 51–52.

52. *PJ*, 1:11.

53. Sherman Paul, *The Shores of America: Thoreau's Inward Exploration* (Urbana: University of Illinois Press, 1958), 28.

54. Thoreau, *Walden*, 103–4.

55. Hadot, *Philosophy*, 275.

56. Quoted in Hadot, *Philosophy*, 275.

CHAPTER 3: OF TIME AND THE RIVER

1. *PJ*, 1:371.

2. *PJ*, 1:447.

3. Henry David Thoreau, *A Week on the Concord and Merrimack Rivers*, ed. Carl F. Hovde (Princeton: Princeton University Press, 1980), 3. Subsequent references to this edition are cited parenthetically by page in the text.

4. Robert D. Richardson, *Myth and Literature in the American Renaissance* (Bloomington: Indiana University Press, 1978), 90.

5. The most thorough account of the book's composition is by Linck C. Johnson, *Thoreau's Complex Weave: The Writing of "A Week on the Concord and Merrimack Rivers"* (Charlottesville: University of Virginia Press, 1986).

6. Quoted in Henry David Thoreau, *A Week on the Concord and Merrimack Rivers* (Boston: Houghton Mifflin Company, 1906), xliii.

7. Thoreau spent the last ten years of his life mapping the Concord, Sudbury, and Assabet Rivers and documenting the impact of the dams, which were preventing the spawning of fish and flooding farmers' hay fields. See Robert M. Thorson, *The Boatman: Henry David Thoreau's River Years* (Cambridge: Harvard University Press, 2017).

8. Ethel Seybold, *Thoreau: The Quest and the Classics* (New Haven: Yale University Press, 1951), 15.

9. Franklin Sanborn, *Recollections of Seventy Years*, vol. 2 (Boston: Gorham Press, 1909), 451.

10. James Turner, *Without God, Without Creed: The Origins of Unbelief in America* (Baltimore: Johns Hopkins University Press, 1985), xii, 163. For a similar argument, see Leigh Eric Schmidt, *Restless Souls: The Making of American Spirituality* (San Francisco: HarperCollins, 2005).

11. Henry Thoreau, *Collected Poems of Henry Thoreau*, ed. Carl Bode (Chicago: Packard and Company, 1943), 230–31.

12. William James, *The Varieties of Religious Experience* (New York: Longmans, Green, and Co., 1925), 380–81.

13. David M. Robinson, *Natural Life: Thoreau's Worldly Transcendentalism* (Ithaca: Cornell University Press, 1994), 57–58.

14. See, for example, "Pond Scum," an essay by Kathryn Schulz that appeared in the October 11, 2015, edition of *The New Yorker*.

15. The record of his friends is mixed. In his eulogy of Thoreau, Emerson wrote, "'I love Henry,' said one of his friends, 'But I cannot like him: and as for taking his arm, I should as soon think of taking the arm of an elm-tree.'" *The Collected Works of Ralph Waldo Emerson*, vol. 10, ed. Ronald A. Bosco and Joel Myerson (Cambridge: Harvard University Press, 2013), 416.

16. F. B. Sanborn, *Henry David Thoreau* (Boston: Houghton Mifflin Company, 1917), 454.

17. Could this have been the inspiration for the enigmatic fable in *Walden*, "I long ago lost a hound, a bay horse, and a turtle-dove, and I am still on their trail"? Henry David Thoreau, *Walden*, ed. L. Lyndon Shanley (Princeton: Princeton University Press, 1973), 17.

18. *PJ*, 3:26.

19. Jeffrey S. Cramer, *Solid Seasons: The Friendship of Henry David Thoreau and Ralph Waldo Emerson* (Berkeley: Counterpoint Press, 2019), 67.

20. Γηγενεις means sprung from the earth, or earth-born.

21. Schools for teaching teachers were once called normal schools.

22. Seybold, *Thoreau*, 7.

23. Jonathan Bishop also highlights the sacred/profane polarity in his interpretation of *A Week*. Jonathan Bishop, "The Experience of the Sacred in Thoreau's *Week*," *ELH* 33, no. 1 (1966): 66–91.

24. Mircea Eliade, *The Sacred and the Profane: The Nature of Religion*, trans. Willard R. Trask (New York: Harcourt, Brace and Company, 1959), 28.

25. Eliade, *The Sacred and the Profane*, 63.

26. Eliade, *The Sacred and the Profane*, 70.

27. Seybold, *Thoreau*, 10–11.

28. Mircea Eliade, *Patterns in Comparative Religion*, trans. Rosemary Sheed (New York: Sheed and Ward, 1958), 99–100.

29. Mircea Eliade, *Images and Symbols: Studies in Religious Symbolism*, trans. Philip Mairet (New York: Sheed and Ward, 1969), 51.

30. John C. Broderick also calls attention to this pattern in his essay "The Movement of Thoreau's Prose," *American Literature* 33, no. 2 (May 1961): 133–42.

31. Mircea Eliade, *Myths, Dreams, and Mysteries: The Encounter between Contemporary Faiths and Archaic Realities*, trans. Philip Mairet (New York: Harper and Brothers, 1960), 66.

32. Lucretius, *The Way Things Are*, trans. Rolfe Humphries (Bloomington: Indiana University Press, 1968), 52.
33. See Pierre Hadot, *Philosophy as a Way of Life*, trans. Michael Chase, ed. Arnold I. Davidson (Malden, MA: Blackwell Publishing, 1995), 238–50. In this light, consider also Thoreau's description of the ant war in *Walden*, 228–32.
34. See Robinson, *Natural Life*, 61.

CHAPTER 4: BEGINNING TO LIVE

1. *PJ*, 2:155.
2. *PJ*, 1:296–97.
3. *PJ*, 1:347.
4. F. B. Sanborn, *Henry David Thoreau* (Boston: Houghton Mifflin Company, 1917), 211.
5. Robert D. Richardson Jr., *Henry David Thoreau: A Life of the Mind* (Berkeley: University of California Press, 1986), 154.
6. Henry David Thoreau, *Walden*, ed. L. Lyndon Shanley (Princeton: Princeton University Press, 1973), 90–91. Subsequent references to this edition are cited parenthetically by page in the text.
7. J. Lyndon Shanley, *The Making of "Walden"* (Chicago: University of Chicago Press, 1957), 7.
8. *PJ*, 4:170.
9. Mircea Eliade, *Myth and Reality*, trans. Willard R. Trask (New York: Harper and Row, 1963), 1.
10. Martha C. Nussbaum, *The Therapy of Desire: Theory and Practice in Hellenistic Ethics* (Princeton: Princeton University Press, 2009), 3.
11. *PJ*, 1:365.
12. In his commencement speech at Harvard he said that, instead of working six days a week for one day of leisure, we should reverse the order, enjoying six days of leisure for one day of work.
13. Mircea Eliade, *Patterns in Comparative Religion*, trans. Rosemary Sheed (New York: Sheed and Ward, 1958), 379.
14. Mircea Eliade, *Images and Symbols: Studies in Religious Symbolism*, trans. Philip Mairet (New York: Sheed and Ward, 1969), 49–50.
15. Pierre Hadot, "There Are Nowadays Professors of Philosophy, but Not Philosophers," *Journal of Speculative Philosophy* 19, no. 3 (2005): 233.
16. Mark G. Vasquez, *Authority and Reform: Religious and Educational Discourses in Nineteenth-Century New England Literature* (Knoxville: University of Tennessee Press, 2003), 30.
17. See Joseph F. Kett, *The Pursuit of Knowledge under Difficulties: From Self-Improvement to Adult Education in America, 1750–1990* (Stanford: Stanford University Press, 1994), 110–25.
18. The margins of books in his day were often much larger than those today.
19. This isn't actually true; several others, including Irish laborers and an alcoholic named Hugh Coyle, lived within the radius of one mile. See Laura Dassow Walls, *Henry David Thoreau: A Life* (Chicago: University of Chicago Press, 2017), 199–200.
20. The Five Points was a rough section in what is now lower Manhattan.
21. Charles R. Anderson, *The Magic Circle of Walden* (New York: Holt, Rinehart and Winston, 1968), 91.
22. Sherry Turkle, *Reclaiming Conversation: The Power of Talk in a Digital Age* (New York: Penguin, 2015), 47.

23. For more on this curious criticism, see Brent Ranalli, "Laundry!," *The Concord Saunterer*, n.s. 29 (2021): 1; and Rebecca Solnit, "Mysteries of Thoreau, Unsolved," *Orion* 32, no. 3 (2013).

24. Eliade, *Patterns*, 195.

25. Anderson, *Magic Circle*, 222.

26. *PJ*, 4:144.

27. John Farmer is an imaginary everyman, whereas John Field, mentioned in the "Baker Farm" chapter, was evidently a real person.

28. Victor Carl Friesen examines this distinction at length in *The Spirit of the Huckleberry: Sensuousness in Henry Thoreau* (Edmonton: University of Alberta Press, 1984). See especially chap. 2, "A Body All Sentient."

29. Marcus Aurelius, *Meditations*, 148, 161.

30. Hadot, *Philosophy*, 245.

31. Elise Lemire, *Black Walden: Slavery and Its Aftermath in Concord, Massachusetts* (Philadelphia: University of Pennsylvania Press, 2009), 10.

32. Eliade, *Patterns*, 196.

33. Literature on nature religion in America is extensive. Two fine surveys are Catherine L. Albanese, *Nature Religion in America: From the Algonkian Indians to the New Age* (Chicago: University of Chicago Press, 1990); and John Gatta, *Making Nature Sacred: Literature, Religion, and Environment in America from the Puritans to the Present* (New York: Oxford University Press, 2004).

34. Henry David Thoreau, *A Week on the Concord and Merrimack Rivers*, ed. Carl F. Hovde (Princeton: Princeton University Press, 1980), 65; Thoreau, *Correspondence*, 2:153. For discussions of Thoreau's pantheism, see Alan D. Hodder, *Thoreau's Ecstatic Witness* (New Haven: Yale University Press, 2001), 131–34; William J. Wolf, *Thoreau: Mystic, Prophet, Ecologist* (Philadelphia: United Church Press, 1974), 171–73.

35. On the personhood of God, consider this passage from *A Week*: "It is remarkable, that almost all speakers and writers feel it is incumbent on them, sooner or later, to acknowledge the personality of God," he wrote. "It is a sad mistake" (77–78).

36. See Andrea Wulf, *Magnificent Rebels: The First Romantics and the Invention of the Self* (New York: Knopf, 2022); and Samantha C. Harvey and Rochelle L. Johnson, "Coleridge, Thoreau, and the Transatlantic 'Riddle of the World,'" in *Thoreau at Two Hundred: Essays and Reassessments*, ed. Kristen Case and K. P. Van Anglen (Cambridge: Cambridge University Press, 2016), 155–69.

37. Hodder, *Thoreau's Ecstatic Witness*, 161.

38. Thoreau, *Correspondence*, 2:183–84.

39. Alan D. Hodder, "Concord Orientalism, Thoreau, and the Artist of Kouroo," in *Transient and Permanent: The Transcendentalist Movement and Its Critics*, ed. Charles Capper and Conrad Edick Wright (Boston: Massachusetts Historical Society, 1999), 213–14.

40. Lucretius, *The Way Things Are*, trans. Rolfe Humphries (Bloomington: Indiana University Press, 1968), 200.

41. See Walter Harding, *The Days of Henry Thoreau* (New York: Alfred A. Knopf, 1965), 224–25.

42. *PJ*, 4:275.

CHAPTER 5: AFTER WALDEN

1. Walter Harding, *The Days of Henry Thoreau* (New York: Alfred A. Knopf, 1965); 221.

2. *PJ*, 7:123.

3. "H. D. Thoreau's Book," *New-York Daily Tribune*, June 13, 1849, reprinted in *Emerson and*

Thoreau: The Contemporary Reviews, ed. Joel Myerson (Cambridge: Cambridge University Press, 1992), 342.

4. Henry David Thoreau, *Early Essays and Miscellanies*, ed. Joseph J. Moldenhauer and Edwin Moser (Princeton: Princeton University Press, 1975), 8–9.

5. William Rossi, "The Journal, Self-Culture, and the Genesis of 'Walking,'" *Thoreau Quarterly* 16, nos. 3 and 4 (Summer–Fall 1984): 137.

6. *PJ*, 5:219. There are three books dealing especially with Thoreau's journal: Sharon Cameron, *Writing Nature: Henry Thoreau's Journal* (New York: Oxford University Press, 1985); William Howarth, *The Book of Concord: Thoreau's Life as a Writer* (New York: Viking Press, 1982); and Malcolm Clemens Young, *The Spiritual Journal of Henry David Thoreau* (Macon, GA: Mercer University Press, 2009).

7. Lawrence Buell, *Literary Transcendentalism: Style and Vision in the American Renaissance* (Ithaca: Cornell University Press, 1973), 135–36.

8. *PJ*, 4:177.

9. Pierre Hadot, *The Inner Citadel: The Meditations of Marcus Aurelius*, trans. Michael Chase (Cambridge: Harvard University Press, 1998), 31–33.

10. Young, *Spiritual Journal of Thoreau*, 83.

11. *PJ*, 1:151.

12. *PJ*, 1:204.

13. Mircea Eliade, *Myth and Reality* (New York: Harper and Row, Publishers, 1963), 1.

14. *PJ*, 3:94.

15. Owing to the fact that no copy of Fuller's marriage certificate has been found, some of her contemporaries suspected that she and Ossoli were not officially married. Fearing that Ossoli's staunchly Catholic family would disown him if they knew he had married a Protestant, she insisted on keeping her marriage and the birth of their son a secret. Nevertheless, according to Thomas Wentworth Higginson, "one day after great anxiety, she called Mrs. [William Wetmore] Story to her and confided to her the secret of their marriage, showing her the marriage certificate and those relating to the birth of their child." Thomas Wentworth Higginson, *Margaret Fuller Ossoli* (Boston: Houghton, Mifflin and Company, 1887), 241.

16. *PJ*, 3:95.

17. *PJ*, 3:95.

18. *PJ*, 3:97. Note that in the 1927 Houghton Mifflin edition of Thoreau's journal, "*super natural*" is conflated to "*supernatural*," giving the quotation an entirely different meaning. *JHDT*, 2:46.

19. Henry David Thoreau, *A Week on the Concord and Merrimack Rivers*, ed. Carl F. Hovde (Princeton: Princeton University Press, 1980), 379, 382, 380.

20. *PJ*, 3:97.

21. *PJ*, 3:368.

22. *PJ*, 3:305–6.

23. *PJ*, 3:306.

24. David M. Robinson, *Natural Life: Thoreau's Worldly Transcendentalism* (Ithaca: Cornell University Press, 2004), 19.

25. *PJ*, 3:354–55.

26. *PJ*, 4:76.

27. *PJ*, 3:251. Having walked at night numerous times myself, I can attest to the veracity of Thoreau's remarks. On one occasion I walked from central Concord to Walden Pond

at night, encountering no obstacles in making my way through the woods to the site of his cabin. I was rewarded by the sight of moonrise over the east end of the pond. The experience is not as eerie or difficult as it might seem. Our eyes have both rods (scotopic vision) and cones (photopic vision). Rods are responsible for nighttime vision, cones for seeing in daytime. If we allow our vision to adjust, without any extraneous light (such as a flashlight), it is remarkable how well we are able to see.

28. *PJ*, 3:272.
29. *PJ*, 3:261.
30. *PJ*, 5:217.
31. *PJ*, 1:129.
32. *PJ*, 2:112.
33. May Sarton, *Journal of a Solitude* (New York: W. W. Norton & Company, 1973), 11.
34. *JHDT*, 9:246–47.
35. *PJ*, 7:30.
36. Amos Bronson Alcott, *Concord Days* (1872; repr., Carlisle, MA: Applewood Books, 2011), 13.
37. *The Collected Works of Ralph Waldo Emerson*, vol. 10, ed. Joel Myerson (Cambridge: Harvard University Press, 2010), 419.
38. *JHDT*, 9:208–9.
39. *PJ*, 1:266.
40. *PJ*, 3:95–96.
41. *PJ*, 5:412.
42. *PJ*, 5:344.
43. *PJ*, 6:30.
44. *PJ*, 6:204.
45. *PJ*, 1:348.
46. Emerson, *Collected Works*, 1:160.
47. M. H. Abrams, *Natural Supernaturalism: Tradition and Revolution in Romantic Literature* (New York: W. W. Norton and Company, 1971), 29.
48. Emerson *Collected Works*, 1:43.
49. *PJ*, 4:3.
50. *PJ*, 3:380.
51. *PJ*, 4:51–52.
52. *PJ*, 4:52–53.
53. *PJ*, 4:54–55.
54. See Richard Primack, *Walden Warming: Climate Change Comes to Thoreau's Woods* (Chicago: University of Chicago Press, 2015). Primack, professor of biology at Boston University, has used Thoreau's phenological studies to demonstrate that spring arrives several weeks earlier now than in Thoreau's time.
55. See Kristen Case, "Thoreau's Kalendar," *Thoreau Society Bulletin*, no. 321 (Spring 2023): 1–3.
56. See Robert M. Thorson, *The Boatman: Henry David Thoreau's River Years* (Cambridge: Harvard University Press, 2017).
57. *PJ*, 5:469–70.
58. *JHDT*, 12:171.
59. *PJ*, 7:268.
60. Quoted in Robert D. Richardson Jr., *Henry David Thoreau: A Life of the Mind* (Berkeley: University of California Press, 1986), 209.

61. Lawrence Buell, *The Environmental Imagination: Thoreau, Nature, and the Formation of the American Canon* (Cambridge: Harvard University Press, 1995), 119.

62. *JHDT*, 14:306–7.

63. Buell, *Environmental Imagination*, 138.

64. *JHDT*, 14:304.

65. Thoreau, *Correspondence*, 1:358. The most accessible volume of Thoreau's letters to Blake is *Letters to a Spiritual Seeker*, ed. Bradley P. Dean (New York: W. W. Norton & Company, 2004).

66. Thoreau, *Correspondence*, 1:359.

67. Thoreau, *Correspondence*, 1:360.

68. Thoreau, *Correspondence*, 1:361.

69. Thoreau, *Correspondence*, 1:361.

70. Thoreau, *Correspondence*, 1:362.

71. Thoreau, *Correspondence*, 1:369.

72. Thoreau, *Correspondence*, 1:370.

73. Thoreau, *Correspondence*, 2:43.

74. Thoreau, *Correspondence*, 2:43.

75. Thoreau, *Correspondence*, 2:54–55.

76. Thoreau, *Correspondence*, 2: 54–55.

77. Thoreau, *Correspondence*, 2:55–56.

78. Thoreau, *Correspondence*, 2:58–59. The life-everlasting is a flowering herb, *Sedum telephium*, also known as orpine.

79. Thoreau, *Correspondence*, 2:60.

80. Thoreau, *Correspondence*, 2:78–79.

81. Thoreau, *Correspondence*, 2:127.

82. Thoreau, *Correspondence*, 2:140.

83. Thoreau, *Correspondence*, 2:142.

84. Thoreau, *Correspondence*, 2:143.

85. Thoreau, *Correspondence*, 2:183.

86. Thoreau, *Correspondence*, 2:184.

87. Thoreau, *Correspondence*, 2:332.

88. Thoreau, *Correspondence*, 2:348.

89. For example, Adam Smith, author of the influential text *The Wealth of Nations* and a major figure in the Scottish Enlightenment, taught moral philosophy at the University of Glasgow and Balliol College, Oxford.

90. Thoreau, *Correspondence*, 2:446–47.

91. Thoreau, *Correspondence*, 2:487–88.

92. Thoreau, *Letters to a Spiritual Seeker*, 156. The Princeton edition of Thoreau's correspondence does not include any letters written or received after 1856.

93. Thoreau, *Letters to a Spiritual Seeker*, 158–59.

94. Henry David Thoreau, *Excursions*, ed. Joseph J. Moldenhauer (Princeton: Princeton University Press, 2007), 45–46.

95. Thoreau, *Letters to a Spiritual Seeker*, 181–83.

96. Thoreau, *Letters to a Spiritual Seeker*, 25.

CHAPTER 6: YEARS OF DECISION

1. Bernard DeVoto, *Year of Decision: 1846* (Boston: Houghton Mifflin Company, 1961), 4.

2. DeVoto, *Year of Decision*, 212–13.

3. Ralph Waldo Emerson, *Journal*, vol. 7, ed. Edward Waldo Emerson and Waldo Emerson Forbes (Boston: Houghton Mifflin Company, 1900), 219.

4. Henry David Thoreau, *Reform Papers*, ed. Wendell Glick (Princeton: Princeton University Press, 1973), 84. Hereafter cited parenthetically by page in the text.

5. *The Journals of Bronson Alcott*, ed. Odell Shepard (Boston: Little, Brown and Company, 1938), 183–84. While Emerson disapproved of Thoreau's action, there is no truth to the oft-reported exchange in which Emerson, arriving at Thoreau's jail cell, asks, "What are you doing in there?" To which Thoreau is said to have replied, "What are you doing out there?"

6. Quoted in William Stuart Nelson, "Thoreau and American Non-Violent Resistance," in *Thoreau in Our Season*, ed. John H. Hicks (Amherst: University of Massachusetts Press, 1962), 14.

7. Martin Luther King Jr., "A Legacy of Creative Protest," in Hicks, *Thoreau in Our Season*, 13.

8. See Kong Lingyu, "Thoreau's Action: Non-violent or Violent?" *IOSR Journal of Humanities and Social Science* 22, no. 7 (July 2017): 56–58.

9. Thomas Wentworth Higginson, *Cheerful Yesterdays* (Boston: Houghton, Mifflin and Company, 1898), 158. The most complete account of the Burns affair is Albert J. von Frank, *The Trials of Anthony Burns: Freedom and Slavery in Emerson's Boston* (Cambridge: Harvard University Press, 1998).

10. Peter Wirzbicki, *Fighting for the Higher Law: Black and White Transcendentalists against Slavery* (Philadelphia: University of Pennsylvania Press, 2021), 10.

11. *JHDT*, 7:400.

12. David S. Reynolds, *John Brown, Abolitionist* (New York: Alfred A. Knopf, 2005), 344.

13. Several sources state that Thoreau delivered his speech at the Concord Town Hall. Bronson Alcott noted in his journal on October 30, 1859, however, "Thoreau reads a paper of his on John Brown, his virtues, spirit, and deeds, at the Vestry this evening." Alcott, *Journals*, 320. I take this to refer to the vestry of First Parish Church. This location is further confirmed by Joel Myerson's account in "Thoreau's Lectures after Walden: Lecture 65," available online from the Thoreau Institute at walden.org.

14. Quoted in Laura Dassow Walls, *Henry David Thoreau: A Life* (Chicago: University of Chicago Press, 2017), 126.

15. Concluding his impromptu speech at the trial, Brown said: "I believe that to interfere as I have done, as I have always freely admitted that I have done on behalf of His despised poor, I did not wrong, but right. Now, if it is deemed necessary that I should forfeit my life for the furtherance of the ends of justice, and mingle my blood further with the blood of millions in this slave country whose rights are disregarded by wicked, cruel, and unjust enactments, I say, let it be done." Reynolds comments: "This speech has won many admirers over the years. Emerson called it and the Gettysburg Address the two greatest American speeches." Reynolds, *John Brown*, 354–55.

16. A press report on Brown's execution stated that as he descended the jailhouse steps, he spotted a Black woman in the crowd, holding her child. Bending over, he kissed the child. Of this episode, Reynolds writes: "This final gesture of his love for blacks had

an irresistible appeal to those sympathetic to Brown. The anecdote appeared in many speeches, poems, and essays about Brown." Reynolds, *John Brown*, 394.

17. Taylor Stoehr, *Nay-Saying in Concord: Emerson, Alcott, and Thoreau* (Hamden, CT: Archon Books, 1979), 19.

18. Reynolds, *John Brown*, 215.

19. *The Complete Works of Ralph Waldo Emerson*, vol. 7, ed. Edward Waldo Emerson (Boston: Houghton Mifflin Company, 1904), 427.

20. See Reynolds, *John Brown*, 427.

21. Henry David Thoreau, *A Week on the Concord and Merrimack Rivers*, ed. Carl F. Hovde (Princeton: Princeton University Press, 1980), 73.

22. Hannah Arendt, *Crises of the Republic* (New York: Harcourt Brace & Company, 1972), 60.

23. Arendt, *Crises of the Republic*, 63.

24. Henry David Thoreau, *Walden*, ed. L. Lyndon Shanley (Princeton: Princeton University Press, 1973), 90.

25. Jack Turner, *Awakening to Race: Individualism and Social Consciousness in America* (Chicago: University of Chicago Press, 2012), 35.

26. Turner, *Awakening to Race*, 27.

27. Jack Turner, "Performing Conscience: Thoreau, Political Action, and the Plea for John Brown," *Political Theory* 33, no. 4 (August 2005): 453.

28. Moncure Conway, *Autobiography: Memories and Experiences*, vol. 1 (Boston: Houghton Mifflin and Company, 1904), 141.

29. Thoreau, *Walden*, 108–10.

CHAPTER 7: EXCURSIONS

1. Henry David Thoreau, *The Maine Woods*, ed. Joseph J. Moldenhauer (Princeton: Princeton University Press, 1972), 47.

2. Thoreau, *Maine Woods*, 61.

3. Thoreau, *Maine Woods*, 64.

4. Thoreau, *Maine Woods*, 70.

5. Aldous Huxley, *Collected Essays* (New York: Harper and Brothers Publishers, 1958), 1.

6. Thoreau, *Maine Woods*, 71.

7. Henry David Thoreau, *Early Essays and Miscellanies*, ed. Joseph J. Moldenhauer and Edwin Moser (Princeton: Princeton University Press, 1975), 98.

8. Rudolf Otto, *The Idea of the Holy*, trans. John W. Harvey (Oxford: Oxford University Press, 1924), 19, 31.

9. Mircea Eliade, *The Sacred and the Profane: The Nature of Religion*, trans. Willard R. Trask (New York: Harcourt, Brace and Company, 1959), 11.

10. Thoreau, *Maine Woods*, 64.

11. Thoreau, *Maine Woods*, 88.

12. Thoreau, *Maine Woods*, 108–9.

13. Thoreau, *Maine Woods*, 122. Thoreau was incensed when James Russell Lowell, editor of the *Atlantic Monthly* magazine, objected to Thoreau's pantheism in depicting the pine tree as immortal and wanted the passage removed. Joseph J. Moldenhauer, "Textual Introduction," in Thoreau, *Maine Woods*, 361.

14. Thoreau, *Maine Woods*, 156.

15. Thoreau, *Maine Woods*, 185.

16. Thoreau, *Maine Woods*, 215–16.

17. Thoreau, *Maine Woods*, 296.

18. Lawrence Buell, *Literary Transcendentalism: Style and Vision in the American Renaissance* (Ithaca: Cornell University Press, 1973), 135.

19. On March 19, 1841, he wrote, "The religion I love is very laic." *PJ*, 1:289.

20. Henry David Thoreau, *Reform Papers*, ed. Wendell Glick (Princeton: Princeton University Press, 1973), 156, 58.

21. Thoreau, *Reform Papers*, 161.

22. Thoreau, *Reform Papers*, 165.

23. Thoreau, *Reform Papers*, 169.

24. Thoreau, *Reform Papers*, 164.

25. Thoreau, *Reform Papers*, 156.

26. Thoreau, *Reform Papers*, 173.

27. Thoreau, *Reform Papers*, 178.

28. Jonathan van Belle and John Kaag, "What Thoreau Can Teach Us about the Great Resignation," *Fast Company*, November 11, 2021, https://www.fastcompany.com/90695132/what-thoreau-can-teach-us-about-the-great-resignation.

29. Henry David Thoreau, *Excursions*, ed. Joseph J. Moldenhauer (Princeton: Princeton University Press, 2007), 166, 181–82.

30. This event is described in Randall Fuller, *The Book That Changed America: How Darwin's Theory of Evolution Ignited a Nation* (New York: Viking, 2017), 3–6.

31. *JHDT*, 13:77.

32. Henry David Thoreau, *Faith in a Seed: The Dispersion of Seeds and Other Late Natural History Writings*, ed. Bradley P. Dean (Washington, DC: Island Press, 1993), 102.

33. Henry David Thoreau, *Wild Fruits: Thoreau's Rediscovered Last Manuscript* (New York: W. W. Norton & Company, 2000), 4.

34. Thoreau, *Wild Fruits*, 168–69.

35. Thoreau, *Wild Fruits*, 238–39.

36. Alan D. Hodder, "The Gospel According to This Moment: Thoreau, Wildness, and American Nature Religion," *Religion and the Arts* 15 (2011): 460.

37. Thoreau, *Excursions*, 185.

38. John Hanson Mitchell, *The Wildest Place on Earth: Italian Gardens and the Invention of Wilderness* (Washington, DC: Counterpoint, 2001), 13.

39. Thoreau, *Excursions*, 187.

40. Thoreau, *Excursions*, 186. By comparison, consider what Emerson writes in his essay "Self-Reliance": "I shun father and mother and wife and brother, when my genius calls me." *The Collected Works of Ralph Waldo Emerson*, vol. 2, ed. Alfred R. Ferguson and Jean Ferguson Carr (Cambridge: Harvard University Press, 1979), 30. Also what Jesus says in the Gospel of Matthew (10:35): "I have come to set a man against his father, a daughter against her mother, a young wife against her mother-in-law."

41. Thoreau, *Excursions*, 189.

42. Thoreau, *Excursions*, 190.

43. David Robinson, "Walking the Mythical Path: Thoreau's Old Marlboro Road," in *Narratives of Place in Literature and Film*, ed. Steven Allen and Kirsten Mollegaard (New York: Routledge, 2019), 82.

44. Thoreau, *Excursions*, 193.

45. Thoreau, *Excursions*, 194.

46. Robinson, "Walking the Mythical Path," 94.

47. Thoreau, *Excursions*, 195.

48. Rebecca Solnit, *Wanderlust: A History of Walking* (New York: Viking, 2000), 267.

49. Amos Bronson Alcott, *Concord Days* (Boston: Roberts Brothers, 1872), 13.

50. For definitions of Tao in Confucianism and Taoism, see Zhang Dainian, *Key Concepts in Chinese Philosophy*, trans. Edmund Ryden (New Haven: Yale University Press, 2002), 11–26; and Yi Wu, *Chinese Philosophical Terms* (Lanham, MD: University Press of America, 1986), 103–8.

51. *The Complete Works of Zhuangzi*, trans. Burton Watson (New York: Columbia University Press, 2013), xii.

52. Zhuangzi, *Complete Works*, 114.

53. Thoreau, *Excursions*, 195.

54. Zhuangzi, *Complete Works*, 9.

55. Carl J. Dull, "Zhuangzi and Thoreau: Wandering, Nature, and Freedom," *Journal of Chinese Philosophy* 39, no. 2 (June 2012): 230.

56. Henry David Thoreau, *Walden*, ed. L. Lyndon Shanley (Princeton: Princeton University Press, 1973), 53.

57. D. B. Johnson, *Henry Hikes to Fitchburg* (Boston: Houghton Mifflin Company, 2000).

58. Erling Kagge, *Walking: One Step at a Time*, trans. Becky L. Crook (New York: Pantheon Books, 2019), 17.

59. Thoreau, *Excursions*, 202.

60. Thoreau, *Excursions*, 203.

61. Thoreau, *Excursions*, 205.

62. See "Mending the Inborn Nature," chap. 16 of Zhuangzi, *Complete Works*, 122–26.

63. Thoreau, *Excursions*, 213

64. Edward Abbey, *Down the River* (New York: Plume, 1991), 38.

65. Thoreau, *Excursions*, 217.

66. Thoreau, *Excursions*, 214–15. The Boston Society for the Diffusion of Knowledge was founded in 1828.

67. Thoreau, *Excursions*, 215.

68. Thoreau, *Excursions*, 215–16.

69. Thoreau, *Excursions*, 209.

70. R. W. B. Lewis, *The American Adam: Innocence, Tragedy, and Tradition in the Nineteenth Century* (Chicago: University of Chicago Press, 1955), 21.

71. Thoreau, *Excursions*, 218.

72. Thoreau, *Excursions*, 220.

73. Thoreau, *Excursions*, 222.

74. Lawrence Buell, *The Environmental Imagination: Thoreau, Nature, and the Formation of the American Canon* (Cambridge: Harvard University Press, 1995), 115.

75. John Burroughs, "Another Word on Thoreau," in *The Last Harvest* (Boston: Houghton Mifflin Company, 1922).

76. *PJ*, 3:368.

77. Robert Richardson, "The Rooster's Philosophy," in *Thoreau at 200: Essays and Reassessments*, ed. Kristen Case and K. P. Van Anglen (New York: Cambridge University Press, 2016), 249.

78. Thoreau, *Excursions*, 256.

79. Thoreau, *Excursions*, 224.

80. Thoreau, *Excursions*, 241–42.

81. Thoreau, *Excursions*, 259.

82. *JHDT*, 12:344.

83. Quoted in Kathy Fedorko, "Revisiting Henry's Last Words," *Thoreau Society Bulletin*, no. 295 (Fall 2016): 2.

CHAPTER 8: PILGRIMAGE

1. *The Collected Works of Ralph Waldo Emerson*, vol. 10, ed. Joel Myerson (Cambridge: Harvard University Press, 2010), 431.

2. See Walter Harding, *The Days of Henry Thoreau* (New York: Alfred A. Knopf, 1965), 466–68.

3. *The Journals of Bronson Alcott*, ed. Odell Shepard (Boston: Little, Brown and Company, 1938), 425–26.

4. Henry David Thoreau, *Walden*, ed. L. Lyndon Shanley (Princeton: Princeton University Press, 1973), 107–8.

5. *The Lost Notebooks of Loren Eisley*, ed. Kenneth Heuer (Boston: Little, Brown and Company, 1987), 231–32.

6. Emerson, *Collected Works*, 10:429.

7. See, for example, François Specq, Laura Dassow Walls, and Michael Granger, eds., *Thoreauvian Modernities: Transatlantic Conversations on an American Icon* (Athens: University of Georgia Press, 2013); and François Specq, Laura Dassow Walls, and Julien Nègre, eds., *Thoreau beyond Borders: New International Essays on America's Most Famous Nature Writer* (Amherst: University of Massachusetts Press, 2020).

8. Edwin Way Teale, *The Thoughts of Thoreau* (New York: Dodd, Mead & Company, 1987), x.

9. Roderick Nash, *Wilderness and the American Mind* (New Haven: Yale University Press, 1982), 257.

10. Nash, *Wilderness and the American Mind*, 85–86.

11. John Burroughs, *Time and Change* (Boston: Houghton Mifflin Company, 1912), 265.

12. See, for example, Jack Turner, ed., *A Political Companion to Henry David Thoreau* (Lexington: University of Kentucky Press, 2009).

13. Thoreau, *Walden*, 90.

14. Alan Hodder, "Thoreau and the New American Spirituality," in *Thoreau at 200: Essays and Reassessments*, ed. Kristen Case and K. P. Van Anglen (New York: Cambridge University Press, 2016), 230.

15. See K. P. Van Anglen, "Transcendentalism and Religion: The State of Play," *Literature Compass* 5–6 (2008): 1010–24.

16. Hodder, "Thoreau," 232.

17. For the former, see David Faflik, *Transcendental Heresies: Harvard and the Modern American Practice of Unbelief* (Amherst: University of Massachusetts Press, 2020); Robert A. Gross, "'That Terrible Thoreau': Concord and Its Hermit," in *A Historical Guide to Henry David Thoreau*, ed. William B. Cain (New York: Oxford University Press, 2000), 181–241; and Robert A. Gross, *The Transcendentalists and Their World* (New York: Farrar, Straus and Giroux, 2021). For the latter, see Alda Balthrop-Lewis, *Thoreau's Religion: Walden Woods, Social Justice, and the Politics of Asceticism* (New York: Cambridge University Press, 2021).

18. Balthrop-Lewis, *Thoreau's Religion*, 270.

19. *PJ*, 3:62.

20. *PJ*, 1:348.

21. *JHDT*, 12:159.

22. See especially Alan D. Hodder, *Thoreau's Ecstatic Witness* (New Haven: Yale University Press, 2001).

23. William James, *The Varieties of Religious Experience* (New York: Longmans, Green, and Co., 1925), 380–81.

24. *PJ*, 3:251–52.

25. Andreas Hess, "Purposeful Solitude: Reading Thoreau in a Lockdown," *Open Democracy*, April 28, 2020.

26. Thoreau, *Walden*, 323–24.

27. Emerson, *Collected Works*, 10:416.

INDEX

Darwin, Charles, 1, 143–44
Dean, Bradley P., 116, 143
Declaration of Independence, 120–21
development theory, 143–44
DeVoto, Bernard, 117
Dharma Shastra, 50
The Dial: Blake's interest in, 109; "Ethnical Scriptures," 18, 20, 26–41, 148; Thoreau's early writing for, 19, 42. *See also* "Ethnical Scriptures" (*The Dial*)
Dillard, Annie, 160
Diogenes, 92, 103
divine marriage, Romanticism on, 105
The Divine Pymander (Hermes Trismegistus), 38
"Divinity School Address" (Emerson), 45, 48, 109
Doctrine of the Mean (Confucian literature), 27, 36
double consciousness problem, 105–6, 164
"Down the River with Henry Thoreau" (Abby), 150–51
Dred Scott case (1857), 129
Dull, Carl J., 149
Duston, Hannah, 56–57

Eastern philosophy. *See* Confucius and Confucianism; Hinduism; Taoism
Echoes of Harpers Ferry (book), 128
Eclectic school, 10
economics, commerce, and simple living: bank failures (1857), 115; California Gold Rush, 140; Carlyle on Mechanical Age, 22; economics as moral philosophy, 114; environmental impact of materialism, 107–9, 134, 159–61, 174n7; Panic of 1837, 11; Thoreau on love of life and contentment, 67–69, 90–91, 112, 166; Thoreau on personal fulfillment from work, 140–42; Thoreau's Fitchburg train vs. walk example, 149; Thoreau's Harvard commencement speech on commercialism, 11–12; Thoreau's legacy of simple living ethic, 161–62; Transcendentalism on "simple living and high thinking," 103, 161
ecstasies, Thoreau on, 99, 106, 114, 163–67

Edinburgh Review, Carlyle's articles in, 22
ego, transcending, 29–31, 39, 91, 164–66. *See also* spirituality and religion
Eisley, Loren, 158
Eliade, Mircea: on myth, 152; *Myth and Reality*, 64, 97; on Otto's work, 137; *Patterns in Comparative Religion*, 61, 69, 78, 86; *The Sacred and the Profane: The Nature of Religion*, 59–60
Emerson, Edith (daughter), 94
Emerson, Edward "Eddy" (son), 94, 117, 127
Emerson, Ellen (daughter), 94
Emerson, Lidian (wife), 12, 13, 93, 94, 118
Emerson, Phoebe (grandmother), 84
Emerson, Ralph Waldo: as abolitionist, 118, 120, 122, 126, 129; and Blake's correspondence with Thoreau, 109; on Brown, 181n15; burial of, 156; and Carlyle, 22; on Christianity, 131; European travel by, 93, 94; and Fuller's death, 98; journal of, 95; scholarly study of, 5; on self-culture, 14–16, 25–26, 100; Thoreau's early influence by, 18–20; Thoreau's eulogy by, 157, 159, 168, 175n15; Thoreau's friendship strained with, 56; and Thoreau's life on Walden Pond, 63, 77, 82, 84, 88, 93; Thoreau's philosophical influence by, 24–26, 33, 38–40; on Thoreau's poll tax protest (jail stay), 118, 181n5; Thoreau's spiritual influence by, 3, 5, 6; Thoreau's work at home of, 18, 93, 94; writing style of, 139, 150
Emerson, Ralph Waldo, written works: "Courage," 129–30; "Divinity School Address," 45, 48, 109; "Human Culture" lectures, 97; "Indian Superstition," 25; *Nature*, 2, 10, 12–13, 62, 105; "The Over-Soul," 105; "Persian Poetry," 38–39; "Self-Reliance," 183n40; "The Transcendentalist," 105
Emerson, Waldo, Jr. (son), 42
Emerson, William (brother), 23, 42
Emerson, William (grandfather), 23, 84
Epictetus, 32
Epicureanism, 29–33, 68–69, 71, 91
Epicurus, 29, 68–69, 91
Esau (biblical figure), 140

INDEX 193

"Ode" (Wordsworth), 100
"The Old Marlboro Road" (Thoreau),
146–47
On the Origin of Species (Darwin), 1, 143–44
"On the Rights and Duties of the Individual
in Relation to Government" (Thoreau), 118
"On the Shortness of Life" (Seneca), 33
The Orient in American Transcendentalism
(Christy), 36
Ossoli, Giovanni, 98, 104, 155, 178n15
Otto, Rudolf, 137
"The Over-Soul" (Emerson), 105

pacifism vs. nonviolent resistance, 35, 120–
22, 125, 129. *See also* nonviolent resistance
Pan (Greek god), 75
pantheism, 75, 87–88, 182n13
Parker, Theodore, 48, 123
passive mystical experience, James on, 52
passive resistance. *See* nonviolent resistance
Patterns in Comparative Religion (Eliade),
69, 78, 86
Paul, Sherman, 39–40
Paul (apostle), 81
Pauthier, Jean-Pierre-Guillaume, 35, 148
Peabody, Elizabeth Palmer, 118, 121, 122
Persia, philosophy influence on Thoreau,
38–40, 47
Persius (Aulus Persius Flaccus), 18
*The Phenix: a Collection of Old and Rare
Fragments*, 27
Phillips, Wendell, 123
*A Philosophical Enquiry into the Origin of Our
Ideas of the Sublime and Beautiful* (Burke),
137
philosophy: Alcott on Thoreau as "peripatetic philosopher," 103, 147; Eclectic
school, 10; Epicureanism, 29–33, 68–69,
71, 91; pantheism, 75, 87–88; Reason, 10,
62, 105–6, 112; Romanticism, 87–88, 105;
Stoicism, 29–33, 68–69, 71; Taoism, 148,
174n44; as Thoreau's way of life, 26–33;
virtue ethics, 26, 36, 126, 148, 173; *Walden*
and influence of, 26, 28, 31, 33, 36, 37, 40,
66–67. *See also* Confucius and Confucianism; moral philosophy; self-culture;
spirituality and religion; Thoreau, Henry

David, written works and lectures;
Transcendentalism; *individual names of
philosophers*
Philosophy as a Way of Life (Hadot), 29, 83
Pih E (Bo Yi), 37
Pillsbury, Parker, 156
"A Plea for Captain John Brown" (Thoreau),
126–28, 131, 181n13
Plutarch, 31
Polis, Joe, 138–39
poll tax protest, by Thoreau, 65, 77, 117–18,
131, 181n5
Pope, Alexander, 112
Primack, Richard B., 159
Puranas, 50, 75
"Purposeful Solitude: Reading Thoreau in a
Lockdown" (Hess), 167

Quoil, Hugh, 84
quotes by Thoreau. *See* Thoreau, Henry
David, quotes

Rammohun Roy, 34
reading, *Walden* on, 71–72
reality vs. appearance, 105–6, 111–12
Reason: Coleridge on, 10, 105, 112; Transcen-
dentalists on Understanding vs. Reason,
62; vs. Understanding, 105–6
*Reclaiming Conversation: The Power of Talk
in a Digital Age* (Turkle), 76
reclusion, 37, 173n41
"Reform and the Reformers" (Thoreau), 132
Reform Papers (Thoreau), 121, 142, 160
"Resistance to Civil Government" (Tho-
reau), 118
*Restless Souls: The Making of American
Spirituality* (Schmidt), 3
Reynolds, David S., 126, 129, 181–82nn15–16
Reynolds, Grindall, 157
Richardson, Robert D., 16, 19, 43, 153–54
Ripley, Ezra, 7–8
Robinson, David, 6, 54, 100, 146–47
Roman philosophy. *See* Stoicism
Romanticism, 87–88, 105. *See also* Coleridge,
Samuel Taylor
Rossi, William, 95
Rousseau, Jean-Jacques, 147